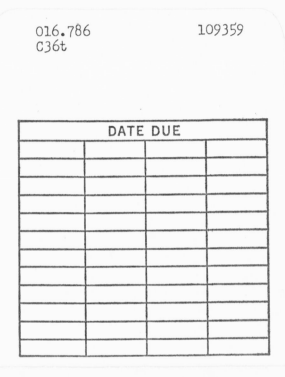

TEAM PIANO
REPERTOIRE

*A Manual of Music for Multiple Players
at One or More Pianos*

by
Frederic Ming Chang
and
Albert Faurot

The Scarecrow Press, Inc.
Metuchen, N.J.   1976

Library of Congress Cataloging in Publication Data

Chang, Frederic Ming, 1930-
  Team piano repertoire.

    1. Piano music (4 hands)--Bibliography. 2. Piano
music (Pianos (2))--Bibliography. I. Faurot, Albert,
joint author. II. Title.
ML128.P3C48   016.786.4'9   76-14927
ISBN 0-8108-0937-0

Dedicated to our Partners,

Jan and Ruth Marie

CONTENTS

ACKNOWLEDGMENTS

The authors are grateful to the staff of the following libraries and music stores for their courtesy and assistance:

Music Division of the New York Public Library, and the Research Library of the Performing Arts at Lincoln Center

Music Division of the Library of Congress

Music Library of Columbia University

The Newark Public Library

G. Schirmer's, especially Mr. William Kulkman

The Patelson Music House

INTRODUCTION

Of all man-made musical instruments, the piano lends
itself best to solo playing. A single person with only ten
fingers can, by activating the eighty-eight keys fixed in a
four-foot manual, produce melody, accompaniment, rhythm,
counterpoint, atmospheric effects and background music, si-
multaneously. In fact the potential of the instrument is so
great that the temptation at once arises to add more hands
and fingers to realize it. The very length of the keyboard
invites companionship. These two factors, the urge for greater sonority, and the craving to share the fun of producing it,
have led to a large literature of music for multiple players.

Music for "two at one," commonly known as four-
hand music, has from the beginning tended toward the
intimate and the entertaining. The setting was the "parlor,"
and the first heyday of duet playing was nineteenth-century
Vienna, with its glorification of "gemütlichkeit," the comfort
of the prosperous middle-class home. Here friends brought
their fiddles and flutes, and after the trios and quartets, took
turns pairing off at the keyboard, playing duets for their own
enjoyment and for that of the sympathetic group of family and
friends. Many an affair of the heart must have flowered as
hands touched on the keys. Children, too, were encouraged
to participate, and another type of duet grew up, designed to
glamorize the thin sounds of the beginner. In our own day,
when a family with two members who can play piano is a
rare phenomenon, this music can be enjoyed in the home on
fine records, but the fun of mutually discovering and creating
the sound is lost. In the eighteenth century, one of the de-
terrents, according to that tireless musical tour guide,
Charles Burney, was the lady's hoop skirts and crinolines,
which kept everyone at too great a distance for duets.

The lavish attire and sumptuous salons of the eighteenth-century aristocracy produced another type of team music. Two or more harpsichords and later the new-fangled
fortepianos were to be found in princely courts, as well as

the public room of the Three Swans in Leipzig and Vauxhall's Hanover Square Rooms in London. Here a more showy and superficial type of duet for players at two instruments grew up. It presupposed the presence of a critical audience waiting to be titillated and dazzled, and certain to make invidious comparisons. The music took on a showy, virtuoso character in keeping with the baroque and rococo setting and the sense of competition. Unfortunately (or, perhaps, fortunately), little of this music has survived, though the few pieces which have been preserved, by Couperin the Grand of The Sun King's Court, the Roman Pasquini from the Borghese Palace, and the great J. S. Bach of the Leipzig Collegium make us wish for more.

More works for two keyboards appeared with the advent of the piano, adopted by the sons of Bach, and Mozart. They were attracted by the brilliant interplay of passage-work possible by two players, each with an entire keyboard, as well as by the richer texture of twenty-note chords, and the contrast of staccato and legato from two sets of pedals. Often two klaviers were featured as guest soloists with an orchestra, and concertos for multiple keyboards were written, one specifically for the combination of the venerable cembalo and the upstart fortepiano. A few teachers welcomed the presence of two instruments in the homes of their aristocratic pupils, and Mattheson of Hamburg wrote sonatas to play with the English Legate's son, while Padre Soler accompanied the Spanish Infanta Gabriel at the Escorial in duets on two unspecified keyboard instruments.

With the notable exceptions of Schubert and Brahms most of the great nineteenth-century romantic composers did not write very much piano music for multiple players. After turning out one or two pieces for four hands or two pianos, they usually returned to the more challenging orchestra or the more marketable solo piece. Some pianist-composers, like Chopin and Liszt, preferred to display their own wares without competition from a second player. At the end of the nineteenth century, Brahms realized the full potential of both the four-hand and the two-piano medium in a series of masterpieces which he sent off to Clara Schumann, works which pave the way for the great twentieth-century boom.

In the last fifty years two-piano music has come into its own. A vogue for duo-piano playing swept the country in the thirties and teams were presented on concert circuits, on radio and records, and even in the great orchestra halls of the world's musical capitals. Sometimes two pianists,

each famed as soloist, would team up, with sensational results. A few of these memorable occasions have been preserved on records, though many more impromptu performances at midnight gatherings must have been lost. Rachmaninoff and Horowitz, Rachmaninoff and Gabrilowitsch, Gabrilowitsch and Bauer, Bauer and Hess, Lipatti and Boulanger,
have all played together.

Professional two-piano teams devoted exclusively to
duet playing became popular. Some toured the country with
their own instruments in specially built automobile trailers,
recalling the fabulous feats of Gottschalk in the early days of
the railroad and the opening of the West. The finest teams
are often family members--husband and wife, father and son,
siblings--who understandably feel a mutual empathy that makes
for fine ensemble. Igor Stravinsky and son Soulima played
together briefly. The Spanish pianist, Jose Iturbi, sometimes
played with his sister Amparo. Olivier Messiaen toured with
his wife, Yvonne Loriod, playing his great two-piano masterpiece, before returning exclusively to composing. Artur
Schnabel occasionally appeared with son, Karl Ulrich. The
three Casadesus, father, mother and son, have played and
recorded on two and three pianos. Joseph Lhevinne, noted
for his fine solo playing, was often joined by his wife Rosina,
later to become one of the great teachers of our day. Among
the couples who have made a career of duo-pianism are Vronsky and Babin, Luboschutz and Nemenoff, Bartlett and Robertson, Morley and Gearhardt, and others.

To these teams we owe a great debt, and not only for
many hours of pleasant listening to the masterpieces of the
repertoire in concert hall and on records. They have also
inspired and commissioned the composition of many splendid
new works. Many of the sonatas, concertos, suites and variations reviewed here were written for such famous teams as
Wittemore and Lowe, Gold and Fizdale, Maier and Pattison,
Appleton and Field, Dougherty and Ruzicka, Ferrante and
Teicher. Their fine partnerships have encouraged not only
a sizable body of new two-piano music, but also a plethora
of arrangements and transcriptions and several concertos for
two pianos with orchestra. This book will discuss only original two-piano and duet music, though a list of selected arrangements is included.

All devotees of duet playing will wish to own Ernest
Lubin's recent book, The Piano Duet (Grossman, 1970). It
is written con amore and will undoubtedly awaken a like fer-
vor for four-hand playing in musical readers. But it touches

only lightly on contemporary duet music, and is frustrating to use as a reference work, as each item must be looked up in three places for full information.

The first and only book-length study of two-piano playing is Hans Moldenhauer's Duo-Pianism, which appeared in 1950 and is still available from the author (Moldenhauer Archives, 1011 Comstock Court, Spokane, Wash., 99203). A third of the book deals with the history of two-piano playing, including harpsichords; another large part discusses the medium from an artistic, creative, and educational point of view. Only eighteen pages are devoted to the literature. Many of the items catalogued are occasional works, no longer of interest after twenty-five years, a condition which will undoubtedly apply to the present book in future years. Other items are out of print or no longer available. Some of the latter which might be of interest if they can be secured have been included here.

Team Piano Repertoire takes up where Faurot's Concert Piano Repertoire (Scarecrow Press, 1974) left off with solo music, and continues to list, evaluate and discuss music for multiple players and multiple instruments. The alphabetical composer listing is continued. Since, however, most people using such a manual will be looking for music for a team of a specific size, the material is divided into categories according to the number of players and pianos required. Music for mass piano performances is not included, since such stunts usually use duet or two-piano material, with a Barnum and Bailey emphasis on size and volume.

1. Two at One (Music for two players, four hands, at one piano).

2. Two at Two (Music for two players, four hands, at two pianos).

3. Three or Four at Two (Three or four players at two pianos; six- or eight-hand music).

4. Three at Three and Four at Four (Three players at three pianos, and four at four pianos).

5. Arrangements and Transcriptions.

6. Recordings.

Only music originally composed for these combinations

is discussed, exceptions being made when the composer has written both a solo and a duet version of the same piece. The large literature of duet music for children and for teaching is left for another occasion. No music for Three at One has been included. Though there are many pieces of six-hand music, they are all for very small people, and are on an elementary level. Solo concertos with an orchestra reduction for second piano are not duets and are not included; they deserve a book to themselves. Concertos for two or more pianos are discussed only if the orchestra can be dispensed with and the orchestra accompaniment successfully incorporated into the piano parts. A selected list of four-hand and two-piano arrangements from solo music, chamber music or orchestra scores, which are of recital or concert calibre, appears in Part 5. Part 6 is a list of recordings. Only published works have been included, and publishers have been listed. Although some of the titles are out-of-print, they are still available in libraries.

In buying music for two pianos it is important always to notice whether the publisher provides a set of two parts (set), or whether it is necessary to buy two separate copies (sep). In the former case, some European houses cheat by printing only the music for Piano I in one score, that for Piano II in the other (like orchestra parts), leaving each pianist to guess what the other is playing and making rehearsals extremely frustrating.

The relative difficulty of the music is rated from the moderately easy (Mod. E.) level of the Moszkowski Spanish Dances, through the progressively more difficult Grieg Norwegian Dances (Mod. Dif.), to Brahms Hungarian Dances (Dif.) and such virtuoso works as Stravinsky's Concerto for Two Solo Pianos (Vir.). Opinions about the music have grown out of the authors' years of listening, playing, teaching, and collecting of scores and records. For a book of this nature, completeness would have been an impossible aim, and apologies are offered for the inevitable omissions. A more important goal has been to make known worthy music that has been overlooked, and to inspire performance of it in the home, the studio and the concert hall.

Frederic Ming Chang

Albert Faurot

xi

TABLE OF ABBREVIATIONS

AD	A. Drago, Magenta, Italy
AF-CPR	A. Faurot, <u>Concert Piano Repertoire</u> (Scarecrow Press, Inc., Metuchen, N.J., 1974)
AFo	A. Forlevesi, Florence
AL	Alfred Legnick & Co., London
ALe	Alphonse Leduc, Paris
AME	American Music Editions, N.Y.
AMI	Affiliated Musicians Inc., Los Angeles
AMP	Associated Music Publishers, N.Y.
An	Anthology
APS	A. P. Schmidt, Boston
Arg	Argentina
Aug	Augener, London
Aus	Austria
Ausl	Australia
AVV	Ars Viva Verlag, Mainz
Ba	Barry, Buenos Aires
B&B	Bote & Bock, Wiesbaden
B&H	Boosey & Hawkes, London, New York
Bar	Barenreiter, Kassel
BB	Broude Bros., N.Y.
Bel	Belgium
Bes	Bessel et Cie, Paris
BM	Belwin, Inc., N.Y. (also Belwin-Mills)
BMC	Boston Music Co., Boston
BMI	Broadcast Music, Inc., Toronto
BMP	Bomart Music Pub., Long Island, N.Y.
Bon	Bongiovanni, F., Bologna, Italy
Bos	Bosworth, London
Br&H	Breitkopf & Haertel, Weisbaden
Bra	Brazil
BSe	B. Senff, Leipzig
BSS	B. Schott Sohne, Mainz (<u>see also</u> SS)
Can	Canada
Car	Carisch, S. P. A., Milan (also A. & G. Carisch)

CBDM	Centre Belge de Documentation Musicale, Brussels
CF	Carl Fischer, N.Y.
CFo	C. Foley, N.Y.
CFP	C. F. Peters, N.Y. (Leipzig)
CFS	Clayton F. Summy, Chicago
Ch	Chappel & Co., N.Y.
Chi	Chile
Cho	Choudens, Paris
col	collection
CPE	Composer/Performer Editions, Davis, Cal.
CPS	C. P. Spehr
CS	Carl Simon, Berlin
Cu	Cuba
Cyp	Cyprus
Czech	Czechoslovakia
D&B	Dubois and Bacon, N.Y.
Den	Denmark
Don	Donemus, Amsterdam
DP	Dover Publications, N.Y.
DR	D. Rahter, Hamburg
Dur	Durand & Co., Paris (also Durand fils, A. Durand, Durand & Cie)
EAM	Editorial Argentina de Música, Buenos Aires
EB	E. Baudoux & Cie, Paris
EBM	E. B. Marks Music Corp., N.Y.
EC	Edizioni Curci, Milan
ECK	E. C. Kirby, Ltd., Toronto
ECo	Editions Costellat, Paris
ECS	E. C. Schirmer, Boston
EFK	E. F. Kalmus Edition, N.Y.
EFM	Editions francais de musique, Paris
Egy	Egypt
EHL	Editions H. Lemoine, Paris
Elk	Elkin & Co., Ltd., London
EL-PD	Ernest Lubin, The Piano Duet (Grossman, N.Y., 1970)
EM	Edition Musica, Budapest
EMM	Editions Mexicanas de Musica, Mexico City
EMS	Editions M. Senard, Paris
EMT	Editions Musique Transatlantique, Paris
EMu	Edition musicus, N.Y.
En	Enoch & Cie, Paris
ES	Edward Schuberth & Co., N.Y.
Est	Estonia
ET	Edition Tonos, Darmstadt
EV	Elkan Vogel, Bryn Mawr, Pa.

FECL	F.E.C. Leuckart, Leipzig
FH	Friederic Hofmeister, Leipzig
Fin	Finland
FK	F. Kistner, Leipzig
Fr	France
FW	F. Whislling, Leipzig
GB	Great Britain
GBil	Gerard Billaudot, Paris
Ger	Germany
GH	G. Heinze, Leipzig
GMC	Galaxy Music Corp., N.Y.
GME	Galliard Music Editions, London
GMP	General Music Publishing Co., N.Y.
GR	G. Ricordi, Milan, N.Y.
Gr	Greece
GS	G. Schirmer, N.Y.
HE	Hinrichsen Edition, London
Hei	Heinrichshofen, Magdeburg
Heu	Heugel & Cie, Paris
HF	Harold Flammer, N.Y.
HM-DP	Hans Moldenhauer, Duo Pianism (Moldenhauer Archives, 1011 Comstock Court, Spokane, Wash., USA, 99203)
HS	H. Sikorski, Hamburg (see also MHS)
Hun	Hungary
HV	Henle Verlag, Geneva
HWG	H. W. Gray, N.Y.
IM	Izd-vo Muzyka, Moscow
IMC	International Music Corp., N.Y.
IMI	Israeli Music Institute, Tel-Aviv
IMP	Independent Music Pub., N.Y.
Isr	Israel
It	Italy
J&WC	J. & W. Chester, London
Jap	Japan
JAV	J. Aibl Verlag
JC	J. Curwen & Sons, London
JCh	John Church, Cincinnati
JF	J. Fischer & Bros., N.Y.
JH	J. Hamelle, Paris
JHai	J. Hainauer, Breslau
JJ	Jean Jobert, Paris
JMC	J. M. Chester, Inc., London
JMRB	J. M. Reiter-Biederman, N.Y.

JSM	Jack Spratt Music Co., Stamford, Conn.
JW	Joseph Weinberger, London
JWi	J. Williams, London
L&K	Lauterbach & Kuhn, Leipzig
LD	Ludwig Dobblinger, Vienna
Lit	Litolff Collections, Frankfurt
LPC	Leeds Publishing Co., N. Y. (Also Leeds Music Corp.)
MaM	Marks Music Corp., N. Y.
MAP	Musical Arts Press, Burbank, Cal.
Math	Mathot, Paris
MCA	Music Corp. of America, N. Y.
MEE	Max Eschig Editions, Paris
MeM	Mercury Music Corp., N. Y.
Mex	Mexico
MH	Musica Hispana, Madrid
MHS	Musikverlag H. Sikorski, Hamburg (see also HS)
MMC	Mills Music Co., N. Y.
MPB	M. P. Belaieff, Leipzig
MPC	Music Publishing Co., N. Y.
MuM	Murdoch, Murdoch & Co., London
MW	Maxwell Weaner (Axelrod), N. Y.
Neth	Netherlands
NM	New Music, N. Y.
Nor	Norway
Nov	Novello & Co., London
NWM	New World Music Co., N. Y.
NZ	New Zealand
OB	O. Bornemann, Paris
OD	Oliver Ditson, Bryn Mawr, Pa.
ONT	Ongaku no Tomo, Tokyo
OP	Out of Print
OxU	Oxford University Press, London
Pan	Panama
PAP	Pro Art Publications, Westbury, N. Y.
PE	Philippo Editions, Paris
PIC	Peer International Corp., N. Y.
PJ	P. Jurgenson, Moscow
Pol	Poland
PR	Puerto Rico
PWM	Polskie Wydannictwo Muzyzne, Warsaw
RA	Ricordi Americana, Buenos Aires

RDR	R. D. Row, Boston
RF	Rob. Forberg, Leipzig
RL	Rouart, Lerolle & Cie
RM	Russischer Musikverlag, Moscow
RoM	Rongwen Music, Inc., N.Y.
Rou	Roumania
Roz	Rozsavolgyi & Cie, Budapest
RSMP	Russian State Music Publications, Moscow
RuS	Russischer Staatsverlag, Moscow
Rus	Russia
S&G	Schroeder and Gunther, N.Y.
SAf	South Africa
Schl	Schlesinger, Berlin
Scho	Schott and Co., Ltd., London
SE	Salabert Editions, Paris
Si	Sirene, Cop. Paris
Sim	Simrock, N., Leipzig
SM	Suddestscher Musikverlag, Heidelberg
SMC	Seesaw Music Corp., N.Y.
SME	Section Musicale des Editions d'etat, Moscow
SMP	Southern Music Publishers, N.Y.
SP	Shawnee Press
Sp	Spain
SS	Schott's Sohne, Mainz (see also BSS)
SV	Steingraber Verlag, Weisbaden
Swe	Sweden
Swi	Switzerland
SZ	Suvini Zerboni, Milan
TBH	T. B. Harms, N.Y.
TP	Theodore Presser, Bryn Mawr, Pa.
TR	Th. Rattig, Vienna
Tur	Turkey
UE	Universal Edition, Vienna, London, New York
UMC	Universal Music Corp., N.Y.
UMCC	Universal Music Co., Chicago
UME	Union Musical Espagnola, Madrid
Ur	Uruguay
Urb	Urbanek & Sons, Prague
USA	United States of America
USSR	Union of Soviet Socialist Republic
Ven	Venezuela
WB	W. Bessel, St. Petersbourg
WH	Whilhlm Hansen, Copenhagen

WMC	Willis Music Co., Cincinnati, Ohio
WmH	Wm Hall, N.Y.
WZ	W. Zimmermann, Frankfurt
Zen	Zenmukiado, Budapest

PART 1

TWO AT ONE

Music for two players
at one piano (known
as four-hand music)

AKIMENKO, FIODOR S.   (Rus-Fr 1876-1945)
    Six pièces ukrainiennes, op. 71 (RL, 1925). Pupil of
Rimsky-Korsakoff, and professor at Petrograd Conservatory,
FSA lived in Paris after the Russian revolution.   These at-
tractive miniatures are diatonic and full of folk flavor.   1.
Dumka; 2. Do Tanzu; 3.   Diznya; 4. Vessilia; 5.   Listopad;
6.   Gretchaniki.   35 pages.   Mod.

ALKAN, CHARLES   (Fr 1813-1888)
    Trois Marches, piano à quatre mains, op. 40 (ECo).
These three marches by the pianist-composer are all in flat
keys and in a driving tempo.   No. 1 and No. 2 are brilliant
and sonorous; No. 3 is rather quiet except for a forte ending.
No. 1 and 3 are only moderately difficult, but No. 2 requires
full virtuosity to play at the marked tempo.   42 pages.

ANDRE, JOHANN ANTON   (Ger 1775-1842)
    Divertimento in A Minor (CFP, 1961).   An amiable
duet of two short movements: Andantino moderato; Allegro
moderato.   13 pages.   Mod.

ARNELL, RICHARD   (GB 1917-)
    Sonatina for Piano, Four Hands, Op. 61 (Scho, 1951).
Active composer of ballet, TV and film scores, whose latest
is a multi-media spectacle called Combat Zone, wrote this
as a ballet score, with four contrasting scenes.   A short
majestic Andante introduces a terpsichorean Allegro, tonal
but mildly dissonant.   Third movement restates opening material enhanced with new figures but retaining the dancer's
firm beat.   Poco presto kicks up its heels with mobile figures against static poses.   Pianistic and effective with or
without Ballanchine.   Mod.

BACH, JOHANN CHRISTIAN   (Ger 1735-1782)
    The youngest of the Bach dynasty settled in London,
where the Mozart children played duets for him in 1765.
This may have inspired him to compose the first extended

3

set of pieces ever written for piano, four hands.

Sonatas for Four Hands (CFP).   Three two-movement
works in an elegant graceful classical style.   The Bach-Mo-
zart influence seems to have been a two-way current, and
these are remarkably like early Mozart, lacking only WAM's
bold dramatic clarity.   Worth exploring.   Mod.

BACH, P. D. Q.   See SCHICKELE, PETER

BACH, WILHELM FRIEDRICH ERNST   (Ger 1759-1845)
          Andante in A Minor (GS).   Chiefly of interest because
it is by a grandson of J. S. , and the last of the line.   It is
a one-movement romance in rococo vein, genial and slightly
sentimental.   Published with the Sonata by W. E. Wolf.
                                                           Mod. E.

BARBER, SAMUEL   (USA 1910-   )
          Souvenirs, Op. 28 (GS, 1954).   The original four-
hand version of what was to become a ballet suite.   Six
dances from pre-WWI, they are meant to be a sentimental
recollection, not a satire.   Very low-key, whether nonsense
or nostalgia, they need instrumentation for color.   20 minutes,
67 pages.   Mod.

          There is an arrangement of this for two pianos by
Gold and Fizdale (GS).

BEETHOVEN, LUDWIG VAN   (Ger 1770-1827)
          This giant of the keyboard left no music for two pi-
anos and only a few duets for four hands, which were mostly
early and immature.   They are all available in one volume
from IMC.

          Sonata in D, Op. 6 (1796-1797) (IMC).   Simple work
of LVB's youth, in two movements, Allegro Molto and Rondo
Moderato.   Mod. E.

          Three Marches, Op. 45 (1802-1803).   From the peri-
od of the Eroica, these echo the bold masculine military
mood.   Best are Nos. 1 and 3.   Mod. Dif.

          Variations.   Two sets of early works, written for
friends or sweethearts, are interesting if not arresting.
Variations on An Air of Count Waldstein (1791-1792) is overextended and innocuous.   The other set, Six Variations on
the Song "Ich denke dein" (1799 and 1803), is to a tune writ-

ten in the album of the Brunswick sisters, under a line of
Goethe verse.   Properly ingenuous and feminine.   Mod.

Grosse Fugue, Op. 134.   Transcription by LVB of the
Finale which he rejected for the B-flat Quartet, Op. 130.
The first impulse was right, and few will care to resurrect
this moribund experiment.   There is a version for two pianos,
arranged by Harold Bauer (see Part 5).   Dif.

BENNETT, RICHARD RODNEY   (GB 1936-   )
Capriccio, Piano Duet (UE, 1968).   Fast-moving, one-
movement atonal work with fortissimo ending, on four simul-
taneous glissandi (two on black keys, two on white, both going
up and down).   23 pages, 11 minutes.   Mod. Dif.

BERKELEY, LENNOX   (GB 1903-   )
Sonatina for Piano Duet (J&WC, 1954).   Modestly titled
Sonatina, this has a full-scale Allegro with development section, an unpretentious but winsome Andante, and a snappy
third movement Allegro, which makes attractive use of mirror imitation, fast scales in fourths, and irregular meters.
20 pages, 7 min. 30 sec.   Mod.

BERNERS, LORD GERALD TYRWHITT   (GB 1883-1950)
Valses Bourgeoises (J&WC).   A modern spoof on the
"noble" waltzes of the nineteenth century, by a nobleman who
was a talented and sophisticated amateur composer.   His sly
dissonances and wry wit won him the soubriquet, the British
Satie.   Three brilliant extended works full of sudden contrasts,
alternating ardor and languor.   Written without key signature,
they make much use of bitonality and polytonality for a wrong-
note humorous effect.   The third is called "Strauss, Strauss
et Strauss. "   Dif.

BIZET, GEORGES   (Fr 1838-1875)
Jeux d'enfants, Op. 22 (IMC).   This staple of the duet
repertoire by the composer of Carmen stems from Schumann's
music about childhood, and paves the way for a spate of
French albums on the subject.   The twelve duets are spirited
and boisterous, as befits children's games, with gentler movements for the "Wedding" and "Doll's Lullaby. "   They are di-
versified by inventive use of trills, scales, and accompaniment chords.   Requires drive and a good finger technic.   Not
for infants.   Mod.

BORODIN, ALEXANDER   (Rus 1833-1887)
Polka; Tarantelle (LPC).   The nationalist revival of

"The Mighty Heap" did not touch these duets. The Polka is the traditional nineteenth-century up-down dance; the Tarantelle a long concert work requiring good technic and fire to reify.   Mod.

BRAHMS, JOHANNES (Ger 1833-1897)
   Variations on a Theme by Schumann, Op. 23 (IMC). This superb duet adumbrates much that is to come in the great solo and two-piano variation sets (the Handel, Op. 24, was written immediately after this), yet it is a fully realized work. The simple serene theme could have been from Schumann's youth, instead of his last sad days. The nine transformations retain the binary form and the basic harmony, but only vestiges of the tune, adding flowing counter-subjects, pianistic figures and accompaniments, piquant rhythmic motifs, all fresh and amiable. The closing variation is in JB's favorite energico mood, rapid octave scales on the pick-up beats, which have the panache of an actor's gestures. Should be rescued from oblivion. 15 minutes.   Mod. Dif.

   Waltzes, Op. 39 (Sim, EFK, GS, CFP). This North German fell under the spell of the Viennese waltz, and used it frequently to lighten the profundity of his natural style. The sixteen dances in this set were arranged by him for solo piano, but need the brilliance and scope of the original four-hand setting. The linked set has a key cycle mostly in the upper sharp keys, major and minor; only three waltzes are in flat keys. Though secondo parts play mostly the oom-papa figure of the dance band, they have great harmonic variety, subtle rhythmic variations and occasional counter-melodies. The sentimental and playful moods give way to more vigor and excitement from No. 13 on, with possible Magyar influences. JB arranged five of these (Nos. 1, 2, 11, 14, 15) for two pianos (CFP).   Mod. Dif.

   Liebeslieder Waltzes, Op. 52 (Sim, EFK, CFP). This set of eighteen is even more sparkling and exuberant, made unique by the addition of a quartet of singers to the team, singing romantic verses by Daumer. Moods of tenderness and passion, of despondency and yearning, of teasing and scolding alternate. The piano writing is brilliant and complex, but the music is incomplete without the vocal quartet, though JB wrote a version for piano only, and Guy Maier arranged twelve for two pianos (JF).   Dif.

   Neue Liebeslieder, Op. 65 (EFK, CFP). This uses leftover matter from the first set, in fourteen more waltzes

and an Epilogue in 9/4 to a poem by Goethe.   Several are
for solo voice and are almost operatic; others treat the vocal
quartet in a polyphonic manner, though never losing the waltz
lilt.   The Epilogue is a set of variations on a ground bass,
with central passages of rich polyphony.   Though as fine as
the first set, these are darker and less popular in appeal.
                                                                    Dif.

          Twenty-one Hungarian Dances (GS, HV, CFP).   Some
good four-hand music here, if one is not bothered by the fact
that they are not Hungarian but arrangements of Gypsy music;
or by the overfamiliarity of the few constantly murdered on
Muzak in arrangements for saxophone, organ, harmonica, et
cetera.   The best are the original ones in the third and
fourth books: Nos. 11, 14, 15, 17.   All have a driving
verve alternating with passages of melting languor, requiring
subtle rubato and nuance.   Mod.

BRAITHWAITE, SAM HARTLEY   (GB 1883-1947)
          Pastorale (Aug, 1937).   An academic work by an Acad-
emician of the Royal Academy of Music, London.   Well-
wrought and meticulously annotated, using fanfares and themes
derived from them.   Marked Frescamente, it is rather stale.
9 pages.   Mod.

BRUCH, MAX   (Ger 1838-1920)
          Swedish Dances, Op. 63 (Sim).   Rare piano music
from a great violinist, these fifteen duets, in two books, are
pianistic in a traditional nineteenth-century way, uninspired
but competent.   Each book is linked like a chain of waltzes.
                                                                    Mod.

BRUCKNER, ANTON   (Aus 1824-1896)
          Quadrille (1854) (Hei, 1944).   Rare keyboard work by
the symphonist who was a rival of Brahms.   The three parts
are all in ternary form with a trio, contrasting legato flowing figures, expressive chordal writing and staccato passages.
                                                                    Mod.

BURNEY, CHARLES   (GB 1726-1814)
          Sonatas for Two Performers upon One Instrument.
(Sonata in F, Scho; Sonata in E-flat, TP).   This musical
Baedeker, the Lowell Thomas of eighteenth-century music,
is to be thanked for the pen portraits of great musicians
whom he sought out in his travels.   Hearing the Mozart
Geschwestern play duets in London inspired him to try his
hand.   He claims (incorrectly) that his Sonatas are the first

duets ever to be printed, and writes an amusing Apologia to
introduce them (CB's prose is superior to his music). His
famous daughter Fanny wrote of "Duet concerts a la mode"
and of "Duets a quatre mains" which the family enjoyed on
the new six-octave pianoforte which CB had ordered built.
Only two are now in print, but they are enough to show us
that CB solved the problems of four-hand playing neatly, but
had little musical inventiveness or incisiveness. Repetitious,
plodding and pedestrian.   Mod. E.

BUSONI, FERRUCCIO (It 1866-1924)
       Two Finnish Dances (CFP). There is more of FB,
the keyboard giant, than of ethnic dance in these ponderous,
lugubrious numbers. The mood evoked is that of the Land
of the Midnight Sun at noon in winter.   Dif.

CARLTON, NICHOLAS (GB 15??-1630)
       A Verse, for Two to Play on One Virginal or Organ
(Scho). This, with the companion piece, A Fancy by Thomas
Tomkins, is undoubtedly the oldest duet music extant. In
fact it is the only four-hand music to survive from the harp-
sichord age, when the short keyboard discouraged team work.
(See the contemporary Farnaby, under Two at Two.)

       Autographs of the two duets are preserved in a music
manuscript book of Tomkins' now in the British museum.
They were published together by Schott in 1949 as Two Eliza-
bethan Keyboard Duets. Tomkins was a noted organist and
madrigalist, best known of a large family of composers.
Carlton was listed among the children at the St. Paul Cathe-
dral foundling home. At the end of his short life he named
as executor of his will (the most valuable legacy of which
have been this duet), Thomas Tomkins of Worcester, "my
singular and esteemed good friend." The two duets may well
have been a unique tribute to their friendship.

       Tomkins' is the better piece. Called A Fancy, it is
an English form of Ricercare, more choral than instrumental
in texture. It moves in grave stately steps, Secondo answer-
ing Primo in canonic imitation, then the two players and
four hands doubling in passages of parallel thirds, with frequent 6/4 chords, modulating smoothly from A minor to d,
g, C and A. The Carlton Verse, based on a plainsong chant,
is similar but less clear-cut. They convey a faint but delicate fragrance of a bygone age.

       This version was edited by Frank Dawes and differs

slightly from the original, which was reprinted in "The Earliest Keyboard Duets" by Hugh M. Miller, in Musical Quarterly, October, 1943.   Mod. E.

CASELLA, ALFREDO (It 1883-1947)
Pupazzetti (GR, 1916, reprinted 1973).   AC suggests either one or two pianos, but it can all be comfortably played at one keyboard. His subtitle, "5 Pezzi Facili," is misleading, as the pieces demand mature musicianship and a hand span of a ninth. Little March, Berceuse, Serenade, Little Nocturne and Polka are the conventional titles of the highly original pieces, iridescent in harmony, rich in touch and dynamic contrasts. 19 pages.   Mod.

CHABRIER, EMMANUEL (Fr 1841-1894)
Souvenir de Munich (ECo, AMP). Composer of innocuous salon music, after a visit to the Wagner theatre at Munich, Chabrier let off steam by fitting the lush music of Tristan's love-death into the strait jacket of a quadrille. This must have been sidesplitting for the ardent Wagnerites; today's youth will be more amused by the inane, frenetic galloping that passed for duet-making among our grandfolks.
                                                              Mod.

CHOPIN, FREDERIC (Pol-Fr 1810-1849)
Variations sur un air national de Moore (PWM, 1965; EBM). A recently discovered set from FC's sixteenth year, this must take its place beside the Op. 2 and Op. 12 sets of solo variations as a historical record of the unpromising first steps of one who was to become the greatest master of his instrument. The theme is the familiar Carnival in Venice, which FC mistakenly attributed to Moore. Pianistic and showy, with dashing scales in 64th notes, a passing-note variation in parallel sixths, a funeral march, it is harmonically and melodically drab. 20 pages.   Mod.

CLEMENTI, MUZIO (It-GB 1752-1832)
Seven Sonatas (Br&H). Pianists still addicted to the Sonatinas and the Steps to Parnassus may wish to try these. More difficult than the Sonatinas, they are well crafted and entirely predictable.   Mod.

CUNDICK, ROBERT
Prelude & Fugue (CF, 1973). Attractive new duet combining tradition and innovation. The one-page Prelude is modal, in 3/4 with measures of 5/4, and has an archaic flavor. It returns in Secondo for the coda, under the fugue

theme. The four-voice fugue, two for each player, is neatly
set forth in running staccato figures, with an added imaginative legato countersubject.   Mod.

DEBUSSY, CLAUDE   (Fr 1862-1918)
    Petite Suite (Dur, GS, IMC).   This set of four num-
bers, modestly called "small," is very viable duet music,
though early CD.   The opening Andantino, called "In a Boat,"
gives Secondo a flowing undulating figure while Primo plays
the melody in single notes, parallel thirds or trumpet triads.
The Cortège depicts an outdoor processional, festive and
joyous, full of fanfares and racing thirds.   The Menuet has
a stately antique dance tune, almost buried in a busyness of
notes.   The closing Ballet is a bumptious 2/4 dance tune,
which must be played very fast and rhythmically, framing an
insouciant valse.   Mod.

    Six Epigraphes antiques (Dur).   Though not on a par
with CD's finest solo music, these must rank high among
modern four-hand works.   The six are well laid out, and
show little trace of their improvised origin, as background
music for a reading of the Chanson de Bilitis.   No. I is
called "To invoke Pan, god of the summer wind," and is in
the bucolic mood of Preludes No. 8, Book I and No. 5, Book
II.   The modal writing is effectively "antique." II, "For a
nameless tomb," is to be played slow and sad, and is written
entirely on the whole-tone scale, with a wailing tritone figure.
III, "That the night be propitious," spreads many layers of
independent parts, blending them for a mesmeric incantatory
sound.   IV is a more rhythmic, staccato dance movement
largely on white keys, "For the dancing girl with crotales"
(ancient Assyrian shell-cymbals).   V, "For the Egyptian,"
returns to the spirit world with a syncopated pedal bass under
ululations and melismas.   VI is the best of the set, "Thanks-
giving for morning rain."   A delightfully varied rain-drop
figure is shared by the players with melody sometimes above,
sometimes below, and a return to the Pan theme for a fade-
out.   Mod. D.

    Marche ecossaise (JJ).   Few potboilers have risen to
the level of this superb duet, commissioned (through a trans-
lator) by the Earl of Ross, whose Scots clan song is heard
throughout, imaginatively accompanied by skirling trills, bagpipe drones, modal harmony, building to an exciting acme,
all well-deployed for two players.   Deserves to be played and
heard.   Mod.

Ballade (JJ).   The composer's arrangement of an early
solo work, originally titled Ballade Slav, which gives a clue
as to influences.   Vapid and derivative with no adumbrations
of the great innovations to come.   Mod.

Cortège et air de dance, from L'enfant prodique (OP).
Recently recorded in an album of the complete duet music of
CD and Ravel, this excerpt from the Prix de Rome cantata
is not without charm.   Mod.

DEL TREDICI, DAVID   (USA 1937-)
Scherzo for Piano, Four Hands (1960) (B&H).   Written
by the composer-pianist on a Naumburg Foundation award
commission, this is a brilliant one-movement duet.   DDT
uses a modified dodecaphonic texture in a complex pattern of
polyrhythms.   The three-part piece frames a slow expressive
core with two scintillating and propulsive movements.   6
minutes.   Recorded recently by the composer and Robert
Helps (see part 6).   Dif.

DEMUTH, NORMAN   (GB 1898-1968)
Sonatina (1954) (MMC, 1956).   English authority on
modern French music wrote an attractive three-movement
sonata in a neo-classic French style.   The transparent linear
writing of the Allegretto has a melody in octaves over broken
chords, the players reversing the parts for the recapitulation.
The two-page Andante tranquillo has an archaic folkloric
sound, with freely altered scale tones in a D major tonality.
The Con brio is a peasant dance, alfresco, bouncing and
genial. 14 pages.   Mod. E.

DIERCKS, JOHN   (USA 1927-)
Suite No. 1 (MCA, 1972).   A simple but playable work
in four movements, March, Dance, Song, Finale.   The writing is tonal throughout; the one-page Song has a modal quality.
The spirited Finale, to be played "Fast and joyously," has
echoes of Kabalevsky.   Mod. E.

DONIZETTI, GAETANO   (It 1797-1848)
Sonatas (ECK).   This contemporary of Schubert's became known for his sparkling operas, more than a hundred
of which were produced during his short lifetime.   These
early works are all in one movement, and lean on Weber,
the Bach boys and the early Vienna masters, though the form
is more often Scarlatti's binary movement.   They have the
melodic grace of opera arias, but the harmony and keyboard
figuration are thin and pale.   Best are the bumptious Presto

movements, as euphonic as a comic opera overture, if the
players egg each other on to top speed.   Four have been
edited by Douglas Townsend and published by E. C. Kerby,
Ltd. , of Toronto, available through Joseph Boonin, Inc.
                                                    Mod. Dif.
        Tre pezzi per pianoforte a 4 mani (GR, 1971).

DUREY, LOUIS (Fr 1888-)
        Two Pieces, Op. 7 (SE).   Early work by this veteran
composer.   The style is romantic-impressionist, with traditional keyboard figures.   The pieces are picturesque and expressive, though overextended.   Carillons requires large
hand span for the bell effects; Niege, technical control for
a delicate, atmospheric effect.   Mod.

DUSSEK, JOHANN LUDWIG (JAN LADISLAUS) (Czech 1760-
1812)
        Sonata in C, Op. 43 (Heu).   Prolific keyboard com-
poser, overshadowed by his great contemporaries, wrote sixteen works for duet, of which this brilliant facile work is
representative.   Other easier Sonatas were intended for instruction.   Mod.

DVOŘAK, ANTONIN (Czech 1841-1904)
        Legends, Op. 59 (Sim).   Among the choicest of the
four-hand sets, these ten pieces in two books combine the
best elements of nineteenth-century romanticism: narrative
and emotional power, folk and national flavor, and a rich
keyboard idiom.   Melodic and rhythmic motifs are shared by
the two players and balanced by imaginative counterparts.
Each piece is a well-shaped unit, with numerous key and
tempo changes suggesting the elements of legend without re-
course to titles.   Separate pieces from Book I make good
program numbers.   Book II is even more inspired and has
an orchestral quality.   The entire book can be played as a
suite.   Mod.

        Slavonic Dances, Op. 46, Op. 72 (Sim, GS, etc.).
Two sets of eight dances each, familiar through AD's own
orchestra transcription, were originally four-hand music.
They are eminently playable, and any for whom the music is
still fresh will enjoy them.   They range from the bucolic to
the furious, the graceful to the bumptious.   Besides the
numerous time shifts a subtle rubato is needed to give them
an authentic Czech flavor.   Mod.

        From the Bohemian Forest, Op. 68 (Sim).   A later

set of six extended duets with programmatic titles.   More
complex and less inspired than the dances or legends.
                                                          Mod. Dif.

ELLIOTT, ROBERT
      Fantaisie sur un motif de sarabande, Op. 3 (Nov,
1957).   Short slow piece with a wistful melody in E minor
with frequently altered scale tones, harmonized with parallel
triads.   Well laid out on the keyboard.   4 pages.   Mod. E.

FAURE, GABRIEL   (Fr 1845-1924)
      Dolly, Op. 56 (IMC).   The fortunate dedicatee of this
demure suite was Debussy's stepdaughter, the "Little Cab-
bage-Head" of his Children's Corner.   Both works are for
children to hear, not to play, though GF makes only modest
technical demands.   Musically the pieces are subtle and evocative and richly varied, and call for a sensitive touch and
dynamic control.   Like so many of the best four-hand music,
this has been transcribed for orchestra by a well-meaning
admirer.   Mod.

FELDMAN, MORTON   (USA 1926-   )
      Piano Four Hands (CFP, 1962).   See Two at Two.

FERNANDEZ, OSCAR L.   (Bra 1897-1948)
      The Fantastic Horseman (PIC, 1945).   Short recital
piece in the nineteenth-century genre style, diatonic and
triadic with few surprises.   5 pages.   Mod. E.

FERROUD, PIERRE OCTAVE   (Fr 1900-1936)
      Serenade (Dur, 1927).   Short-lived composer who an-
ticipated Poulenc with his blend of popular and neo-classical.
This three-part suite contrasts a linear contrapuntal Berceuse
with an expressive Pavane and a lively, jazzy Spiritual.
                                                              Mod.

FLOTHUIS, MARIUS   (Neth 1914-   )
      Valses Nobles, Op. 52 (Don, 1954).   Useful set of six
valses with coda, from an eminent Dutch composer who writes
in a neo-romantic style.   21 pages.   Mod. E.

FRICKER, PETER RACINE   (GB 1920-   )
      Nocturne and Scherzo, Op. 23 (Scho, 1958; AMP).
Extended work for two musically mature players, in two
movements.   The Nocturne creates and sustains an air of
mystery with rocking couplet figures later urged into triplets
and sixteenths under and around a chromatically ambiguous

chorale. The Scherzo is less successful in evoking a mood,
though it generates excitement with its vivace 5/8 rhythm,
its scurrying linear figures, its climactic build up.   10
minutes.   Mod. Dif.

FRID, GEZA (Hun-Neth 1904-)
     Kermesse à Charleroi (SMP, 1964). Fairs and carni-
vals make popular duet subjects, with four busy hands to suggest constant colorful activity. This has little content, but
the repeated motor figures and fanfares are well employed to
compose an effective and brilliant program number.   19
pages.   Mod.

GILBERT, HENRY FRANKLIN (USA 1868-1928)
     Three American Dances (BMC, 1919). Contemporary
of MacDowell, HFG lacked an individual style, but employed
jazz, Afro-American rhythms and folk material. These are
called Ragtime Dances, and the composer indicates that they
are to be played with nonchalant grace and in moderate time.
The first is called Uncle Remus and is bold and driving, with
a climax. Delphine is light and playful. Brer Rabbit contrasts three moods.   Mod. Dif.

GLINKA, MIKHAIL (Rus 1804-1857)
     Capriccio sur des themes russes (LPC). More valu-
able as historical document than as music, this is among the
earliest concert pieces to use ethnic material. Three Russian
tunes developed in a rather opaque manner. Several other
duets are included in the album published by Leeds. Mod. E.

GODOWSKY, LEOPOLD (Rus-USA 1870-1938)
     Miniatures (CF). LG's dual career as a pianist and
pedagogue combined to produce works like these four books
of duets for teacher and pupil. Carefully crafted, the pupil's
part is simple but interesting, while the teacher's is varied
and imaginative.   E. and Dif.

GRAINGER, PERCY ALDRIDGE (Ausl-USA 1882-1961)
     Harvest Hymn, Piano Duet (GS, 1940). "The root-
form of this tone-work is for Elastic Scoring (2 instruments
up to massed orchestra, with or without voice or voices),
all other versions (piano duet, piano solo, and so on) are off-
shoots from the root-form. " 5 pages.   Mod.

     Let's Dance Gay in Green Meadow; 'Neath the Mould
Shall Never Dancer's Tread Go' (GS, 1967). Faeroe Island
Dance-Folksong, collected by Hjalman Thuren, set for piano,

four hands by Percy Grainger.   9 pages.   Mod.

See also Two at Two.

GRIEG, EDVARD   (Nor 1843-1907)
     Four Norwegian Dances, Op. 35 (CFP).   One of the
first to use ethnic material in concert music, EG captured in
his four-hand music the essence of the spirited country dance
band: an old fiddler, an accordion and percussion.   Though
all four are in a driving duple meter, there are quieter trios,
and a subtle rubato is needed.   The seventh and ninth chords
that were so striking in the Concerto appear, and chromaticism lends a lyric note.   Still fresh and folksy, in spite of
the orchestral transcriptions that have made them hackneyed.
A later set of duet dances, Op. 64, suffered the same fate,
and is known today only under the title "Symphonic Dances."
                                                             Mod.

     Valses-caprices, Op. 37 (CFP).   The subtle, delicate
originality of EG's harmony and ornamentation raises these
two above the mediocrity of nineteenth-century parlor music.
                                                             Mod.

HAUER, JOSEF MATTHIAS   (Aus 1883-1959)
     Labyrinthischer Tanz (1952) (UE, 1953).   Late work
by the theoretician who challenged Schoenberg as inventor of
dodecaphony.   Not serial and frequently tonal, the duet makes
use of the four-hand idiom to weave a labyrinth of themes.
Actually, however, only four short motifs are introduced
through the work, which is written in an unchanging 3/4 beat,
and limited to the middle octaves of the keyboard.   Without
dynamic variation or contrasting section, the music palls
long before the seven dense pages are finished.   The best
contribution of the moribund work is the device used at the
end of each page, of a cue for each player, in small type,
of what is to come on the next page, a practice recommended
to all duet writers.   11 pages, 5 minutes.   Mod.

HAYDN, FRANZ JOSEPH   (Aus 1732-1809)
     Il Maestro e lo scolare (BSS).   The first composer
to write extensively for piano, FJH has left a duet that is a
classic to be found in most anthologies and collections of
four-hand music.   A set of seven simple variations on a ten-
measure Andantino, the "master" leads off in the treble, to
be imitated exactly by the "scholar" an octave lower.   Variations are all ornamental or rhythmic, the melody being sub-
divided into triplets, 16ths, 32nds, expanded into scale and

arpeggio figures.   Arranged for two pianos by G. Maier.
                                                                    E. to Mod.

Partita for Four Hands (GS, Col).   Recently published
for the first time, in the GS anthology, a two-movement duet
in the manner of the early sonatas.   Mod. E.

HEIDEN, BERNHARD   (Ger-USA 1910-)
Sonata for Piano, Four Hands (1946) (AMP, 1953).   I.
Allegro moderato; II. Ostinato, very fast; III. Fantasia -
Variations, begins very slowly, but ends Vivace (15/8) with
four hands playing same notes at different octaves in rapid
tempo.   Dissonant but tonal.   Well-crafted and euphonious.
Presently on the faculty of Indiana University, BH spent his
early years in Germany where he studied with Hindemith at
the Berlin Hochschule.   43 pages.   Mod. Dif.

HELPS, ROBERT   (USA 1928-)
Saccade (CFP, 1969).   A non-serial work that seems
to aspire to the ambiguous sound of serial music by assidu-
ously avoiding any tonal gravitation and employing only sevenths, fourths and seconds.   An opening chordal melody of
four measures is boldly articulated, first in Primo, then in
Secondo, and later overlaid with complex but comfortable keyboard figures derived from the same chords.   The arcane
title, nowhere explained, will puzzle most pianists, though a
violinist might know it as a term meaning "sharply accented,"
and borrowed from an equestrian direction to "jerk" the horse
to a stop.   The chords are all heavily accented (with inverted
V and written acciaccatura), thus creating a "jerked" sound
with the Second piano played on the beat.   A single movement without tempo changes; accelerandos and crescendos out-
line the form which mounts to a powerful acme, then sub-
sides.   15 pages, 7 1/2 minutes.   Dif.

HILLER, FERDINAND   (Ger 1811-1885)
Operette ohne Text, Op. 106 (Aug).   Forgotten opera
composer has a unique operetta for piano, four hands, which
tells its own story in a series of duets in the standard opera
forms: Overture, Maiden's Prayer, Hunter's Chorus, Hero's
Romanza, Duet, Drinking Song, Women's Chorus, Ballet and
Grand Finale.   Amusing and imaginative parody in traditional
nineteenth-century romantic style.   Mod.

HINDEMITH, PAUL   (Ger-USA 1895-1963)
Sonata for Piano, Four Hands (1938) (ES).   Three-
movement neo-classic sonata, "weighty and earnest" (see last

movement) as are all of PH's works, eschewing all show
and sedulously avoiding the familiar and the predictable.
First movement flows in steady 3/4 quarters and eighths with
a dotted mazurka motif for second theme. Running triplets
and sixteenths form a development with the two players ex-
changing parts. Second movement is a lively 2/2, pitting
staccato against legato, with measures of 3/2 and 5/4 for
surprise. Dynamics range from ff to ppp "without the shov-
er" as the Germans so aptly term the soft pedal. Though
the tempo of the third movement is Adagio, it is marked
"quietly moving" and has a restless wailing quality to the
themes. A severe lurching dotted figure in Secondo is soft-
ened by a rapid weaving line high in the treble. A section
in compound rhythm, "fast but always earnest and important,"
plays chord trills against meandering lines. The reprise
ends, as does the first movement, with one of PH's melting
resolutions to an E major chord, a modern use of the tierce
de Picardie that brightens so many a minor-key prelude or
fugue of Bach's. The difficulties are musical and rhythmical,
and are considerable.   Dif.

HUMMEL, JOHANN NEPOMUK (Aus 1778-1837)
        Sonata in E-flat, Op. 51 (CFP). Contemporary and
rival of Beethoven now largely forgotten. This three-movement divertissement opens with a plodding March, follows
with a lightweight Andante and an over-extended Rondo con
brio.   Mod.

        Grande Sonata in A-flat, Op. 92 (CFP). From the
pen of a virtuoso pianist this is a show piece for two players. Pompous introduction followed by long brilliant Allegro,
dancey Andante with showy trio, monotonous and intermin-
able Rondo. If you two happen to have two friends who play
horns, there is another duet with horn obligato, in the form
of a Nocturne, with variations, Op. 91.   Mod. Dif.

HUSA, KAREL (Czech-US 1921-)
        Eight Czech Duets (SS, 1958). Orchestra and chamber
music composer and Pulitzer Prize winner has written a set
of duets simple enough for gifted children, but vivid enough
for program items. The style owes as much to Kodály's
piano pieces as to Bartók. An Elegie on the song, "Waters
ripple and flow" (No. 5), in parlando style, heightens the
bold bumptious vigor of the Slovak Dance and Little Scherzo.
36 pages.   E. to Mod.

JOHNSTON, BENJAMIN (USA 1926-)

Knocking Piece, for Piano Interior (2 Players) (CPE,
1967). "For two percussionists to play on the inside of a
grand piano. The sustaining pedal can and should be used,
ad lib. Pitch should be used only as color, if at all.
Typical piano sound should be avoided..."--composer's
note. 6 pages in portfolio. A piano piece for non-
pianists.

JONGEN, JOSEPH (Bel 1873-1953)
Jeux d'enfants, Op. 120 (1941) (CB, 1966). Prolific
Belgian composer, director of Brussels Conservatory. A
work for students in the nineteenth-century French tradition.
Two Andantes flank a lively dance. Facsimile score. 25
pages, 11 minutes.   Mod. E.

Cocass March, Petite Berceuse et Divertissement, op.
129 (CBDM, 1965). The first two pieces were written in 1945
(9 and 6 pages); the Divertissement in 1950 (10 pages).
Rhythmic and appealing pieces of moderate difficulty.

JUON, PAUL (Rus-Ger 1872-1940)
Tanzrythmen, Op. 14, 24, 41 (Schl). This distinguished Berlin professor has left seven books of duets, all
exploring various dance rhythms, more scholarly than imaginative. Some rhythmic experiments parallel the folk dances
used by Bartók, and the mathematical formulae of Boris
Blacher. Not easy.   Mod. to Dif.

KASEMETS, UDO (Est-Can 1919-)
Squares (BMI, 1969). "Each of the 30 squares has to
be played once, the individual player deciding the order of
their appearance." 2 pages.

KOECHLIN, CHARLES (Fr 1867-1950)
Quatres Sonatines Françaises (OxU). Once famous
writer, lecturer and composer, now seldom heard. The four
neo-classical works are French in their lucid, diaphonous
linear quality, mildly modern in idiom.   Mod.

KOHN, KARL (Aus-USA 1926-)
Recreations (1968) (CF, 1973). No doubt this busy
composer found writing these a pleasant recreation from his
heavy chamber music. For two serially oriented players the
text of the four pieces is not difficult reading, though it requires computer-like counting to reassemble its fractured
figures. The hearer may find them more in the nature of
Interferences or Interruptions than Recreations, with their

sedulous avoidance of consonance, cadence and memorable
melodic line.   23 pages, 15 1/2 minutes.   Mod.

A well-written duet suite for children by KK, called
Castles and Kings (CF, 1965), would be a good introduction to
non-tonal music.

KRIEGER, EDINO   (Bra 1928-   )
Sonata (PIC).   Second generation Brazilian composer
who has deserted dodecaphony for neo-classic writing with
ethnic flavor.   In one movement (eight minutes), the duet is
winsome and refreshing, though the harmony is largely traditional and triadic and the piano figuration conventional.   Well
deployed, the dialogue is carried out in fluent passages that
build to cumulative and opulent climaxes.   Mod.

LAMBERT, CONSTANT   (GB 1905-1951)
Trois pièces nègres (1949) (OxU, 1950).   Important set by the short-lived conductor and composer of ballets.
Both the whimsical humor and the harmonic idiom suggest
Satie.   The three "Black Pieces, for the White Keys" use jazz
or Latin rhythms, for an Aubade, Siesta, and Nocturne.
The chords and melodies are fresh and imaginative and remarkably varied, considering the restriction.   Only briefly
in the Nocturne is a standard tonic-dominant bass used, where
it has the effect of a pedal point; more often the melody is
in parallel major sevenths, the chords built on seconds,
fourths, ninths, elevenths, or thirteenths.   8 minutes. Mod.

LA MONTAINE, JOHN   (USA 1920-   )
Sonata, Op. 25 (EV, 1967).   Three-movement work
modeled after Hindemith's sonatas for four hands and two
pianos.   Weighty Preamble; bright Scherzo harmonically ambiguous and meandering; scholarly Fugue.   Musically demanding.   27 pages, 8 minutes.   Dif.

LANZA, ALCIDES   (Arg 1929-   )
Plectros (1962-II) for One or Two Pianos.   See Two
at Two.

LYBBERT, DONALD   (USA 1923-   )
Movement (CFP, 1967).   A well-intentioned five-minute
Allegro intrepido, with a brief Lento deciso passage.   The
keyboard figures, tremolos on ninths, two-hand chord trills,
parallel sixths, are effective at first but become monotonous
as they run on and on.   Mod. Dif.

MacDOWELL, EDWARD   (USA 1861-1908)
     Three Poems, Op. 20 (GS). Two sets of four-hand
pieces (both out-of-print) belong to MacDowell's early period,
before he developed a personal idiom.   All have picturesque
or literary titles and are in a late romantic style.   Night by
the Sea, A Tale from Knightly Times, Ballade are the three
poems.   Mod. Dif.

     Lunar Pictures, Op. 21 (JHai).   Five more genre
pieces with titles from Hans Christian Andersen's "Picture
Book Without Pictures": The Hindu Maiden (Larghetto), Story
of the Stork (Allegretto giocoso), In the Tyrol (Moderato
placido), The Swan (Andantino calmato), Visit of the Bears
(Allegretto semplice).   Mod. to Mod. Dif.

MASON, DANIEL GREGORY   (USA 1873-1953)
     Birthday Waltzes, Op. 2 (BMC).   Musicologist and
educator who occasionally wrote piano pieces in a nineteenth-
century style.   This cheerful set has echoes of Grieg and
Brahms.   Mod.

MASSEUS, JAN   (Neth 1913-   )
     Zoological Impressions, Op. 24 (1954) (Don, CFP,
1954).   Suite of six pieces modeled after Saint-Saëns' Carnival in form, but impressionistic in texture.   Aquarium uses
a watery wash of broken chords around a floating melody
largely based on ninth chords.   A slow dotted rhythm suggests Sea Anemones.   The Camel moves on plodding bass
fifths.   Chameleon shifts from a Tango to a Scherzo to
Vivace and Molto tranquillo.   De Slang is one of the animals,
Misterioso, in jazz blues.   Apes closes the cycle.   Well written with rather common-place material.   Facsimile score.
23 pages, 11 minutes.   Mod.

MENDELSSOHN, FELIX   (Ger 1809-1847)
     Allegro Brillante, Op. 92 (IMC).   This single duet by
Mendelssohn combines his fairy music style, his scherzo
style, and his concert performer style.   Requires full technic for velocity, staccato and brilliant coda ending.   Dif.

     There is a four-hand transcription of a set of solo
variations (Op. 83a), lengthy and difficult.

MOSCHELES, IGNAZ   (Czech-Ger-GB 1794-1870)
     La Belle Union, Op. 76; Grand Duo, Op. 102; Sonate
Symphonique, Op. 112 (OP).   The current fad for forgotten
nineteenth-century music may see reprinted some of these

flashy, shallow duets by the teacher of Mendelssohn and rival of Chopin. The reason for their neglect is evident in
their rhetorical and dreary redundancy.   Mod. Dif.

MOSS, LAWRENCE (US 1927-)
        Omaggio (EV, 1967). Avant-garde duet in "spatial
notation," with single-note patterns of sevenths, ninths, seconds, sprinkled with trills, glissandi, mashed-note tremolandi,
sputtering from ppp to fff. Written entirely in 32nd notes
"as fast as possible," it should be over in three, four, or
five minutes. The duettists take turns standing at the side of
the piano, tickling the insides (a second copy of the music
must be bought for this person, though he needn't be a pianist, if he has good fingernails, and is handy with a spoon).
The homage is to Mozart, though few players or hearers will
be able to identify the quotes from the four-hand Sonata in
B-flat, or the even more arcane series of key signatures
from the first six quartets. The effect of the brief piece is
atmospheric, lacey and delicate, and more akin to the Impressionists than to the classic master. 10 pages.   Vir.

MOSZKOWSKI, MORITZ (Ger-Fr 1854-1925)
        Spanish Dances, Op. 12 (GS, BM, etc.). Generations
of duettists have cut their collective teeth on this set of
Spanish dances by the German with the Russian name who
lived in Paris. They remain hardy and delectable for future
youth. Though easy, they have authentic Hispanic rhythms,
both the fiery and the languorous. A second set, New Spanish Dances, Op. 65, is somewhat less original.
                                                E. to Mod. E.

        From Foreign Lands (GS). Another lightweight suite,
good for teaching.   E. to Mod.

MOZART, WOLFGANG AMADEUS (Aus 1756-1791)
        The precocious talent of both WAM and his sister
Nannerl, two years older, led to the early discovery of the
joys of duet playing, and to the production of much fine four-
hand and two-piano music.

        Sonata in C, K. 19d (OxU, HV). Only recently dis-
covered, this work of the nine-year-old WAM for the London
tour is remarkably good, though better on the two-manual
harpsichord or on two pianos, because of overlapping parts.
Three movements, Allegro, Menuetto and trio, and Rondo
allegretto, of which the best is the second. In the last,
WAM has already discovered the game of sneaking in the re-

frain, and startling the audience with new themes.
                                            E. to Mod. E.

Sonata in D, K. 381 (GS, HV, CFP). Written by the
sixteen-year-old in his Salzburg home, this bears traces of
the Italian visit. Lightweight and entertaining, it is very
playable, with neat exchanges between players.   Mod. E.

Sonata in B-flat, K. 358 (GS, HV, CFP). Two years
later the Geschwestern Mozart are working out the frustra-
tions of their monastic life in ever more exciting keyboard
antics. The first movement is only a Sonatina allegro, with
an eleven-measure development, but it is balanced by an extended coda, inventive and attractive. The Adagio demands
a slow tempo for its expressive complexities, and the closing
Molto presto must be dashed off in a spirit of rivalry, the
two players egging each other on.   Mod. Dif.

Sonata in F, K. 497 (GS, CFP, HV). This is mature
Mozart, ranking with the greatest of his keyboard works, for
its soulful introductory Adagio, and brilliant extended Allegro
di molto. As in the solo sonatas, the second repeat is
usually ignored. The Andante has three disparate themes,
richly developed across the keyboard. The delightful Rondo
has an elusive form, an eleven-measure ritornello, five +
six, gleefully interrupting three other bold themes. It should
have the climactic feeling of the vocal sextets that cap each
act of the operas being written at this time--Figaro and Don
Giovanni. A fine program number. 27 minutes.   Dif.

Sonata in C, K. 521 (GS, HV, CFP). This, last of
the duet sonatas, might sound better for two pianos (con-
sidered by WAM), but the players would lose the intimacy
and rapport of four-hand playing. Concertante in form and
texture, it reflects WAM's mature work, the concertos and
symphonies. Players must "orchestrate" to contrast ensemble and duet passages. The Andante is really an Adagio in-
tricately embellished, with extended passages accompanied
by flowing 32nd notes. Though less original, the closing Allegretto is brilliant and has surprises. 20 minutes.   Dif.

Sonata in G, K. 357 (HV). The Henle Verlag collection of four-hand music contains this two-movement work,
only a sketch for which was left by WAM, probably late.
Completed by Julius Andre in 1853, using largely material
from the WAM fragments, it is a work of more importance
to historians than to musicians. Allegro and Andante (a Rondo
with rather thin variations).   Mod.

Andante and Variations in G, K. 501 (GS, CFP).
WAM's only set of variations for four hands, these are simpler than the Sonatas. An expressive 26-measure Andante is
displayed five times (once in minor), each player sharing the
melody and the cumulatively elaborate decorations.   Mod.

Fugue in G Minor, K. 401 (GS, CFP). Less successful
than the two-piano fugue, this experimental work might sound
better for strings, as the larger one in C Minor does.
Mod. E.

Two Fantasias in F minor, K. 594, 608 (HV, GS,
CFP). Written as potboilers in 1790 for a mechanical-organ
builder ("my watchmaker"), these two are best known in the
four-hand arrangement. (Busoni arranged them for two pianos, and there are other instrumental versions.) They have
qualities. The first frames an F major Allegro in French
overture style with an expressive Adagio in F minor, 3/4.
The second (K. 608) is an inspired work which sounds best
for organ with chime registration. WAM seems to have
omitted a tempo indication, as the opening eight bars are a
stately introductory sinfonia requiring a slow beat (Largo
maestoso?), and the faster Allegro enters at bar 9 with a
four-voice fugue effective for four hands. An Andante in A-
flat, 3/4, forms a solid middle movement with a return of
the sinfonia and fugue for finale.   Mod. Dif.

NIEMANN, WALTER   (Ger 1876-1953)
Kocheler Landler, Op. 135 (CFP, 1934). Twelve
short waltzes, composed in 1933 by this author-composer
who was a pupil of Humperdinck. Similar to those by Brahms.
In simple keys--one sharp or one flat. 27 pages.
E. to Mod.

ORE, HARRY   (GB 1885-)
Three Latvian Folk Songs, Op. 27 (JC, 1958). Busy
Hong Kong educator and impresario found time to write duets
for his pupils. These three use simple but effective keyboard
figures that retain the mood and modes of the Slavic songs,
with their liturgical overtones. The last builds a big climax
with full chords and sweeping scales. 11 pages, 5 1/2 minutes.   Mod. E.

A simpler set of two is called Album Leaf and Old
Russian Polka (JC, 1960). 6 pages and 8 pages.

PAPINEAU-COUTURE, JEAN   (Can 1916-)

Rondo (1945) (PIC, 1960).   A neat duet, each
player comfortably accommodated within the middle octaves
of the keyboard.   Though without key signature, it begins in
a clear E minor, and ends in E major.   The lively tempo
is polymetric, with numerous changes of meter growing
naturally out of the melodic episodes.   Largely linear with
transparent chordal harmony.   16 pages.   Mod.

PERSICHETTI, VINCENT   (USA 1915-)
Concerto for Piano, Four Hands (EV).   This is a large
work, large in format (a facsimile edition) and in form, con-
sisting of a Lento-andante-presto-larghissimo-coda in a single
linked movement.   It is an occasional work, written for the
Pittsburgh International Contemporary Music Festival in 1954,
and is sedulously festive and contemporary.   Though not
strictly serial, it has the acidulous harmony and ambiguous
melodic line of such music.   A series of sharply etched rhythmic motifs stand out in a web of running sixteenths.   The
row is effectively compressed for a brilliant close to the first
section, where it is played Presto in unison by the four hands,
then in canon.   An exciting Coda wraps up the work with a
furious accelerando built on the row.   More brilliant than
the 1940 Sonata for Two Pianos (see Two at Two), and less
ingratiating.   Dif.

PHILLIPS, BURRILL   (USA 1907-)
Serenade for Piano, Four Hands (SMP, 1963).   Omaha-
born composer and teacher, BP studied with Howard Hanson
at the Eastman School of Music and later became a faculty
member there.   Dedicated to Dorothea and Vincent Persichetti, Serenade is in four movements: I. Lyric overture
(Molto moderato, with a diatonic folksong-like melody in
Piano I). II. A game with tones (Allegro molto sempre staccato); III. Air (Andante); IV. Christmas in Biloxi (Allegro
ritmico).   Linear and light textured, occasionally bitonal.
27 pages.   Mod. Dif.

PLEYEL, IGNAZ JOSEPH   (Aus-Fr 1757-1831)
Sonata in G Minor (1815) (CFP, 1961).   Contemporary
of Mozart who lived to see the arrival of Chopin in Paris.
The Pleyel piano and Recital Hall have preserved his name
for posterity better than his music.   This lightweight classical
work is genial and pleasant to play and hear.   The Allegro
transposes the entire recapitulation to major.   The Largo
espressivo is too conventional to be moving, but the closing
Minuet, more of a Scherzo, is animated and amusing.   17
pages.   Mod. E.

POSER, HANS (Ger 1917-1970)
Sonate für Klavier zu vier Händen, Op. 17 (HS, 1962).
Three movements, clear textured, melodic and lyrical. Allegro non troppo with fff ending, followed by a short Allegro grazioso, alla valse, and a lengthy and rhythmic Larghetto, with climactic ending. Much use of fourths and fifths melodically and harmonically. 37 pages.   Mod. Dif.

POULENC, FRANCIS (Fr 1899-1963)
This facile keyboard writer is seldom profound or innovative, yet always fresh and pianistic. He has one duet in each category, four-hand and two-piano.

Sonata for Piano, Four Hands (J&WC). Written when FP was nineteen, this is a fun piece full of felicitous highjinks, the two players crowding each other at the keyboard and egging each other on to louder and faster fun. Modere seems a misnomer for the first movement, written alla breve; FP suggests 152 per quarter, which is only slightly slower than the 160 of the Tres Vif Finale. A folksy tune that sounds modal by avoiding the tonic is driven along by relentless hammered chords, but there are brief lyric interludes, marked sweet and sad, and much dynamic contrast. In Rustique, a five-note tune provides both melody, figuration and an ostinato bass. It is played entirely on the white keys, and has a tongue-in-cheek "nymphs and shepherds" mood. In the Finale (all movements are in duple meters) the same material is dashed off, spiced with a few flats, as an introduction to a pseudo fugue, building excitement with crescendo and accelerando, for a return of both opening and second-movement themes and a coda.   Mod.

RACHMANINOFF, SERGEI (Rus-USA 1873-1943)
Six Pieces for Piano, Four Hands, Op. 11 (IMC, 1956).
Like that other pianist-composer, Chopin, SR preferred to write solo pieces which he could play alone in concerts.
This single duet set is bold and fresh and deserves to be better known. Barcarolle is 4/4 with unusual syncopated eighth-note figures, later urged into triplets and septolets. Little melody, but much chromatic harmonic movement which creates a swaying, hypnotic effect. The light staccato Scherzo, à la Mendelssohn, must be played as fast as possible, and is quite stunning. Best are the two Russian movements: No. 3 on a Russian theme similar to the Volga Boat Song, and the closing Slava (Glory) on an Orthodox chant. SR here eschews chromaticism for a bold triadic style enriched with trills and bell sonorities ranging from pppp to fff. 61 pages.
                                                                            Mod.

RAPHLING, SAM   (USA 1910-   )
   Four-Hand Sonata (GMP, 1970). Brief, simple, yet
original duet piece in four short movements, which might
better have been called Sonatina.   First movement is Lively
(two pages), which set forth two related themes in a three-
part song-form.   Middle movements, Moderately Slow (one
page) and Slowly Expressive (one page) explore subtle dynamic and touch variations with chords of fourths, fifths and
sevenths.   Closes with a bright dancey tune.   Mod. E.

RAVEL, MAURICE   (Fr 1875-1937)
   Ma mère l'oye (Dur).   A set of miniatures on "Mother Goose" nursery tales, naive, winsome and technically undemanding, though written the same year as the transcenden-
tal Scarbo.   The four-hand layout is ideal, though most peo-
pleple now recognize the music from the orchestra transcription.   A twenty-measure Pavane opens, this time not for a
Dead Princess, but for a Sleeping Beauty.   Simple linear
writing with only two black keys; soft chimes suggest courtiers
slowly weaving about the bed of the beautiful dreamer.   In
No. II, Hop o' My Thumb seems to have a companion (like
Hansel and Gretel), for the meandering scales go hand in
hand in thirds looking in vain for the lost crumbs while
birds chirp quietly overhead.   III: "A thousand exotic instruments play as the Empress of Pagodas steps into her bath."
Largely black-key pentatonic for an Oriental effect, the brilliant and amusing sketch poses tricky ensemble problems.
IV, Beauty and the Beast, is a demure valse lente, so re-
strained that even the beast's roar is a muted bass triplet
tritone, later altered as, with a glissando slide, the Beast
becomes Prince Charming.   V, The Fairy Garden, begins
with suave four-voice writing, two lines for each player, then
shimmers with rolled chords, and ends in a burst of color
with triadic fanfares and high, rhythmic glissandi.   Not for
children.   Mod. E. to Mod. Dif.

RAWSTHORNE, ALAN   (GB 1905-1971)
   The Creel (OxU).   Distinguished British composer
whose piano music is most often in suites of short pieces.
The four pieces in this set take their titles from Izaak Walton, contrasting four moods in dissonant and imaginative
idiom, well laid out for two players.   The prelude is stately:
The Mighty Pike Is Tyrant of the Fresh Water.   A neat but
playful two-voice canon in double octaves is called The Sprat,
A Fish That Is Ever in Motion.   The Carp Is Queen of the
Rivers, a tranquil cantabile movement.   The Leap or Sommer-
sault of the Salmon closes with a clever surprise ending.
                                 Mod. Dif.

REBIKOV, VLADIMIR   (Rus 1866-1920)
     Petite Suite (PJ).   Contemporary and rival of Debussy,
VR claimed to have originated whole-tone music.   Seven extended and rather pedestrian dances.   Mod.

REINECKE, CARL   (Ger 1824-1910)
     Nutcracker and Mouse King, Op. 46 (GS).   Suite of
sixteen related fantasy pieces, Schumannesque in inspiration
and texture.   Long but not difficult.   Mod.

     From the Cradle to the Grave, Op. 202 (ES).   Sixteen
more in the same vein.   Mod.

     Improvisations on a Gavotte from Orpheus, Op. 125
(CFP).   One of many transcriptions of this much-put-upon
dance.   Also arranged for two-pianos.   Mod.

RIMSKY-KORSAKOV, NIKOLAI   (Rus 1844-1908) and others
     Paraphrases on Chopsticks (CFP).   Any who have not
been driven insane by hearing chopsticks played ad nauseam
by indolent children or youth incapable of five minutes serious practice may enjoy exploring this amazing work.   The set
started with a polka by Borodin accompanied by the Chopsticks
figure.   RK added to it, and persuaded Cui and Liadov to
join in the fun.   While someone hammers out the Chopsticks
pattern, the pianist plays a set of twenty-four highly imaginative variations, followed by the polka, a funeral march, waltz,
berceuse, galop, gigue, and even a fugue on the B. A. C. H.
theme.   If you have soundproofing, draw the curtains, and
pitch in.   E. and Dif.

RUBINSTEIN, ANTON   (Rus 1829-1894)
     Six Characteristic Pieces, Op. 50 (GS).   Contrasts of
rhythm, mood, texture for a Nocturne, Scherzo, Barcarolle,
Capriccio, Berceuse and March.   Mod.

     Bal Costume, Op. 103 (PJ).   Brilliant and extended
suite now largely forgotten.   The dances attempt to suggest
both ethnic and period styles, but end up as nineteenth-century salon music, with some echoes of Russian nationalist
composers.   Dif.

     There is also a well-structured Sonata (OP).

RUSSELL, ROBERT
     Places; Suite for Piano, Four Hands, Op. 9 (1964)
(GMP, 1968).   Contents: New York, N. Y.; Brooklyn Bridge

(harp effect achieved by having Secondo depress the hammers without striking the strings, while Primo strums the strings with fingernails); Orchard Street; The Cloisters; Central Park Green; The Bay at Dusk; Perambulation.   Light textured miniatures, dissonant but euphonious.   27 pages.   Mod.

SAINT-SAËNS, CAMILLE   (Fr 1835-1921)
        Pas redouble, Op. 86 (Dur, GS, An).   Sprightly and genial, this spoof on a dance form has been anthologized.
                                                                    Mod.

        Berceuse, Op. 105 (Dur, 1896).   A simple duet that uses a triplet figure that rocks in and out of the tonic and dominant chords, first in Primo, then in Secondo, and finally in both parts.   7 pages.   Mod. E.

        Other four-hand music, available from the French firm, Durand & Co., are: Ballade, Op. 59; March, Op. 25, and an arrangement of the third symphony.   There are also six duets for harmonium and piano, Op. 8.

SATIE, ERIK   (Fr 1866-1925)
        Like his solo music, ES' duets are simple enough for students, but have a subtle charm and humor that demand maturity.

        Trois Morceaux en forme de poire (1903) (SE).   This genial suite (actually seven pieces) is ES' reply to a charge that his music was formless.   The full title might be translated: Three Pear-Shaped Pieces, with a Kind of Opening, A Continuation of the Same, Still More, and a Rehash.   There is more variety in tempo changes and sharp sudden dynamic bursts than the titles might imply.   ES did not write program music, and his titles are never to be taken seriously.   The Secondo sometimes becomes soporific, with its continuous octave-chord syncopation, but the treble sparkles with sharp incisive motifs, chordal or melodic.   Fun to play, pleasant to hear.   Mod.

        Aperçus désagréables (1908-1912) (MEE, AMP, 1967). Not actually disagreeable, just rather boring.   The directions are more amusing than the music: Look! Don't turn around; Slow down, I beg you; Speak; Don't speak; Visible; Necessary; Smile; Scratch; Plenty; More.   The three pieces are a Pastorale, a one-page Chorale, and a three-page fugue, with some mild surprises.   Mod. E.

Trois Petites Pièces montées; La Belle excentrique
(ME, AMP). In the album with the above four-hand work are
two others which are arrangements or sketches of orchestra
works. The subtle satire of the early works is gone, and
these are pure cafe or street-corner music, vulgar and triv-
ial.   Mod. E.

En habit de cheval (1911) (RL, 1911). "It fits me
very well" was the comment of ES on "The Attire of a
Horse." Also intended for orchestra, this suite with two
Fugues and two Chorals is tepid and innocuous on piano. The
second Fugue is sprightly and has odd turns, but ends quietly.   Mod. E.

SCHÄFFER, BOGUSLAW (Pol 1929-)
4H/1P; Music for Piano; Four Hands, One Piano (Sim,
1968). Chance composition, divided into many short sections.
The performers are given the freedom to choose the duration
of notes within each section. They are also given the oppor-
tunity to execute glissando with forearm, improvise with
finger tips on piano strings, etc. 15 pages. Total duration
recommended by the composer: 9 min. 45 sec., minimum
8 minutes, maximum 12 minutes.

SCHICKELE, PETER (USA 1935-)
The Civilian Barber, Overture for Piano, Four Hands
(EV, 1963). Better known as P.D.Q. Bach, this satirist is
a professionally trained musician. The humor of the duet,
which is in quite proper sonatina form, is in the juxtaposi-
tion of unlikely keyboard cliches, unmusical modulations.
Fun to play and hear, once.   Mod.

Toot Suite, S. 212, by P.D.Q. Bach (TP). A fun
piece, with program notes in PS' wittiest style. Originally
for calliope (!), the three-part suite opens with a Preloud,
in which Primo wakes up now and then to blow a whistle;
O.K. Chorale spoofs harmonic writing, and Fuga Vulgaris
develops a fughetta on the Volga Boat-song.   Mod. E.

SCHMITT, FLORENT (Fr 1870-1958)
Musiques Foraines, Op. 23 (JH). Distinguished and
prolific composer now largely forgotten outside France shared
the Impressionists' attraction to the circus. This large-
scale work has six movements that include clowns, horses,
trained elephants, pythons and parades. Brilliant and difficult in a late Impressionist style.

Une semaine du petit elfe ferme l'oeil (Dur).   Yet another French childhood suite, this one based on Hans Christian Andersen's less familiar stories.   Imaginative and evocative Secondo with the Primo limited to five-note patterns that
can be played by a musical child.   E. and Mod.

Reflets d'Allemagne; valses pour piano à 4 mains,
op. 28 (Math, 1912).   1. Heidelberg.   2. Coblentz.   3. Lü-
beck.   4. Werder.   5. Vienne.   6. Dresde.   7. Nuremberg.
8. Munich.   57 pages.   Mod.

SCHUBERT, FRANZ   (Aus 1797-1828)
Music for Piano, Four Hands (GS, 3 vol.; CFP, 3;
UE, 3; HV, 3; EFK, 5 vol.).   The greatest master of music
for friends--singer and pianist, four string players, two
pianists--has greatly enriched the duet repertoire.   The homes
where he spent all his mature years, either as guest or as
boarder, seldom had more than one piano, so all of the music is for one piano, four hands.   Five of the standard publishers offer the complete duets, Kalmus in five volumes, the
others in three.   The most recent, Henle Verlag, contains
several early works not in the others.

Sonatas.   This contemporary of Beethoven and successor of Mozart and Haydn in the city of Vienna felt compelled
to write in this form, though he was not as at ease in it, as
he was in dance and small genre forms.   Sonata in B-flat,
Op. 30 (D. 617) is a youthful work of little originality, loose
and prolix in form, though fluent and pianistic for both players.   Grand Duo in C, Op. 140 is also known as Sonata in
C (D. 812).   This is the capstone of FS' duet music, rated by
Schubert fans as the equal of the solo sonatas.   The name
Grand Duo, borrowed from Mozart, stresses both the equality
of the players, and the large scale of the work.   It is so
orchestral that some critics maintain that it is a score reduction, yet it is pianistic throughout.   Boldly structured, plung-
ing at once into the Allegro, it is also compactly written,
avoiding cliches and giving musical significance to all passages.   Three of the four movements are in C major; and
though there are many key changes, minor is seldom used,
and the mood is cheerful and sanguine.   The Andante is in
A-flat and has the serenity of the second movement of Beethoven's Fifth.   A must for Schubert addicts.   Mod.

Fantasias.   The Fantasie in F Minor, Op. 103 (D. 940)
borrows both its key from Mozart's duet Fantasias, and its
form from the great solo Fantasia in C minor.   The series

of short contrasting linked movements is, however, predom-
inantly lyrical, rather than dramatic, as is Mozart's.   There
are three immature early experiments in Fantasia form in
the Henle collection.   Mod.

        Marches.   These are spirited, original, remarkably
varied, and pleasant to play.   They require more drive than
musicality, and only moderate technic.   Trois Marches
heroiques, Op. 27 (D. 602) were written when FS was twenty.
The first is the best, as sparkling as ballet music.   The other two chatter away too long.   Six Grandes marches, Op. 40
(D. 819) are all on a large scale with contrasting Trios in related keys.   Most are in minor, some suggest orchestra or
Magyar instruments.   Trois marches militaire, Op. 51 (D.
733) opens with the familiar D Major, made into a rattling
virtuoso solo by Carl Tausig.   But FS was right in using
four hands for his grand military band effects.   Op. 55 is a
Grand Marche funebre (D. 859) for the death of Alexander I of
Russia, stirringly evocative of a royal cortége; and Op. 66,
Grand Marche heroique (D. 885) is the coronation march for
his successor.   Both large-scale serious pieces deserve an
occasional hearing.   Deux Marches caracteristiques, Op. 121
(D. 886) are both Allegro vivace in C, 6/8, and are overextended, but spirited and fun.   There is also a fine duet
march from a Hungarian Divertissement, Op. 54 (D. 818) and
a one-page duet for the ten-year-old son of his host (D. 928).
                                                         Mod.

        Dances.   Among the many dance duets, the freshest
are the Six Landler, Op. 67, that rustic ancestor of the
Waltz.   There are numerous Waltzes, both " Sentimental"
and plain, all rather insipid.   National dances include Polonaises and Ecossaises.   With the wealth of fine ethnic-based
dance duets available, these will have little appeal, though
the Polonaises are rhythmically intriguing.   Mod.

        Variations.   There are five sets, some of which are
effective.   Variations on a French Air (D. 624) marked Op.
10, and FS' first published work, was a favorite of Beethoven.
Variations on an Original Theme in A-flat, Op. 35 (D. 813)
is one of the finest of the duets, alternating brilliant and
lyrical episodes skillfully deployed for two players.   Mod.

        Miscellaneous Pieces include several Rondos, a Fugue,
and a French Divertissement.   There is also an Allegro in
A Minor, Op. 144 (D. 947) subtitled Lebensstürme, an im-
passioned work from the last tragic year of Schubert's life,

and a Rondo with the intriguing title, Notre amitie est invari-
able.

Overtures and Transcriptions.   In those pre-recording
days, every orchestral, chamber or operatic score was offered to the public as a piano duet.   Now that they are available in the original form at the turn of a switch, the duets
have little appeal.   FS himself transcribed his many opera
overtures, entreacts and ballet scenes.   The incidental music
to the opera Rosamunde is a good sample, and since few will
ever hear the opera, good to know.   The music is titillating
to play, and offers the pleasures of rediscovery and recreation as a shared experience.

German Dances in E Major and G Major (1818) (JC,
GS, 1958).   Written in 1818 while FS was music master of
the three children of Count Esterhazy, possibly for his pupils.
The score was discovered by Brahms fifty-four years later,
and was not printed until 1909.   The current edition by Curwen was edited by Jack Werner.   Mod.

SCHUSTER, GIORA   (Ger-Isr 1915-   )
Mimos I, for Piano, Four Hands (IMI, 1970).   This
short, airy work of three sections was composed in 1966.
The light expressive middle section, Con tenerezza, is
framed by two fast outer movements, Vivo grazioso and
Vivace.   Moderately dissonant.   9 pages.   8 minutes.   There
are two other versions: one for flute, clarinet and violin;
the other for flute, clarinet (or viola) and piano.   Mod.

SHAPERO, HAROLD   (USA 1920-   )
Sonata for Piano, Four-hands (AMI, 1941).   Appealing
work in extended three-movement form.   All parts have a
clear ringing bell-like sonority making much use of triads,
open fourths and fifths, and evoking American folk music.
The metronome mark for the introduction, Very Slowly, is
surely incorrect.   The material is enriched and swells to a
grand climax in the middle movement.   Closes with a crackling finale, pitting lean legato lines against a chordal tapping,
both players rapping out the pattern for a coda.   Mod.

SHIFRIN, SEYMOUR   (USA 1926-   )
The Modern Temper (1959) (Lit; CFP, 1961).   The
name is well chosen, though the subtitle, A Dance, seems
unlikely.   Avant-garde, row-oriented work for two specialists.
Short angular motifs scattered among the four hands at the
opening later solidify into chords in a staggered rhythm.   The

rapid-fire dynamic changes used with such largesse by avant-
garde writers are kept to a minimum here, and the single-
movement work seems to progress organically to a finish.
6 minutes.   Dif.

SINDING, CHRISTIAN (Nor 1856-1941)
        Suite, Op. 35 (CFP). Two marches, an Allegro and
a Finale adroitly deployed for four hands, require drive and
incisive rhythm, but only moderate technic. Traditional in
harmony and figuration but imaginative and fresh. Mod. Dif.

        Norwegian Dances and Melodies, Op. 98 (CFP).
These numbers, "after Grieg," alternate a lyric mood (the
Melodies) and a bucolic boldness for the dances.   Mod.

SPIEGELMAN, JOEL (USA 1933-)
        Morsels ("Kousochki") (MCA, 1967). Harpsichordist
and electronics specialist here uses the piano to suggest bell
sonorities, inspired by Russian twelfth-century monastery
chimes. (Why "Morsels"?) The tone row permeates the
piece, alternately tolled out in six-note chords tossed from
player to player, and spelled out in tintinnabulating patterns.
The third part introduces an element of chance with a series
of short phrases to be arranged in any order by each player.
Dynamics tax both the instrument and the player to the limits
of power. 16 pages.   Dif.

STARER, ROBERT (Aus-USA-Isr 1924-)
        Fantasia Concertante (1959) (MCA, 1966). A brilliant,
lengthy movement for concert use, commissioned by the team
of Lillian and Irwin Freundlich. RS has found an original
and authentic voice, basically tonal but highly chromatic,
often suggesting tone rows. Clear-cut, detached motifs, often
in octaves or unison, give a proclamatory, heraldic sound,
while half-step progressions in a mosaic of flexible figures
capture the Middle Eastern melismatic wail, which so often
eludes the keyboard composer. An important and fine work,
technically and musically demanding. 31 pages.   Dif.

STRATEGIER, HERMAN (Neth 1912-)
        Suite for Piano, Four Hands (1945) (Don, 1946). All
duettists should have the catalog from this prolific house. In
Holland home music-making is still very much alive, and the
six movements of this suite are all dedicated to young duet
teams. The music is genial and melodious, not exacting but
often exciting in a traditional style. 23 pages. Mod. E.

STRAVINSKY, IGOR   (Rus-USA 1882-1971)
    Three Easy Pieces for Piano Duet (1915) (Omega,
1949; GS, Col). The best piano music from the great twentieth-century innovator of ballets, symphonic and chamber
works is his music for various piano teams. The impresario,
Diaghilev, who gathered about him in Paris a brilliant coterie
of artists, must have envied duettists the intimacy of four-
hand playing. Since he could not play the piano, IS wrote
for him, between ballets, a duet which required only one repeated bass chord, while his partner played in the treble a
witty Polka full of wry wrong-notes, (a pompous caricature
of the Impresario himself). Alfredo Casella was so delighted
with the bit of "pop-corn" from the bombastic neo-primitive,
that IS wrote for him a March with a similar innocuous bass,
and a complex dissonant treble, with fanfares and measures
in triple time thrown in. Between the two he put a waltz
for Erik Satie, less lugubrious than Satie's Grecian dances
but using similar modal harmony (two chords for Secondo this
time, while Primo sparkles with unusual figuration). The
title of the set is deceiving, as even the three-finger bass
requires maturity for the ensemble, and the first part is
moderately difficult. 7 pages (Omega).   E. and Mod. Dif.

    Five Easy Pieces for Piano Duet (Omega; GS, Col;
IMC, 1970). Written to teach his two children "music and
piano playing," these have a somewhat more difficult treble
(for the child) and a delightfully whimsical Secondo. Three
were suggested by family travels, and the quiet opening
Andante and closing Galop round out a fine set for teacher
and first-year pupil. 16 pages (IMC).   E. and Mod.

TCHAIKOVSKY, PETER I.   (Rus 1840-1893)
    Russian Folk Songs (LPC, CFP). Though these are
only transcriptions of songs in arrangements simple enough
for children, they should be known for their wealth of rich
source material. Plundered already for many a symphony
or quartet movement, they still contain fresh tunes in intriguing rhythms and scales that an imaginative composer
could put to good use. They are also attractive teaching material. The Leeds volume contains all fifty, the Peters, a
selection of thirty-six.   E.

TOCH, ERNST   (Aus-USA 1887-1964)
    Sonata, Op. 87 (MMC, 1963). Like Vivaldi, whose
concerto provided so many fine pieces under different titles,
Toch gave his standard work many guises. Nobody will be

fooled into thinking this one is new or modern by the absence
of key signatures. The outer movements, in B-flat, have
similarly inane and innocuous ditties for themes over a
doodling bass. The Andante espressivo is a rechauffe of
Paderewski's celebrated Minuet, without credit to IJP.   31
pages.   Mod.

TOMKINS, THOMAS
    A Fancy. See CARLTON, NICHOLAS.

TOVEY, DONALD FRANCIS (GB 1875-1940)
    Balliol Dances (Scho).   A set of waltzes in a neo-
Brahmsian style, well-wrought but tending to plod or languish.
                                                            Mod.

TOWNSEND, DOUGLAS (USA 1921-)
    Four Fantasies on American Folk Songs (CF, 1957).
Distinguished musicologist here puts his researches to practical use. The five tunes all avoid the leading tone except
one, which flats it. They are harmonized conventionally,
with much modulation and no dissonance, in traditional keyboard figures. Bouncing and genial, they are only moderately difficult.   Mod.

TÜRK, DANIEL GOTTLOB (Ger 1756-1813)
    Tonstücke fur Vier Hände (Scho, AMP). By a con-
temporary of Mozart noted for his teaching pieces, these
simple unaffected duets are both educational and entertaining.
                                                            Mod. E.

VAN WYK, ARNOLD (SAf 1916-)
    Three Improvisations on Dutch Folk Songs (B&H).
South African composer and educator wrote these for the BBC
in 1944, before returning to S. A. Contrasting pieces alternating lively and lyrical, in contemporary technic, but harmonically tonal.   Mod. Dif.

WAGNER, RICHARD (Ger 1813-1883)
    Polonaise in D (Br&H). Early work before RW re-
pudiated all music but opera, adopted the rhythmic motif of
the wedding march as his motto, and succumbed to the lure
of chromaticism. Bold simple dotted rhythms in triadic
harmony.   Mod.

WEBER, CARL MARIA VON (Ger 1786-1826)
    This short-lived composer, remembered today chiefly
for his operas, suffers by comparison with the contemporary

giants. A brilliant pianist, he wrote facile keyboard music,
harmonically pedestrian. Numerous editions of all three
books.

Six Pieces for Piano, Four Hands, Op. 3 (CFP, GS).
Written by the 14-year-old CMVW, these were called "petites
pieces faciles," and are pleasant, unpretentious and uncom-
plicated. The six are a Sonatina (often anthologized), Ro-
manze, Menuetto (marked Presto and better named Scherzo),
Andante con variazione, Marche and Rondo.   Mod. E.

Six Pieces for Piano, Four Hands, Op. 10. Another
set with six movements evidently intended to be played together, like the Viennese serenade. The melody is mostly
in Primo, with Secondo playing the duettist's equivalent of
an Alberti bass or a band's um-pa-pa, though there are occasional passages of more interest for the low man. Mod. E.

Eight Pieces for Piano, Four Hands, Op. 60. More
extended and imaginative, these can be played separately or
as a suite. As in the case of Schubert, the four-hand sets
are often more satisfying than the large solo sonatas.
CMVW's favorite forms are all here, spaced out with two
Allegros, an Adagio and a pleasing Siciliano.   Mod.

Invitation to the Dance, Op. 65. Countless arrangements of this popular programmatic solo have been made,
both for four hands and for two pianos. The Rondos of the
solo Sonatas have also been arranged, and should appeal to
pianists with motorized fingers.

WEINER, LEO (Hun 1885-1960)
Suite; Hungarian Folk Dances, Piano Duet, Op. 18
(Zen, 1965). Hungarian composer and teacher of theory at
the Landesakademie in Budapest wrote these four vigorous
dances. I. Allegro risoluto e ben marcato. II. Allegro con
fuoco. III. Pesante, poco maestoso. IV. Presto. II and
III are introduced by a short Andante poco sostenuto, almost
identical in content though in different keys. Rhythmic and
folkloric. Frequent shifting of tonal centers. 63 pages.
                                                      Dif.

WOLF, ERNST WILHELM (Ger 1735-1792)
Sonata in C (GS). One of the earliest of the duet
Sonatas by an obscure contemporary of Haydn. Well written
and rather pale, in a rococo style. Published with W. F. E.
Bach's Andante.   Mod. E.

WOLFF, CHRISTIAN (Fr-USA, 1934-)
    Duet I; Piano, Four Hands (CFP, 1962).   Chance
composition using diagrammatic score and interior effects.
2 pages of facsimile score and 3 pages of instruction.   See
also Two at Two.

WOOLLEN, RUSSELL (USA 1923-)
    Sonata for Piano Duo (1950) (PIC, 1955).   A three-
movement neo-classic work by a composer of liturgical music.   Three clear-cut themes, mildly chromatic, are set
forth, then developed with progressive intensity to a climax,
without a recapitulation.   The central Adagio moves in a
lilting 6/8 folkloric style spiked with bold sudden dynamic
shifts, and ends in A minor.   A driving Rondo, pianistic
and effective, serves as Finale.   42 pages.   Mod.

WOURINEN, CHARLES (USA 1938-)
    Making Ends Meet (1966) (CFP).   Enormously diffi-
cult work written for the brilliant four-hand duet team, Jean
and Kenneth Wentworth.   The music is in two sections titled
Development and Variations.   The meaning of the title is
obscure, but the problem of making parts meet and play in
ensemble at breakneck speed in dense complex patterns will
be insuperable for all but professionals specializing in serial
reification.   Vir.

WYK, ARNOLD VAN See VAN WYK, ARNOLD

PART 2

TWO AT TWO

Music for two players,
four hands, at two pianos

TWO AT TWO

ABSIL, JEAN (Bel 1893-)
   Rhapsodie no. 5, sur de vieux noëls français, pour deux pianos, op. 102 (CBDM, 1968 set). Professor of harmony at Brussels Conservatory wrote this brilliant one-movement work in toccata style, with contrasting sections of different tempos and dynamics. Much use of chromatic scale and octave passages, punctuated by chords built on fourths. Frequent meter changes from 2/4 to 5/8 to 6/8 etc. Requires octave and fast finger technique. 16 pages. Score is facsimile of manuscript. Dif.

   Asymétries, pour deux pianos, op. 136 (1968) (CBDM, 1969, sep). Three movements: 1. Andante mysterioso et allegro scherzando. 2. Andantino. 3. Allegro vivo. Rhythmical and dissonant. Extensive use of the chromatic scale, doubled an octave apart, and in successions of thirds and chords. 23 pages, 11 minutes. Facsimile score. Mod. Dif.

ANDRIESSEN, JURRIAAN (Neth 1925-)
   Concerto for Two Pianos (Don, 1946, sep). Second generation Dutch composer trained in Paris writes in a neoclassic early Stravinsky style. The large work is well-structured, pianistic and euphonious. Parts compliment each other effectively with flowing passage work balancing chordal melody. Wide ranging dynamics and free rubato mark the expressive Adagio. The "hanonic" unisons of the scurrying Allegro threaten to become comical, till enriched by a broad quarter-note melody. Facsimile score. 43 pages.
                                                              Mod. Dif.

   Dutch Rhapsody for Two Pianos.

ANDRIESSEN, LOUIS (Neth 1939-)
   Séries, pour deux pianos (1958) (Don, 1964, set). One-movement twelve-tone work divided into twelve sections each containing twelve bars. Except for the first and the last, order of the sections is left to the choice of the per-

41

formers. Complex rhythmic patterns for both Piano I and
Piano II, though the duration of each bar is equal to four
quarter notes. Sudden and constant shifting of dynamics between fff and ppp. 10 pages, 9 minutes. Score is facsimile
reduced from manuscript.   Dif.

ANSON, HUGO VERNON (NZ-Eng 1894-1958)
     The Lonely Sailing Ship, for Two Pianos; ed. by Ethel
Bartlett and Rae Robertson (OxU, 1934, set). Born in New
Zealand, HVA received his training at Royal College of Music
and at Cambridge University. "The actual ship which suggested the idea of this piece to the composer was a derelict
vessel, allowed to ride at anchor.... The movement must
be rather dragging and the tempo very slow. "--Editor's note.
Chromatic but tonal. Atmospheric. 4 pages.   Mod.

ARENSKY, ANTON (Rus 1861-1906)
     Suite, Op. 15 (B&H, GS, set). Popular three-move-
ment suite by a distinguished teacher who enjoyed playing
duets with his pupils, (Scriabin and Rachmaninoff were among
them). Romance is a series of variations on an alternating
Allegro-Andante, fresh, lyrical and pianistically deployed.
The familiar Valse was gleefully played prestissimo by Rachmaninoff and Gabrilowitsch, but is only marked Allegro (not
easy). The Polonaise is less inspired and rather ungainly to
perform.   Mod. Dif.

     Silhouettes, Op. 23 (CFP, set). Five contrasting
character pieces of uneven worth. Le Savant is a fine canon,
a form AA handled well; La Coquette is a coy valse; in
Polichinello and La Reveur the rhythmic complexities and keyboard acrobatics swamp the music. La Danseuze attempts
the grace of the famous Valse (see above), but the intricate
figuration in a compound Bolero rhythm is labored.   Mod.

     Suite, Op. 62 (PJ). Six canons for teaching, pleasant
to play.   Mod. E.

ASHTON, ALGERNON (GB 1859-1937)
     Suite, Op. 50 (HE, set). Extended, traditional work
of five movements by the scholarly pianist-composer. 1.
Praeludium. 2. Pastorale. 3. Scherzo. 4. March tri-
omphate. 5. Finale. 71 pages.   Dif.

     Toccata Brillante, Op. 144 (FECL, set). 23 pages.

AUBERT, LOUIS (Fr 1877-1968)

Suite, Op. 6 (Dur).   Once popular work written for
the Paris Exposition of 1900; leans heavily on Debussy and
Ravel.   Mod.

AURIC, GEORGES   (Fr 1899-)
Partita (MEE, 1955, set).   The last surviving member
of "Les Six," GA became known for his scores for ballets
and films (Moulin Rouge), and was appointed director of the
Opera.   He has added two works to the two-piano repertoire.
The three untitled movements of the Partita are in contrasting
tempos, with constantly shifting meters, generously paced
with metronome marks.   A brittle, sophisticated contemporary
sound is sought, with instructions: bien articule, bien rhyth-
me, bien arpege, bien mesure, bien appuye.   One misses the
sensuous harmony and lilting melody of another of the Six,
Poulenc.   The second movement builds from a quiet rocking
berceuse to a grand, elaborate close.   For a third movement
GA uses a row-like theme in a mock-fugal manner, sempre
staccato, single notes widening to chords and octaves for a
final climax.   Dif.

Double Jeux (SE, 1971, set).   Though written sixteen
years later, this might be a continuation of the Partita, with
the same patterns and moods in a single movement.   Mod.

BABIN, VICTOR   (Rus-USA 1908-1972)
Twelve Etudes for Two Pianos (UMCC, set).   From
his years of experience of two-piano playing in the Vronsky
and Babin team, VB wrote these twelve studies, only six of
which have been published.   They develop technics of ensemble playing along with the mastery of idiomatic figures.
No. 4 is an arrangement of Rimsky-Korsakov's Bumble Bee.
                                                               Dif.

Three March Rhythms (1941) (B&H, 1953, set).   I.
Military, in 2/4 meter.   II. Funereal (slow and short, only
5 pages), in 4/4.   III. Processional, in 2/2.   Pianistic and
brilliant work, moderately dissonant with some use of bitonality.   42 pages.   Dif.

Strains from Far-off Lands; Three Pieces for Two
Pianos, Four Hands, Based on Folk Melodies, 1943-45 (Also
known as Three Fantasies on Old Themes) (Aug, 1948).   1.
The Piper of Polmood.   2. Hebrew Slumber Song.   3. Russian Village.

BACH, CARL PHILIPP EMANUEL   (Ger 1714-1788)

Four Little Duets for Two Pianos (GS, 1971, set).
We may thank the team of Gold and Fizdale for rescuing
these charming miniatures. The first is two pages, the others all one page only (all have repeats). They make an effective set, with two slow movements framed by Allegros.
All are in the flowing, florid rococo style of the early days
of the pianoforte, melodious and harmonically simple. The
pianists play parallel parts in thirds or sixths, or answer
each other antiphonally. Good opener.   Mod.

BACH, JOHANN CHRISTIAN (Ger 1735-1782)
        Sonata in G Major, for Two Pianos, Four Hands
(Scho). See also Two at One.   Mod.

BACH, JOHANN SEBASTIAN (Ger 1685-1750)
        Two Fugues from The Art of the Fugue (CFP, set).
In the mighty compendium of fugal writing, composed in
JSB's last years, are two mirror fugues that are a tour de
force of compositional skill. Since they are in three voices,
difficult for one player, even at a two-manual harpsichord,
the practical old pro arranged them for two instruments and
two players, adding an imaginative and fluent fourth part to
keep all hands busy. Good for the explorer, and for occasional performance by two mature players.   Dif.

        Concerto in C Minor for Two Claviers, BWV 1060
(CFP, sep). Disparagers of the keyboard transcription must
come to grips with JSB, one of the first and most prolific
arrangers of all time. He not only transcribed other composers' works, changing the solo instruments, as in the case
of the Four-Cembalo Concerto, based on Vivaldi's for four
violins; he also transcribed his own Concerto for Two Violins
in D Minor, for two pianos. The one in C minor may originally have been for oboe and violin, but the original is lost.
It is possible to play it without string orchestra, but it suffers, as the strings have independent parts and a pizzicato
accompaniment throughout the Andante.   Dif.

        Concerto in C for Two Claviers, BWV 1061 (CFP,
sep). This superior work may have been written as a duet
for two harpsichords, as the orchestra parts appear to have
been added later, and then only to the first and, briefly, to
the last movements. A fine Adagio siciliano for the two keyboard instruments alone is the core of the work, followed by
a spirited Fugue finale.   Dif.

BACON, ERNST (USA 1898-) and OTTO LUENING (USA

1900-)
      Coal Scuttle Blues (AMP, set). Keyboard high jinks
like these, from two facile pianists brought up on jazz but
also serious competent musicians, seldom get transferred to
paper. A big (twenty pages) Andante-Allegro-Andante gives
all the jazz harmonies and keyboard figures a thorough workout. Markings indicate the spirit of the piece: with varnished
gloss, with cautious exactitude, flea bitten and slightly sub-
ordinate, tough, slightly marshmallowy, with veiled impro-
priety, strumpetly trumpety, the fat in the fire, with arro-
gant deliberation, strutting along. Fun to play with a well-
matched friend ingrained in the jazz idiom.   Dif.

BADINGS, HENK (Neth 1907-)
      Balletto Grottesco (1939) (UE, 1942, sep). Born in
Java, this prolific composer continues to turn out opera and
ballet scores. What was grotesque in 1939 is now nostalgic.
Mildly polytonal harmony, chords of seconds, fourths, ninths,
a Funeral March for an Intrada and a Rumba for Finale add
to the humor of this dated work. 28 pages.   Mod. Dif.

BAERVOETS, RAYMOND (Bel 1932-)
      Scherzo, pour deux pianos, 1957 (CBDM, 1972, sep).
Moderately dissonant one-movement work, with simple linear
texture. Most of the time two hands, sometimes three and
even four, are doubling a constantly moving, chromatic
melodic line. 25 pages (widely spaced notes, and only two
lines on each page), 4 minutes. Facsimile score.   Mod.

BALOGH, ERNÖ (Hun-USA 1897-)
      Peasant Dance (JF, 1939, sep). Written for Bartlett
and Robertson, this well-intentioned work uses a variety of
keyboard patterns that lie well under the hand, but musically
it conveys little. Brilliant presto coda with trills, tremolandi and glissandi. 19 pages.   Dif.

BARTOK, BELA (Hun-USA 1881-1945)
      Seven Pieces from Mikrokosmos (B&H, set). Selec-
tions from Books IV and V of the great pedagogical series
arranged by the composer for concert use. The division of
labor is welcome, and the parts are always playable, though
they only double the lines and chords of the original. For
pianists with motorized fingers and an ear inured to unmiti-
gated dissonance.   Dif.

      Rhapsody, Op. 1 (B&H). There is a two-piano ar-
rangement of this early work. It is a reduction of a concerto,

which in turn was an expansion of a solo piece. It is a brilliant, difficult, large-scale work in the nineteenth-century Teutonic style, built on the two sections of a Hungarian dance, lassu and friss.   Dif.

Suite, Op. 4b (B&H, set). The opus number is misleading. The four-movement orchestra Suite, Op. 4 was written in 1905, and represents a watershed in BB's development, using for the last time styles derived from Liszt, Strauss, Debussy and Ravel. In 1941 BB rewrote it as a two-piano suite for performance with his wife. It retains the eclectic character of the original, but is pianistically deployed. The four movements are a lyrical and richly varied Serenata; an horrendous Allegro diabolico, anticipating the solo piece, Allegro barbaro, but in Sonata-form with a fugal development; an atmospheric slow movement called Scena della puszta, with flute and harp effects; and a sanguine, folksy Per finire. About 30 minutes.   Dif.

BB's great contribution to team piano playing, the Sonata for Two Pianos and Percussion, requires a team of four professionals.   Vir.

BATE, STANLEY (GB 1911-1959)
Three Pieces for Two Pianos (AMP, 1943, set). By the once popular pianist and film music composer, a suite in three movements: Prelude, Pastoral, Rondo. Though intended as a unit, they are lacking in variety, and might be played separately, as each is long. A bright neo-classic style, requiring crisp touch and drive.   Mod.

BAX, ARNOLD (GB 1883-1953)
Moy Mell (MuM, set). Most popular work of a prolific composer whose music remained basically nineteenth-century romantic, in spite of attempts to introduce Russian and Irish ethnic music. AB's pieces often have literary references, and this is subtitled The Happy Plain. One movement romantic work, requiring good balance of tone and dynamics.   Mod.

The Poisoned Fountain (MuM, set). Impressionistic effect with traditional keyboard figures, short, colorful.
                                                              Mod.

Hardanger (MuM). Dance dedicated to Grieg. Well wrought, but unoriginal.   Mod.

The Devil that Tempted St. Anthony (MuM, set).   Two
sections contrast a trance-like Lento and a nervous, crackling
Allegro.   Effective.   Mod. Dif.

BEACH, MRS. H. H. A.   (USA 1867-1944)
    Variations on Balkan Themes, Op. 60 (APS, 1906,
1942, sep).   Twelve variations in two books.   Lyric and
traditional, by the composer-pianist whose Gaelic Symphony
was the first symphonic work by an American woman.
                                             Mod. to Mod. Dif.

    Suite for Two Pianos, Four Hands; Founded Upon Old
Irish Melodies (JCh, 1924, set).   Prelude (28 pages); Old
Times (23 pages); Peasant Dance (25 pages); The Ancient
Cabin (34 pages); Finale.   Mod. Dif.

BECK, ARTHUR   (1901-   )
    Sonatine für zwei Klaviere (BSS, AMP, 1956, sep).
In three movements: Allegro, Andante sostenuto, and a light
and fast Rondo.   Sparse and dissonant, with melodic lines
often doubled by two hands an octave apart.   24 pages.   Mod.

BEECHER, CARL   (USA 1885-1968)
    The Jester (OD, 1923, sep).   Pianist and composer
of numerous student pieces.   A standard two-piano duet,
opening and close in a valse caprice style, with broad contrasting middle section spreading rolling arpeggios under a
slow melody.   An elaborate coda.   15 pages.   Mod. Dif.

BENJAMIN, ARTHUR   (Aus-GB 1893-1960)
    Jamaica Rumba (B&H, set).   The greatest all-time
hit of this successful teacher and composer takes only 1 1/2
minutes to play if the gentle relentless 3-3-2 beat is kept up.
Two folksy tunes are tossed back and forth, over the drum-
ming, and the entire piece is played sempre una corda.   It
has been arranged for every conceivable combination, including full orchestra, but is still best for two pianos.   Dif.

    Caribbean Dance on Two Jamaican Folk-Songs, Lin-
stead Market and Hold 'im Joe (B&H, set).   Like Donizetti,
AB never wasted anything, and here, as elsewhere, turns
his vocal folk-song settings to keyboard pieces.   Fun, if you
don't know the much better one above.   Repetitious and unpianistic.

    From San Domingo (B&H, set).   See comments on
Caribbean Dance above.   Mod. Dif.   .

Two Jamaican Street Songs (B&H, 1949).   Ditto.

Jamaicalypso, for Two Pianos, Based on a Jamaican
Folk-song (B&H, 1957, set).   Brisk tempo, rhythmic.   8
pages.   Dif.

BERGER, ARTHUR   (USA 1912-   )
    Three Pieces for Two Pianos (1962).   Noted critic,
editor and composer of chamber music, often for two instruments, AB has moved from atonal writing to neo-classic, and
serial.   These three short works are well-structured, and,
in spite of the aurally complex serial texture, manage a
pleasing lilt.   Mod. Dif.

BERGER, JEAN   (USA 1909-   )
    Caribbean Cruise (BB, 1958, sep).   Pianistic and
imaginative five-minute piece on Latin dance rhythms.   Before Afro-American music became so commonplace, this
must have been exciting.   14 pages.   Mod. Dif.

BERGER, WILHELM   (USA-Ger 1861-1911)
    Variations in E Minor, Op. 61 (CS, 1896, sep).   Set
of variations in traditional style, by the pianist-conductor-
composer who was born in the United States and educated in
Germany.   Pianistic and brilliant, with fast sixteenth-note
passages, octaves, skips.   34 pages.   Mod. Dif.

BERKELEY, LENNOX   (GB 1903-   )
    Polka (J&WC, 1934, set).   Written for Ethel Bartlett
and Rae Robertson, a brilliant and effective work in very
fast tempo.   Performance time only 1 and 1/4 minutes.   5
pages.   Dif.

    Capriccio; Nocturne.   Both published by J. and W.
Chester.

BETTINELLI, BRUNO   (It 1913-   )
    Sonatina, per due pianoforti (AD, 1955, sep).   Three-
movement work by the Italian pianist-composer and critic.
Allegro con semplicita with singing angular melodies is followed by the expressive Andante, with more singing legato
melodies, and a contrasting staccato Vivace.   Linear and
contrapuntal writing with a light and clear texture.   Chromatic and dissonant, but freely tonal.   9 minutes. Mod. Dif.

BLANCHET, EMILE R.   (Swi 1877-1943)
    Ballade, Op. 57 (MEE, sep).   Dedicated to Clara

Haskil, this is a one-movement work in nineteenth-century romantic style, with a cadenza for Piano I before the climactic ending. There is also a version for piano and orchestra arranged by E. Ansermet. 24 pages. Dif.

BOULEZ, PIERRE (Fr 1925-)
Structures for Two Pianos (UE, 1955, set). Genius of the experimental and innovative, whose enormously difficult compositions for piano took him so "far out" that he has given up for the simpler art of conducting. This work has been called serial music's "Art of the Fugue," a compendium of all possible technics of total serialization. As a musical manifesto, it aroused both enthusiasm and protest when it appeared, but is now largely a historical document. Vir.

BOUTRY, ROGER (Fr 1932-)
Trásně, pour deux pianos (SE, 1967). I. Allegro moderato. II. Allegretto. III. Vivace. Rhythmic work with a vitality achieved by syncopation, offbeat accents, and repetition of rhythmic patterns. Extensive use of ninth and eleventh chords. Two hands frequently double the same melodic lines. 18 pages, 5 minutes. Dif.

BOWEN, YORK (GB 1884-1961)
Suite for Two Pianos, Four Hands, Op. 111 (OxU, 1946, 4 sets). Pianistic and euphonious, these are written in a turn-of-the-century-modern idiom, though dating from the forties. The four dances are a Prelude, a Rigadoon, Intermezzo and Tarantella, published separately. The last is longest and most effective. Mod.

Arabesque, Op. 119 (OxU, 1947, set). Augmented triads and ninth chords in graceful keyboard figures shape for the ear the arabesques of the title. One movement with key changes and cumulative variations. 10 pages. Mod.

BOWLES, PAUL (USA 1910-)
Sonata (GS, 1949, set). Large-scale three-movement work in PB's brittle acerbic style. Extensive use is made of a staccato octave motive divided between the players, fun to play and to watch, but banal to hear as the ear unites the divided. A Molto tranquillo movement with a broad meandering melodic line separates the two marked "in strict tempo." The closing movement is played entirely without pedal, and both instruments are treated as percussion, with brash chord clumps in a great variety of rhythmic motifs and wide-ranging dynamics. 33 pages. Dif.

BOZZA, EUGÈNE   (Fr 1905-)
     Sonata pour deux pianos (ALe, 1963, sep).   Lengthy
and difficult work in three movements.   I. Andante maestoso
with grand opening, moving into Allegro moderato, Tranquillo,
and finally Piu vivo and Vivo.   II. Andante molto moderato.
III. Allegro vivo.   Rapid sixteenth-note passages, broken
chords, octaves and chord trills.   Much use of fourths and
fifths harmonically and melodically.   Requires facility and
drive of both players.   51 pages.   Vir.

BRAGGIOTTI, MARIO   (It-USA 1909-)
     Variations on Yankee Doodle for Two Pianos, Four
Hands, in the manner of Bach, Beethoven, Chopin, Debussy,
Gershwin (GS).

BRAHMS, JOHANNES   (Ger 1833-1897)
     Variations on a Theme of Haydn, Op. 56b (CFP, set).
One of the great works of the repertoire, this shows no signs
of having been conceived for orchestra, and is eminently
pianistic in JB's highly idiosyncratic way.   The ideal theme
is St. Anthony's Chorale (used by Haydn in a woodwind di-
vertimento).   The binary division, with repeats and cadences,
is followed in most of the eight variations, as is the curious
five-measure phrase length.   The grave, exalted theme state-
ment is followed by three variations which form a group, two
Andantes gently flowing but richly contrapuntal, separated by
a lively Vivace in minor key.   Variation IV is longer and
more free, a minor lyric of great expressive beauty; V and
VI are in tocatta style with playful complications; Variation
VII is a lilting Siciliano, sometimes lifted out as a solo piece
(arr. by Harold Bauer).   No. VIII is the only one needing
orchestra color.   The Finale is a great Passacaglia building
a magnificent fugal climax over a relentless five-measure
Cantus firmus.   20 minutes.   Dif.

     Sonata in F Minor, Op. 34b (IMC, CFP, set).   This
enormous work is best in its third and final form as a piano-
quintet, where the contrast of piano percussion and sustained
silken string tone gives it the scope of a concerto.   Yet the
second version can give great pleasure to two tough Brahmins
willing to tackle its formidable figures, and sit out its great
length.   Five bold themes are finely contrasted and organized
for the Allegro non troppo.   The Andante is a romantic serenade, but is almost soporific, without the soaring, swelling
strings.   The JB Scherzo is always on a large scale, and
the panache of the bold masculine theme contrasting with the
tender trio makes this one of the best.   The quiet opening

of the finale needs again the strings, though the presto coda
is great for two keyboard athletes.   There should be a counterpart to the Bach Aria Society, to rescue from oblivion
precious nuggets of chamber music, impacted in slabs of in-
ferior oolite.   41 minutes.   Dif.

BRITTEN, BENJAMIN (GB 1913-)
        Introduction and Rondo alla Burlesca, Op. 23, No. 1
(1940) (B&H, 1945, set).   Brilliant large-scale work.   De-
clamatory Introduction in D minor has players echoing each
other in canons spaced by arcs of quiet arpeggios over tapping chords.   The good-humored rondo begins with a cock-
crow theme in one piano, answered by a low wobbling cork-
screw tune in the other, tautening the tension with thickened
chords and multiplied notes.   A fff chord in Piano I directs
Piano II to "avanti," which it tries in a series of spurts;
then back to the somber mood of the introduction, only to
burst again into cock-crows and cork-screws, ending with a
dashing octave scale.   23 pages.   Dif.

        Mazurka elegiaca (1941) (B&H, 1942, set).   Written
during BB's American years, this occasional piece for the
death of Paderewski might well be revived from time to time.
Keeps both players awake with a variety of Polish motifs,
building climax largely through amplification of dynamics.
One waits in vain for the poignant harmonies of Szymanow-
ski's Mazurkas, or of BB's vocal and choral writing.   15
pages.   Mod. Dif.

BROWN, EARLE (USA 1926-)
        Corroboree for Three and Two Pianos.   See Three at
Three.

BRUCH, MAX (Ger 1838-1920)
        Fantasie in D Minor, Op. 11 (Br&H, set).   Tradi-
tional one-movement work with several contrasting sections.
Short introduction followed by Allegro molto energico listesso
tempo, Adagio ma non tropo, and Vivace assai, ma energico.
12 pages.   Dif.

BUCCHI, VALENTINO (It 1916-)
        Racconto siciliano (Da un'idea di Luchino Viconti);
balletto per due pianoforti liberamente tratto dalla novella
Cavalleria Rusticana di G. Verga. (Car, 1968, sep).   This
"ballet for two pianos" has five sections in different tempos.
Simple texture, well-organized and euphonious.   Section IV
has a tone cluster climax.   52 pages.   Mod. Dif.

BURLEIGH, CECIL (USA 1885-)
      Mountain Pictures Suite, Op. 42 (GS, set). By the
teacher and composer who glorified his native Rockies in a
series of chamber music suites, in a late Impressionist style
with craggy leaps and bold chordal melodies in ninths and
thirteenths.   Mod.

BUSONI, FERRUCCIO (It 1866-1924)
      Improvisation on a Bach Chorale (Br&H, 1917, sep).
Massive work (thirty pages) in the lavish style of the solo
transcriptions, with double the resources for dynamics, octave scales, chordal trills. A few choice passages might be
lifted, were it not for the plethora of excellent two-piano
transcriptions of Bach already available.   Dif.

      Duettino concertante nach Mozart (Br&H, 1921, sep).
Pianists should be grateful to FB for not treating Mozart in
the heavy-handed way he does Bach. This rondo is very
Mozarteen in its transparent texture, rococo figuration and
classical structure. But whereas Mozart's simplicity is that
of genius, this is the simplicity of the commonplace. With
the wealth of duet music available from WAM himself, this
is superfluous. 19 pages.   Mod.

BUSSOTTI, SYLVANO (It 1931-)
      Tableaux vivants, avant la passion selon Sade (1966)
(GR, set). Avant-garde composer who combines visual and
aural, literary and pictorial in his mixed media happenings.
Baker describes this work as "his crowning achievement,
which makes use of theatrical effects, diagrams, drawings,
surrealistic illustrations, etc. , with thematic content evolving
from a dodecaphonic nucleus, allowing great latitude for free
interpolations and set in an open-end form in which fragments of the music are recapitulated at will, until the players
are mutually neutralized. The unifying element of the score
is the recurrent motive D-Es-A-D-E, spelling the name De
Sade, interwoven with that of B-A-C-H. The first production
took place in Palermo on Sept. 5, 1965. "   Vir.

CAGE, JOHN (USA 1912-)
      A Book of Music for Two Pianos (CFP, 1944, set);
Three Dances (CFP, 1945, set); Experiences No. 1 for Two
Pianos (CFP, 1966, set). Influential experimental composer-
philosopher and mushroom expert, much discussed and seldom
played. The Book of Music for Two Pianos and the Three
Dances are in JC's most innovative style, the prepared piano.
For a description of such music, see AF-CPR. The prepara-

tion of each piano takes at least two hours, and incapacitates
the instruments for all other playing.   The initial effect of
the music is intriguing, but there is no sense of development,
of organic structure, of accession or climax, and the novelty
of the muted sounds quickly palls.   The enormous labor and
inconvenience of "preparing" a piano are out of all proportion
to the minimal results (as is also the enormous cost of the
music: $35 for the Book, $27.50 for Three Dances).

    Some of the other pieces exemplify another of JC's
innovations, "do-it-yourself" performance kits, without notation, but with loosely defined indications of procedure.   A-
mong such must be listed the piece titled O'OO", "an in-
dempotent to be performed in any way, by anyone," premiered in Tokyo, Oct. 24, 1962.

CARDEW, CORNELIUS (GB 1936-)
    Two Books of Study for Pianists/Music for Two Pi-
anos (HE, 1966, set of three).   Experimental avant-garde
composer who has the distinction of having been elected to
the Royal Academy.   This neatly written, beautifully printed,
totally organized post-Webern pointillistic composition introduces the element of chance by offering each player the choice
of note durations on each page, so long as he completes the
page in one minute by the stopwatch (sixteen minutes, sixteen
pages).   CC compares the process to arranging beads on a
rod which is fixed at both ends.   Some pages contain only
one note, some none, some a bustle of clusters.   Pages ten
to fifteen keep both players hopping and justify the title, as
it will take some study and sweat to be able to read and play
the widely spaced unrelated chords within the time span.
The third book is called "the composer's version," and does
what all responsible composers should do, writes down the
notes where and when they should be played.   Far out avant-
garde.   Dif.

CARMICHAEL, JOHN (USA)
    Tourbillon (Aug, 1961, set).   This valse brillante
might have been written a hundred years ago.   Effective use
of chromatic scales, broken-chord ninths in the style of
Saint-Säens.   12 pages.   Mod. E.

CASADESUS, ROBERT (Fr-USA 1899-1972)
    Dances Mediterraneennes (CF, set).   Pianist with two
team partners in the family.   A spirited set of three dances,
giving the hearer a good time, and the pianists a workout.
The opening Sardana is bright and propulsive.   A quiet Sara-

bande builds to an acme of power.   Closing Tarentelle is a
sparkling toccata-style moto perpetuo.   Dif.

        Six Pieces for Two Pianos (Dur, 1938, set).   Impres-
sionistic pieces of contrasting character and mood: 1. Algérienne (Andantino misterioso). 2. Russe (Pas vite). 3.
Sicilienne (Doux et balance). 4. Francaise (Animé). 5. Es-
pagnole (Viv). 6. Anglaise (Avec beaucoup d'entrain). 51
pages.   Dif.

CASELLA, ALFREDO   (It 1883-1947)
        Pupazzetti.   See Two at One.

CASTALDI, PAOLO
        Anfrage, per due pianoforti (1963) (GR, 1971).   Giant-
sized score made of fragments from other compositions pieced
together.   The bits and pieces seem to be cut and pasted together and the score is a facsimile copy of this collage.   Detailed instructions for dynamics and expression inserted here
and there all over the 18 pages.   26 minutes.   Dif.

CASTELNUOVO-TEDESCO, MARIO   (It-USA 1895-   )
        Duo-pianism; Impromptu for Two Pianos on the Names
of Hans and Rosaleen Moldenhauer (Greeting Cards, Op. 170,
Nr. 19) (AFo, 1959).   Born in Florence, MCT studied composition with Pizzetti, and later settled in Beverly Hills, California.   The names of Hans Moldenhauer (author of Duo Pi-
anism) and his wife Rosaline provide the melodic material
for this piece.   Twenty-five letters of the English language
(x being omitted) are represented by a two-octave chromatic
scale, in both ascending and descending order.   Thus the
name of Hans is E, A, B-flat, E-flat, and D, A, A-flat, E-
flat.   Harmonized with a waltz-like accompaniment, in a
lyric and romantic manner.   Facsimile score.   10 pages.
                                                               Mod.

CASTEREDE, JACQUES   (Fr 1926-   )
        Feux croisés, pour deux pianos (SE, 1968, sep).
Mammoth dissonant work in four movements: I. Quasi una
Marcia. II. Vivamente. III. Lento misterioso. IV. Ani-
mato e martellato.   Requires technical facility.   72 pages.
Facsimile score.   Dif.

CAZDEN, NORMAN   (USA 1914-   )
        Stony Hollow, Op. 47a (JSM, 1962, set).   Music edu-
cator offers a genial work.   Lively and catchy, but tonal and
undemanding technically.   Overextended for a single 2/4 movement.   15 pages.   Mod.

CHABRIER, EMMANUEL   (Fr 1841-1894)
   Espana Rhapsody (BM, set). The most celebrated
orchestra piece by EC has been effectively transcribed by
the composer for both four hands and two pianos. It is
eminently pianistic, and full of dashing glissandi, chromatic
scales and percussion effects. 32 pages.   Mod.

   Trois Valse romantiques (IMC, set). Superior examples of the French nineteenth-century salon valse, never
profound, but always brilliant, ingratiating, pianistic. Good
separately or together. Players should be warned that the
scores contain only individual parts, and each pianist is left
guessing what the other has next.   Mod. Dif.

CHADABE, JOEL A.   (USA   )
   Diversions; for Two Pianos (1966) (CPE, 1967). A-
tonal work with disjunct movements and tone clusters. Dots,
wedges, slashes, etc. are added to the complex score for
different effects. 14 pages.   Dif.

CHAILLY, LUCIANO   (It 1920-)
   Sonata tritematica n. 11 (in un sol tempo) per due
pianoforti, op. 259, 1961 (EC, 1963, sep). A twelve-tone
work with clear linear texture. The Molto adagio introduction is followed by Theme I (Allegro assai), Theme II (Poco
meno ancora, a fugato of four voices), and Theme III which
contains a free and expressive Recitativo. Ends quietly. 34
pages.   Mod. Dif.

CHANLER, THEODORE   (USA 1902-1961)
   The Second Joyful Mystery (AMP, set). Large-scale
one-movement fugue, correct and well-wrought, tonal but
freely chromatic, alternately lyrical and dramatic. Mod. Dif.

CHASINS, ABRAM   (USA 1903-)
   Period Suite (1948) (Ch, 1949, set). Though AC
claims that the six classical movements (fourteen minutes)
feature seventeenth- and eighteenth-century styles and ornamentation in contemporary harmony and sonority, the texture
is largely nineteenth-century, with all twenty fingers kept
busy, and at least one, often two, modulations per measure.
Rhythms are authentic but impacted in chromaticisms. The
lento Pavane is harmonized in Ravellian sevenths. Best is
the relatively lean Sarabande. 14 minutes.   Mod.

   AC has also written paraphrases of Carmen and Die
Fledermaus, à la Liszt.

CHOPIN, FREDERIC   (Pol-Fr 1810-1849)
      Rondo in C, Op. 73 (GS, CFP, sep).   FC not only
spurned all instruments but the piano, he also spurned a
partner in playing it, to judge by his duet output.   The Rondo
is early and unpublished during his lifetime.   It is a long
flashy showpiece, spirited and lively, with contrasting themes
linked by the rondo tune, exploiting both players.   Harmonically pedestrian and rhythmically monotonous, but amusing
for a matched team.   37 pages (GS); 29 pages (CFP).
                                                      Mod. Dif.

CLEMENTI, MUZIO   (1746-1832)
      Two Sonatas in B-flat Major, Op. 12 and Op. 46 (GS).
See also Two at One.   Mod.

COPLAND, AARON   (USA 1900-   )
      Danzon Cubano (1942) (B&H, 1943, set).   Composer
with prodigious influence and exiguous output that combines
jazz and Latin rhythms, folk-song style and atmospheric effects.   This is a propulsive, spastic dance, bold and dashing.   20 pages.   Mod. Dif.

      Billy the Kid (B&H, set).   Composer's arrangement of
the popular ballet suite.   Pianistic but demanding of musical
sensitivity and drive.   Scenes include The Open Prairie;
Street in a Frontier Town; Celebration Dance; Billy's Death.
                                                      Dif.

      Dance of the Adolescent (B&H, 1968, set).   From an
early ballet score, the orchestral origin is apparent in pseudo
timpani rolls, woodwind melodies, pizzicato accompaniments.
In the "lean, spare clinical texture" (Mellers) of AC's early
work, this lacks the popular appeal, and requires highly
sensitive playing to evoke the poetry of mystery and ecstasy.
24 pages.   Dif.

      For other arrangements, see Part 5.

CORDERO, ROQUE   (Pan-US 1917-   )
      Duo 1954 (PIC, 1965, set).   Black composer from
Panama who often writes in serial technic here uses row-
like motifs with great verve and imagination.   The 24-page
work is in a single movement, but the driving Allegro vigoro-
so is broken by an Adagio that is by turns passionate and
mysterious.   After the opening three pages, which could be
four-hand writing, the parts are well distributed and the two-
piano idiom creatively used.   24 pages.   Mod. to Dif.

CORIGLIANO, JOHN   (USA 1938-   )
    Kaleidoscope (1959) (GS, 1961, set).   Brilliant one-
movement work of moderate length in toccata style, premiered at Spoleto.   The coloristic effect suggested by the
title must be achieved by touch and dynamics, as the limited
melodic material is basically triadic and diatonic, though
freely dissonant, moving away from C and back again.   Full
use of the two-piano potential is made in well-wrought parts.
5 min. 30 sec.   Mod. Dif.

COUPER, MILDRED (COOPER)   (Arg-USA 1887-   )
    Dirge, for Two Pianos, Second Piano Tuned One Quar-
ter Tone Higher Than the First (In New Music, a quarterly
of modern compositions, vol. 10, no. 2, 1937).   Teacher of
piano and composer of ballet and incidental music for plays
wrote this quarter-tone work for two pianos.   9 pages. Mod.

COUPERIN, FRANCOIS   (Fr 1668-1733)
    Pieces de clavecin (Dur, sep).   The French clavecin-
ist, known as "the Great," published twenty-seven suites
called "ordres" in four volumes, which contain several pieces
for two players.   Some are written on three staves, with a
subject on one and a counterpart on the second, "if one
wishes."   The composer suggests different instruments (violin, flute?) or two clavecin, in which case players duplicate
the bass.   Others have two complete parts, marked 1st and
2nd clavecin.   Though more effective on harpsichords, they
make interesting two-piano pieces.

    Allemande in A (9th Ordre).   An imposing piece, so
richly ornamented that it must be taken at a very slow tempo.
                                                           Mod. Dif.

    Le Juillet, Rondeau in F (14th Ordre).   In 6/8 time
marked Gaiement, parts are mostly parallel thirds and
sixths.   Mod. E.

    Musettes in A (15th Ordre).   Two of these dances,
named after the French bagpipe, are written on three staves,
the subject and countersubject attractively varied, with trills
and canonic imitations, but the drone bass, rumbling away on
the octave and fifth, soon palls.   Mod. E.

COWELL, HENRY   (USA 1897-1965)
    Celtic Set (GS, set).   The composer's own arrange-
ment of a solo set written in the early years before his inven-
tion of chord clusters, interior effects.   Three movements

using Irish rhythms and tunes, dedicated to that compulsive folk song arranger, Percy Grainger. Reel, Caoine (a lament), and Hornpipe. Contrasting tempos with bagpipe basses; imitative counter-themes building to a dashing close. Traditional with mild surprises.   Mod.

COX, DAVID VASSALL   (GB 1916-)
        Majorca, a Balearic Impression (Elk, GMC, 1957, set). Lyric and modal, it is based on two traditional melodies of the Balearic Islands. 8 pages.   Mod. E.

DAMASE, JEAN-MICHEL   (Fr 1928-)
        Compliment d'anniversaire pour deux pianos (EMT, 1964, sep). "Pour la Princesse Henri de Polignac," by the pianist-composer who made his debut in New York in 1954. Opens with "Happy Birthday" theme, followed by eight short variations. Quite dissonant. Frequent shifting of meters. 16 pages.   Mod. Dif.

DEBUSSY, CLAUDE   (Fr 1862-1918)
        En blanc et noir, Three Pieces for Two Pianos (Dur, set). Written during the war when CD suffered on the sidelines, soon to die of cancer, the first movement is a kind of justification of his genius, and the second a glorious war piece, unequalled till Britten wrote his mighty War Requiem. Players need enormous brio, fine flexibility, a keen sense of balance, though the many changes are clearly marked. The name, Black and White, a misnomer for so colorful a piece, was suggested by the grays of Velazquez paintings. The Lent sombre, tribute to a friend "killed by the enemy," without being in any way programmatic vividly depicts war, with its drums, bugle calls, wisps of folk song and plainchant. Even the use of Luther's chorale for "the enemy" is musically justified. The Scherzando, dedicated to Stravinsky, uses numerous tired cliches and fails to rise to the level of the rest. Each of the three can be played separately. 15 minutes.
                                                        Dif.

        Lindaraja (1901) (Dur, set; JJ, 1926). This shows CD's early interest in Spanish music; many rhythmic and melodic motifs from this immature work are later polished in Soirée dans Grenade and the prelude to Pour le piano. 11 pages.   Mod.

        Prelude à l'après-midi d'un faune (Dur, set). Both CD and Ravel arranged several of their own solo pieces as duets, CD out of necessity, MR from a desire to hear the

music in a new medium. The master orchestrator, Ravel,
has produced a masterpiece of transcription here, and even
one overfamiliar with the original will enjoy the instrumental
imitations. Requires competent and sensitive players.   CD
also arranged this, as well as La Mer and Nocturnes.   Dif.

    Symphony in B Minor (SME, sep). Written by the
young tutor on his summers with Mme. von Meck in Russia,
there is little of CD in this, but echoes of Mme. 's protege,
Tchaikovsky. A classical Allegro with fluent keyboard writing in a nineteenth-century French operatic overture style.
Mod.

DE LEEUW, TON. See LEEUW, TON DE.

DELLO JOIO, NORMAN (USA 1913-)
    Aria and Toccata (CF, 1955, set). Bold, attractive
concert work, not overlong (ten minutes). A three-note motto on an ascending second and a falling third unifies the three
parts, a serene Adagio, a stately Poco piu movimento in
sarabande rhythm fugally developed, and an Allegro con ritmo spiritoso using conventional keyboard figures in an original and effective way.   Mod. Dif.

DIAMOND, DAVID (USA 1915-)
    Concerto (1942) (SMP, 1953, set). Well named, this
unaccompanied concerto has classic structure and key sequence. First movement, Allegro, is treated with sweeping
keyboard panache and scale figures. The Adagio is a simple
C major 4/4 with a dotted melody in parallel thirds, building
a brief dramatic climax with chordal expansion and dynamics.
The Allegro vivace uses much canonic imitation in patterning
staccato figures; then the racing scales return, with a smashing ending "con tutta forza" on the tonic triad of C. 16 1/2
minutes.   Dif.

DOHNANYI, ERNST VON (Hun-USA 1877-1960)
    Suite en valse, Op. 39 (AL, 1948, set). Post-ro-
mantic composer-pianist whose masterpiece is a set of Variations on a Nursery Tune for piano and orchestra. These
four valses, published separately, are called Valse symphonique, sentimentale, boiteuse, and Valse de fete. All are
pianistic in a jaded concert valse style. In four books, the
last is forty pages in length.   Mod. Dif.

DOUGHERTY, CELIUS (USA 1902-)
    Music from Seas and Ships (1941) (GS, 1950, set).

Famous accompanist and songwriter and duo-pianist (with Ruzika) composed this spirited folksy suite of three movements, called Banks of Sacramento, Sea Calm, and Mobile Bay. Sea chanteys provide the melodic material, and the pentatonic tunes are conventionally harmonized in a fluent effective keyboard style. 44 pages.   Mod.

DRING, MADELEINE   (1923-   )
    Three Fantastic Variations on Lilliburlero, for Two Pianos (AL, 1948, set).   Lilliburlero is a seventeenth-century party tune attributed to Henry Purcell. Despite the title, the variations are quite pedestrian. All three are in 4/4, with much use of triplets. The first one is in C major, the second in A minor, and the third is again in C. Melodic lines are doubled by two hands one or two octaves apart. 27 pages.   Mod.

    Sonata for Two Pianos, Four Hands (AL, 1951, set). A three-movement work similar to the Variations in style. The extended Drammatico e maestoso first movement makes much use of dotted rhythm. Second movement is a short, quiet Elégie. Ends with Allegro vigoroso. 43 pages.
                                            Mod. Dif.

DU PLESSIS, HUBERT L.   (SAf 1922-   )
    Prelude, Fugue and Postlude for Piano Duet, Op. 17 (Nov, 1958, sep). Three-movement work by the pianist-composer whose works have been recorded by the South African Broadcasting Corporation (with the composer at the piano). A lyric and melodic Prelude (Andante con moto), a quiet Fugue (Allegretto moderato) and a light and quick Postlude (Allegro). Lots of accidentals, but tonal. 22 pages.
                                            Mod. Dif.

DUVERNOY, JEAN BAPTISTE   (Fr   )
    Feu Roulant, Op. 256 (EBM, set). This French Czerny has provided calisthenics for twenty fingers, and a good exercise in ensemble, as the two pianists play fast chromatic scale figures with right hands in unison, parallel thirds, trill for Piano I and octave tremolo for Piano II. There is also a mammoth Don Juan Fantasy (Op. 284) on the Serenade from Mozart's Don Giovanni. 10 pages. Mod.

ELKUS, ALBERT   (USA 1884-1962)
    On a Merry Folk Tune (JF, 1933, set). Well-known West Coast pianist-educator. Effective recital piece requiring large hands, good staccato and octave technic. 10 pages.
                                            Mod.

ENESCO, GEORGES (Fr 1881-)
    Variations for Two Pianos, Op. 5 (En, B&H, 1899,
set). Dedicated to Edouard Risler and Alfred Cortot, the
variations are in nineteenth-century traditional style. Technical facility required for octaves and skips. Parts for first
and second pianos are on separate scores. 15 pages for
Piano I; 11 for Piano II.   Dif.

ENGELMANN, HANS ULRICH (Ger 1921-)
    Duplum, pour deux pianos, op. 29 (1965) (ET, 1967,
sep). Large complex avant-garde work in one movement,
with many detailed markings for dynamics and expression.
Disjunct keyboard figures. Use of tone clusters, including
free clusters with elbows. Difficult to read. 34 pages.
                                                              Vir.

FAITH, RICHARD (USA)
    Concerto for Two Pianos (SP, 1974, set). Music edu-
cator and composer has written a useful work in neo-classic
form of moderate difficulty, with no octaves in Piano I. Allegro contrasts a bold and a lyrical theme, well developed
with a snappy coda. The brief Andante should sing. The
Vivace owes much to Kabalevsky (see Sonatina in C) in rhythmic and melodic texture, and in the use of accidentals,
sprinkled lightly over the key of A minor. 22 pages. Mod.

FARNABY, GILES (GB 1560-1640)
    For Two Virginals (Dov, sep). This eight-measure
piece in Vol. II of the Fitzwilliam Virginal Book is probably
the earliest extant work for two keyboards. In C major,
alla breve, Virginal I plays a simple hymn-like tune in
three voices, moving in eighths, while Virginal II plays a
more elaborate part in 16ths and 64ths. Of interest historical-
ly to pianists, but playable on two early keyboard instruments.
                                                              Mod.

FELDMAN, MORTON (USA 1926-)
    Two Pieces for Two Pianos (1954); Vertical Thoughts
1. for Two Pianos (1963) (CFP, sep). This Cage-school
avant-gardist attempts an aural equivalent of the abstract ex-
pressionist painting of Philip Guston, de Kooning, Franz
Kline. His instrumental pieces are in sets called Durations,
Extensions, Projections, Vertical Thoughts, Intermissions,
Structures, Intervals (the names are immaterial and inter-
changeable). The catchwords are predetermined indetermin-
acy, unpredictability, metaphysical place. Non-metaphysical
pianists will find little to engage them in the muted, diluted

dissonant sounds spaced out in silence like long-pondered
chess moves. FM's verbalizations are of little help: "the
repeated notes are not musical pointillism, they are where
the mind rests on an image."   Mod.

        Teams of metaphysical pianists, performing for meta-
physical audiences, should not miss FM's pieces for piano,
four hands, and three and four pianos. For recordings of
some of these, see Part 6.

FERGUSON, HOWARD (GB 1908-)
        Partita (1935-36) (B&H, 1937, set). Influential com-
poser and educator writes in a post-romantic, neo-Brahmsian
style, using classical forms. I. Grave - Allegretto pesante.
II. Allegro un poco agitato. III. Andante un poco mosso.
IV. Allegro con spirito. An extended and pianistic work.
49 pages, 21 minutes. There is another version for orchestra. "Each version was conceived for its own medium, so
neither may be said to be an arrangement of the other."--
composer's note.   Dif.

FICHER, JACOBO (Rus-Arg 1896-)
        Three Hebrew Dances for Two Pianos, Four Hands
(SMP, 1964, set). Lively music using folk melodies and
rhythms. 1. Wedding Dance (Allegro moderato). 2. Mystic
Dance (Andante con moto). 3. Hora (Presto). Needs facili-
ties for fast running passages and octaves. 35 pages.
                                                          Mod. Dif.

FISCHER, ERNEST (Ger, 1900-)
        Dancing Masks; Marabu (BSS, 1937, set). Entertain-
ment music of the kind played at Berlin supper clubs in the
thirties. All are alla breve, variations on the fox-trot
rhythm. 12 pages. There are two more called Skidding
Along and Perpetual Motion (BSS, 1935, set). 19 pages.
                                                            Mod. E.

FONTYN, JACQUELINE (Bel 1930-)
        Spirales (PIC, 1974). Large-scale four-movement
avant-garde work, pointillistic in texture with wide-spaced
linear passages, chord trills and tremolandi. The use of
dissonance is so euphonious as to suggest tonal progressions
and cadences. Shifting meters, tempo rubato, wide dynamics,
much pedal, all meticulously marked. If not for the great
length (31 pages) it would be a good introduction to this style
of writing, as the difficulties are not insuperable, and the
effects rewarding. Facsimile score.   Mod. Dif.

FOSS, LUKAS (Ger-US 1922-)
    Ni Bruit ni vitesse (SE, 1974, sep; 4 copies needed).
Successful conductor and composer who experiments with
tape, amplified strings, improvisation. "Nor Noise nor
Haste" is a set of three pieces which requires two grand
pianos with middle sostenuto pedal, two percussionists with
assorted cowbells, Japanese bowls, etc. Each of the twenty-
one pages of the score must be timed with a stopwatch (a
fifth "performer" and another score). As in the case of
Echoi, LF suggests prerecording one part. For two explorers.   Vir.

    Set of Three Pieces (GS, set). Early work by a com-
poser who has moved from traditional to experimental styles.
Neo-classic writing in a stirring March; lyrical Andante, flowing and lengthy; complex final Concertante, pianistic and
euphonious.   Mod. Dif.

FRANÇAIX, JEAN (Fr 1912-)
    Huit danses exotiques (BSS, 1958, sep). Eight dances
in a category future generations may well think of as twentieth-century salon music, its banal superficiality often excused
as "Gallic wit. " Piano II, better labeled Secondo, plays the
same rhythmic bass with chords on syncopated beats through
a variety of similar meters marked Samba, Mambo, Rock 'n'
Roll, the "exotic" of the title. What passes for melody in
Piano I (Primo) is linear, in octaves or unison, or with occasional left-hand chords. It is not clear why it is marked
Pour Deux´ Pianos, as both parts can be played on one instrument except for a few pages. With some alterations, it can
be easily done on one piano. 36 pages.   Mod.

FRANCK, CESAR (Bel-Fr 1822-1890)
    Prélude, fugue et variation, Op. 18 (Dur, 1962, set).
Since Franck left nothing for two pianos, it is good to have
this transcription of an organ work. It has been arranged
as a piano solo, as a four-hand duet, and for violin, harmonium and piano. All the Franck qualities are here, on a
modest scale, the undulating chromaticism, the well-wrought
fugue, the flowing accompaniment figure. Part Three is a
repeat of the Prelude with a varied accompaniment. 15
pages.   Mod. Dif.

FREED, ISADORE (Rus-USA 1900-1960)
    Carnival (TP, set). Music editor, educator and com-
poser wrote a one-movement Allegro, 13 pages, 4 1/2 minutes, brilliant and playable. Though basically tonal (D major-

minor) it is written without signature, in a steady quarter-
note pulse, toccata-style, with two brief lyrical passages.
                                                       Mod. Dif.

      Hard times (Paraphrase on a Folk Theme) for Two
Pianos, Four Hands (TP, 1957). A slow, modal, melancholy
piece with no key signature, but the theme is in D. Frequent
shift of meter from 4/4 to 3/4 to 2/4. 5 pages.   Mod.

FRICKER, PETER RACINE (GB 1920-)
      Four Fughettas, Op. 2 (Scho, 1950, set). Early work
by prolific and much-performed music educator now in California.   Superior neo-classic writing that is pianistically
idiomatic yet suggestive of colorful instrumentation.   Moderato
e pomposo suggests a Handelian overture with ending for full
band.   The second number is a Capriccioso and evokes bas-
soons and woodwinds, with timpani brought in for punctuation.
The Lento is in minor and expressive. Closing Vivo is a
gigue worthy of JSB himself. 17 pages.   Mod. Dif.

FRID, GEZA (Hun-Neth 1904-)
      Prelude and Fugue, Op. 23 (SMP, 1964, set). Com-
bination of the scholarly and the pianistic by a pianist-teach-
er.   Motor patterns and showy chord progressions seem to
have been conceived at the keyboard.   Even the fugue, after
a long and correct exposition, lapses into toccata-like chord
tapping and keyboard calisthenics, with figures borrowed from
the Prelude. 27 pages.   Mod.

FULEIHAN, ANIS (Cyp-USA 1900-1970)
      Toccata (SMP, 1965, set). The late AF divided his
career between the USA and the Mediterranean, and his music is colored by the associations. This brilliant four-movement work might equally well have been called a Sonata,
except that the varieties of touch are of prime importance in
the highly idiomatic keyboard writing. The long Introduction
is like a free modern fugue, and the Finale is another,
marked to be played percussively and with glassy tone. The
Variations in the second movement have a modal quality, and
the slow melody lines suggest Middle Eastern cantillation.
The closing variation is marked Barbaro, and the frequent
two-hand chord trills in irregular meters evoke the Persian
santir or dulcimer. The quiet Interlude has a similar melodic line floating on a gently undulating chordal figure. 50
pages.   Dif.

GENZMER, HARALD (Ger 1909-)

Sonata for Two Pianos (BSS, 1950, set).   Modern
music for people who don't like modern music, this three-
movement work is bold and pianistic, with straightforward
melodic and rhythmic figures, traditional piano textures,
and a harmony (without key signatures) basically tonal, but
spiced with chromatic dissonances.   Mod. Dif.

GERSHWIN, GEORGE   (USA 1898-1937)

Rhapsody in Blue (HF, NWM, sep).   GG was not content to be one of the most successful composers of pop music; he also wanted to be known for his serious music.   He
wrote nothing for duet or two pianos, but his Three Preludes
are standard solo repertoire.   The Rhapsody in Blue and
Concerto in F, both written to be played with orchestra, were
transcribed for two pianos.   The Rhapsody is playable in this
form, though the wailing clarinet, muted trumpets, and romp-
ing trombones are missed, but it is preferable to the solo
piano version.   The orchestra works, American in Paris
and Cuban Overture, have also been transcribed for two pianos.   Mod. Dif.

Short Story (Scho, set).   This attractive duet was
made from material originally intended for the Preludes.   It
was rejected by GG, but arranged first for violin and piano
by Samuel Dushkin; and then by Al and Lee Reiser for two
pianos.   Several melodic and rhythmic fragments are knit
into a short brilliant piece with the lilt of GG's best jazz
songs.   Piano I is soloistic with several cadenzas.   Mod.

Second Rhapsody (HF, sep).   Intended as a second
smash hit for GG to play, in the tradition of the Rhapsody in
Blue, this is an unsatisfactory work, both in its original
form for piano and orchestra, and as arranged for two pianos.   While the Concerto in F suffers from a plethora of
tuneful themes, underdeveloped, this lacks any inspired
themes, and plods.   It is certainly not a match for the first
Rhapsody.   Mod. Dif.

I Got Rhythm (HF, sep).   This originally appeared in
an album of "Improvised variations" for piano solo, along with
a dozen of GG's songs, popularized by Ginger Rogers, Ethel
Merman, and others.   The composer later turned it into the
set of variations for piano and orchestra on which this two-
piano arrangement is based.   Light-hearted entertainment
music, the six variations include a Chinese version, a valse
triste, and the inevitable blues.   Mod.

GIDEON, MIRIAM (USA 1906-)
Hommage a ma Jeunesse (MM, set). Neo-classic
three-movement sonatina, linear, lucid and winsome. Mod.

GLAZOUNOV, ALEXANDER (Rus 1865-1936)
Fantasie, Op. 104 (MPB, set). Post-romantic three-
movement work, dense and intense.   Dif.

GLIERE, REINHOLD (Rus 1875-1956)
Six Pieces, Opus 41, for Two Pianos, Four Hands
(IMC, 1951, set). Traditional, melodic work with Russian
folk flavor. 1. Prelude. 2. Valse triste. 3. Chanson.
4. Basso ostinato. 5. Air de ballet. 6. Mazurka. 27
pages.   Mod.

GODOWSKY, LEOPOLD (Rus-USA 1870-1938)
Contrapuntal Paraphrase on Weber's "Invitation to the
Dance," with an optional accompaniment of a third piano.
(CF, 1922, set). A large-scale work of considerable com-
plexity. Romantic and elaborate, effective concert piece.
A set of two scores for Piano I and Piano II, containing both
parts, each 74 pages. A third score for Piano III only. 27
pages.   Vir.

GOLDMAN, RICHARD FRANKO (US 1910-)
Le Bobino, Burlesque in Three Scenes (SMP, 1950,
set). Written to recapture the sound of the vaudeville thea-
ter orchestra at Le Bobino, in Paris, in the '30s. A suite
of three movements: 1. Overture (with a trio). 2. Entr'-
acte. 3. Le Jazz cold. 19 pages.   Mod.

GRAINGER, PERCY ALDRIDGE (Ausl-USA 1882-1961)
Country Gardens (GS, set). This brilliant pianist
early discovered a profound affinity for folk music and the
common people. He made countless transcriptions of songs
and dances for various instrumental ensembles, thus pre-
serving the ancient music and also uniting people in a common experience of musical recreating not unlike that of the
folk who originally gathered to dance and sing the music.
PG developed an original way of scoring and notation and
used colloquial English for directions: for example, "louden
lots," encircled in a cartoonist's balloon. His most famous
transcription is the boisterous, bouncing Country Gardens,
which he arranged for every conceivable combination of players: solo for one (a simple and a concert version); duets
for two players at two pianos, four players at two pianos,
etc. He organized and encouraged performances of his music

for massed piano ensembles.   All the arrangements require
considerable dexterity and agility.   Other folk-song transcriptions, available in any combination, are as follows (all GS):
Shepherd's Hey; English Dance; Hill Songs, I and II; Spoon
River; Molly on the Shore; Two Musical Relics of My Mother; One More Day, My John; I'm Seventeen, Come Sunday;
Brigg Fair, etc.   See also Three at Two.

GREEN, RAY   (USA 1909-   )
        Jig for a Concert, Two Pianos (AME, 1953, set).
American composer who studied with Albert Elkus and Ernest
Bloch and taught at the University of California wrote this
fast, vigorous dance in 3/2 meter (actually 9 quarter notes
most of the time).   The recurring modal melody, often
doubled two octaves apart, is imitated between the pianos,
and occasionally accompanied by seventh chords.   Broad ff
ending with melody stated in succession of open triads.
Pleasant and effective.   15 pages.   Mod.

GRETCHANINOV, ALEXANDER   (Rus-USA 1864-1956)
        Deux morceaux pour 2 pianos à 4 mains, op. 18
(RSMP, 1925).   No. 1, Poème, is lyric and expressive, with
two-against-three rhythmic pattern between Piano I and Piano
II.   Use of antiphonal effects.   9 pages.   Mod.   No. 2,
Cortège, is a robust march requiring good octave technique.
13 pages.   Mod. Dif.

GRIEG, EDVARD   (Nor 1843-1907)
        Romance with Variations, Op. 51 (CFP, sep).   Mod-
eled after Schumann's Andante, this is a pleasant, if not exciting work to play and hear.   The full title is Variations on
an Old Norwegian Romance and the sentimental romanticism
of the old song permeates the writing, which is pianistic and
effective.   Mod.

        Second-Piano Accompaniments to Sonatas by Mozart
(GS).   It is doubtful if anyone today will care to play these.
Even when they were published by Grieg, they raised a hue
and cry in Germany.   Guy Maier and Wiktor Labunski de-
plore them as glaring examples of bad taste, though other
pianists at one time defended them.   The increasing respect
for authenticity and style, and the growing familiarity with
Mozart's music today make them appear as amusing aberra-
tions of a generation incapable of enjoying the simplicity and
purity of the classical style.

GRUEN, RUDOLPH   (1900-1966)

Scherzo, Op. 4a, No. 2 (AMP, 1936, set).   A very
fast, bouncy, one-movement work in traditional style.   11
pages.   Mod. Dif.

Humoresque, Op. 14, No. 2 (1935) (AMP, 1936, set).
Traditional, one movement.   13 pages.   Mod. Dif.

GRUNN, HOMER   (USA 1880-1944)
Humoresque Negre (GS, 1928, set).   The solo version
is quite negotiable, but is such fun that sharing it with a
partner is urged.   7 pages.   Mod.

GUASTAVINO, CARLOS   (Arg 1914-   )
Tres romances, para dos pianos (EAM, 1951, sep).
The three romances are: I. Las Niñas (Andante), II. Mucha-
cho Jujeño (Andantino), III. Baile (Allegro).   Late nineteenth-
century style, with much chromaticism, frequent modulations,
and a rich thick texture.   51 pages.   Mod. Dif.

GUION, DAVID WENDEL   (USA 1895-   )
The Harmonica Player (GS, 1926, set).   The solo
transcriptions of American folk tunes by this pianist-ethnolo-
gist are almost too elaborate for the tunes to carry or for
the pianist to play.   A division of labor is welcome, but
DWG seems only to have multiplied the difficulties by two.
Good flashy encore number.   7 pages.   Dif.

GUYONNET, JACQUES   (Swi 1933-   )
Polyphonie II; deux pianos (1961) (UE, 1968, sep).
Avant-garde work with very complex rhythms.   Change of
meter from 3/8 to 2/8 to 4/8, 5/16, 5/8, etc. almost
every measure.   Frequent changes of tempo indicated by
metronome marks.   Sudden shifting of dynamics between fff
and ppp.   10 pages.   Dif.

HAHN, REYNALDO   (Ven-Fr 1874-1947)
Le Ruban dénoué, 12 valses à 2 pianos (Heu, 1916).
By the Venezuela-born Paris-educated composer, these waltzes
are written with conventional rhythm, harmony and keyboard
figurations.   Mod.

HAIEFF, ALEXEI   (Rus-USA 1914-   )
Sonata for Two Pianos (Ch, 1945, set).   Large neo-
classic three-movement piece basically tonal (B-flat) but
harmonically free.   There is much linear writing flashing
from one player to the other in sharp rhythmic and melodic
patterns, with battering chordal punctuation.   Central Andante

tries for lyricism but settles for a tissue of trills and scales.
Like late Beethoven the note-black pages look much richer
than they sound. The finale begins with a giddy chatter of
triplets, but thins for a spare angular cantabile melody in
B minor, with cyclic quotes and a hammered coda climax.
Dif.

HALFFTER, RODOLFO (Sp-Mex 1900-)
Musica para dos Pianos, (EMM, 1967, sep). An occasional work that deserves repetition, this proves that serial
writing can be euphonious if that is the composer's aim. Re-
flected Images uses the two-piano medium boldly and musically, constructing from the row contrasting themes that have
coherence, contrast and sufficient repetition to engage the
ear. Cyclic Ratiocinations carries the process still further,
with frequent meter shifts; sustained chordal writing contrasting with percussive toccata patterns. 43 pages.   Dif.

HANDEL, GEORGE FRIDERIC (Ger-GB 1685-1759)
Suite (OxU, 1950, sep). Duo-pianists must be grateful to Thurston Dart for rescuing from obscurity and present-
ing in practicable form this delightful work of GFH's middle
years, of which only Klavier I has survived. The recon-
structed second-piano part seems eminently right, even the
drastic altering of the Chaconne from three half-notes to the
bar, to 3/8. One suspects that if GFH had prepared the
manuscript for publication, he would have discovered that he
had written a Gigue for his closing dance, not a Chaconne,
as in many of his other suites. The editor, a distinguished
harpsichordist, suggests that while the suite sounds well on
two harpsichords, it might sound even better on two pianos.
16 pages.   Mod.

HAUBENSTOCK-RAMATI, ROMAN (Pol-Isr 1919-)
Catch 1, fur Cembalo Solo (Oder à 2), 1968 (UE,
1968). 8-15 minutes. Catch 2, fur 1 oder 2 Klaviere, 1968
(UE, 1968). About 12 minutes (solo), 15-25 minutes (two
pianos). Both are chance compositions with graphic notation and instructions for performance in German and English.
The first one, for harpsichord, can also be performed on
two instruments, "either live by two performers, or solo by
one performer and a tape recording." Catch 2 is for one or
two pianos.

HAYDN, FRANZ JOSEF (Aus 1732-1809)
The Teacher and the Pupil, arranged for two pianos
by Guy Maier (CFS, set). Originally a four-hand number

(see Two at One), this arrangement of three of the seven variations retains the simplicity and charm of the original, and by transposing the range of parts, makes the "lesson" more humorous.   Mod.

HEILLER, ANTON (Aus 1923-)
     Toccata (UE, 1946, sep).   Best known composition of a noted organ and harpsichord player, frequently featured by two-piano teams.   The brilliant six-minute piece pits a zig-zag running figure in fast 9/8 against a bassoon-like staccato theme, which thickens cumulatively to chords and octaves for a spectacular climax.   27 pages.   Dif.

HEMMER, EUGENE (USA 1929-)
     Introduction and Dance (1949) (AME, 1955, set).   The recurring theme in this piece is from an Appalachian folk song, "The Devil's Ten Questions."   Beginning Andantino tranquillo, it builds to a ffz ending.   Use of parallel fourths and fifths and open triads.   12 pages.   Mod.

HENGEVELD, GERARD (Neth 1910-)
     Suite for Two Pianos (SMP, 1971, set).   Bold, fresh and uncomplicated, a three-part suite with a slow Movement di blues for a middle section, framed by a dashing Allegro ma non troppo splashed with quartal chords and seconds, and a Lento-Allegro, with more suggestions of jazz and popular dance.   40 pages.   Mod.

HENKEMANS, HANS (Neth 1913-)
     Sonata for Two Pianos (1943) (Don, 1950, sep).   Psy-chiatrist turned pianist has this gargantuan sonata in four movements, fifty-nine pages.   The brilliant writing is equally distributed, with broad melodies and running passages in an imaginative variety of figures.   Written without key signatures, the outside movements are basically C-sharp major and C-sharp minor, with chords freely altered and polytonal.   Mid-dle movements are an Adagio with a rich melisma and dazz-ling chord trills, and a dashing Allegro vivo, flashing with dynamic shifts.   The expansive sarabande finale fades to a dying coda, Alla marcia funebre.   A virtuoso work.   Requires technical equipment.   Dif.

HENSELT, ADOLPH VON (Ger 1814-1889)
     Romance in B Minor, Op. 10 (Br&H, 1919, set).
Slow, lyric piece of moderate difficulty.   3 pages for Piano I, 2 pages for Piano II.

HENZE, HANS WERNER   (Ger 1926-   )
    Divertimenti (1964) (BSS, 1965, sep).   Inappropriate
title for an enormously difficult and weighty work in four
movements.   Though the keyboard writing is conventionally
idiomatic and the harmony a Hindemithian dissonant tonality,
often triadic, the texture is opaque with thickly overlaid patterns of busy activity for both players.   Scales, arpeggios,
chord trills, octave tattoos tumble after one another with
only a brief Largo respite.   For two thoroughbred steeds,
champing at the bit.   57 pages.   Vir.

HILL, EDWARD BURLINGAME   (USA 1872-1960)
    Jazz Studies (GS, set).   Since the great jazz master,
Gershwin, left nothing for two pianos, it is good to have
these from the pen of one of America's great early moderns.
EBH was a thorough skillful craftsman, and these four are
well-wrought for two pianos, while retaining the spontaneity
of improvised jazz.   Mod. Dif.

HINDEMITH, PAUL   (Ger-USA 1895-1963)
    Sonata for Two Pianos (1942) (BSS, 1942, sep).   Mod-
ern master of the classical sonata form here writes one of
his most tightly structured works, though spread over five
movements and two keyboards.   The four-hand medium lends
itself well to PH's favorite device of four-voice canonic imitation.   All movements here are unified by an upthrusting
five-note motif (modified for the fugue).   First movement is
called Glockenspiel and begins at once, after the chordal
motto, with a canon figure, each hand rippling down three
octaves.   Chords then chime out melody over the orchestra
bells of Piano II.   An enormous Allegro, with four bold
angular themes laced with running unison figures in unpre-
dictable patterns, ranges from C minor to a smashing C
major.   Third movement is a lento Kanon, the motto-melody
and its accompaniment exactly duplicated one measure later
in Piano II, muted except for one brief forte passage.   The
Recitativ has a fourteenth-century anonymous English verse
for epigraph, and the bold declamation of Piano I, punctuated
by chords on Piano II, is non-metrical until the final perora-
tion in 3/4 molto largo.   The work is rounded off with a
great double fugue, using all the devices of counterpoint and
exploiting the twenty fingers and 176 keys to the full.   42
pages.   Dif.

HOVHANESS, ALAN   (USA 1911-   )
    Vijag, Op. 37 (CFP, 1964, set).   Early and late AH
are much of a piece: at their best, exciting to play and hear,

at their worst, slapdash and formless. The "spirit of an
Armenian festival" is well captured in the nine pages (four
minutes) of this single movement. Both pianos have a single
melodic line of continuous sixteenth notes on white keys (with
an occasional black key) divided between the hands, suggesting the middle Eastern santir or dulcimer. Effective. Mod.

      Ko-Ola-U, Op. 136 (CFP, set). From America's
number one Orientalist, an ode to the mountains of Hawaii,
complete with poem by the composer. Written entirely on
white keys, Piano I in triple rhythms against duple in Piano
II, with running figures against quartal chords. Mellers
finds AH's fluency "a joy in a creatively constipated society,"
but wonders if it is not too easy to write and to listen to.
3 minutes.   Mod. E.

      Mihr, for Two Pianos, imitating an orchestra of
knoons (NM, 1946).

HUMMEL, JOHANN NEPOMUK (Aus 1778-1837)
      Introduction and Rondo, Op. Posth. , No. 5 (Br&H,
set). Piano I and Piano II on separate scores, 11 pages
each. See also Two at One.   Mod. Dif.

INFANTE, MANUEL (Sp-Fr 1883-1958)
      Danses andalouses (1921) (SE, 1931, set). Three
rhythmic Spanish dances by the pianist-composer, in three
books. I. Ritmo (13 pages). 2. Sentimento (24 pages). 3.
Gracia (12 pages). Pianistic, brilliant, and effective. Dif.

IRINO, YOSHIRO (Jap 1921-)
      Music for Two Pianos (ONT, 1963, set). Influential
prize-winning Japanese composer and educator, the first to
use serial writing. Derivative work employing two players in
the exposition of tone rows in standard forms.   Dif.

IVES, CHARLES (USA 1874-1954)
      Three Quarter-Tone Pieces for Two Pianos (CFP,
1968, set). These must rank among the most interesting
works of this versatile maverick, though they will seldom
be played. Few will risk putting a piano a quarter-tone lower or higher, in order to learn them, but any who do so will
be rewarded. Others can hear a fine performance on records
(see Part 6). Interest in quarter-tone music dated from
Ives' boyhood experience of playing on tuned water glasses with
his father. About 1903 he seems to have written part of this
music. In 1925 he met the French pianist-composer, Hans

Barth, who played some of Ives' music on a two-manual
quarter-tone piano at a concert in New York. The first of
the three pieces which CI later assembled is Largo, an atmospheric mood poem in which the odd interval adds to the
haunting, tenuous sonority as piano answers piano. In the
second piece, Allegro, the discrepancy in pitch gives a twangy
piquancy to the jazzy syncopated dance tune. Longest of the
three is the closing Adagio: Chorale. Here many of the
technics and textures of serial music are anticipated, with
wide-ranging running figures that avoid note repetitions and
traditional chord-scale patterns, and are enhanced by the
blurred effect. For the first time the two pianos play in
unison in the slow chorale theme, an excruciating spine-
tingling sound. Even with pianos tuned together the pieces
are worth playing. If the authors may indulge in nostalgia,
the two-piano music played in the mountains of China during
the war, when instruments were rare and tuners non-existent,
often had this unique sound. 26 pages.   Dif.

JACOBSON, MAURICE (GB 1896-)
        Ballade, for Two Pianos, Four Hands (Elk, 1939,
set). One movement, with sections in different tempos, keys
and moods. A music publisher as well as composer, MJ was
the director of J. Curwen and Sons. 23 pages.   Mod. Dif.

JONG, MARINUS DE (Bel 1891-)
        Habanera; pour deux pianos, op. 62 (CBDM, 1963,
sep). Lively dance in late nineteenth-century style. 16
pages, about 6 minutes. Facsimile score.   Mod. Dif.

KADOSA, PAUL (Hun 1903-)
        Sonata for Two Pianos, Op. 37 (1946) (Zen, 1962).
Lengthy work by the important Hungarian composer. PK
was a pupil of Kodály but his style is closer to that of Bartók. In his writings he combines a modern idiom with folk
materials. 68 pages.

KETTERING, EUNICE LEA (USA 1906-)
        Rigadoon (GS, 1970, set). Short effective recital
piece with more of the barn dance than of the rococo court
about it. Staccato chords and scales in thirds with a harmony of ninths and sevenths suggest pizzicato strings. Traditional but fresh. 11 pages.   Mod. E.

KHATCHATURIAN, ARAM (USSR 1903-)
        Suite (LPC, 1948, set). Ostinato (melodic line against
a three-note ostinato), Romance (lyric and Armenian in char-

acter), Fantastic waltz (brilliant and sweeping, Armenian
flavor). 32 pages, 10 minutes.   Mod. Dif.

KLEBE, GISELHER (Ger 1925-   )
    Sonata for Two Pianos (1952) (BSS, 1952, sep).   One
of the many German composers who got a start in the Berlin
Radio, GK experiments with many styles, from neo-classic
to dodecaphonic.   A recent ballet-symphony calls for two
pianos tuned a quarter-tone apart.   The Sonata uses jazz
syncopations in a neo-classic structure.   An Andante con
grazia in D minor-major separates a high-spirited but mind-
less Con moto and a frenetic boogie-woogie (Vivo) and serves
as coda.   Much use of ninths, altered sevenths and jazz
chromaticisms lend a tired gaiety.   Mod. Dif.

KLEIN, JOHN (USA 1915-   )
    Three Dances for Two Pianos (1943) (AMP, 1946, set).
Set of three lively contrasting pieces by the composer-organ-
ist: 1. Jig waltz (Vivace), 11 pages. 2. Stoop dance (Moderato), 7 pages. 3. Whirl (Allegro assai), 14 pages. Mod.

KONIETZNY, HEINRICH (1910-   )
    Toccatina für 2 Klaviere (1969) (Sim, 1972, sep).
Written for the well-known team Aloys and Alfons Kontarsky,
this is a vigorous one-movement work with offbeat accents,
to be played as fast as possible. Dissonant. 10 pages. Dif.

LANCEN, SERGE (Fr 1922-   )
    Promenade, pour deux pianos (EFM, 1961, set).
Short and light-hearted piece in simple 2/4 meter, with a
two-page Molto cantabile middle section.   Melody mostly in
Piano I, with Piano II providing the accompaniment.   Traditional harmony.   SL graduated from Paris Conservatory with
first prize in 1949, and was the winner of Prix de Rome
and Hinrichsen Award. 3 Min. 15 sec.   Mod. E.

LANZA, ALCIDES (Arg 1929-   )
    Plectros (1962-II) for One or Two Pianos (Ba, 1963,
sep).   For two players at one or two pianos.   The performers are instructed to strike the piano with the palm, the
edge of the hand or fist, pluck the strings with finger or
plectrum, scratch the strings with nail or strike with drum
stick, play with thimbled fingers.   Two pages of explanation
for four pages of music. 5 min. 30 sec.

LAVAGNINO, ANGELO (It 1909-   )
    Sonatina for Two Pianos (Car, 1949, sep).   In three

movements: Entrata (Ironico: molto moderato); Inno ves-
perale (In nativitate domini), slow, somber, fugal; Parodia in
boogie-woogie (Allegro dinamico), lively and rhythmic. Dissonant but tonal, using chords built on fourths and fifths.
18 pages. 16 minutes.   Mod. Dif.

LAZAROF, HENRI (Bul-USA 1932-)
       Intonazione (1973) (AMP, 1973, set). Composer
trained in Jerusalem writes a large serial work exploring
varied piano sonorities, from silences to interior effects,
chords, figures, all minutely timed and carefully annotated.
For explorers with vast stores of patience and technic. Vir.

LEES, BENJAMIN (USA 1924-)
       Sonata (B&H, 1951, set). Brilliant large-scale neo-
classic work written for the Fromm Foundation. It is eminently playable, with a Giocoso first movement spreading the
amiable melody over rhythmic chords, octave progressions
and scale figures. The lengthy Adagio semplice is linear,
contrapuntal and expressive. The fluent Allegro finale incorporates a fugue. Written without key signatures it is in
a B-flat tonality, modulating freely and richly chromatic.
46 pages.   Mod. Dif.

LEEUW, TON DE (Neth 1926-)
       Sonate (Don, 1950, sep). Early piece by avant-garde
Dutch composer, using dissonant tonality. The long work,
both scholarly and emotionally intense, makes large demands
on the players. The texture is often made up of small ger-
minal motifs developed and woven into a complex tissue.
Four movements are Moderato appassionato, Minuet, Lento
and Allegro non troppo. For the intrepid. 44 pages, 20
minutes. Manuscript facsimile.   Dif.

LEIGHTON, KENNETH (GB 1929-)
       Scherzo for Two Pianos (ALen, 1953, set). One-
movement rhythmic piece with a climactic fff ending. Modal
and tuneful, with a wistful melody shared between Piano I
and Piano II. Contrapuntal, the two piano parts are equally
interesting. 19 pages.   Mod.

LESUR, DANIEL (Fr 1908-)
       Fantaisie, pour deux pianos (1962) (GR, 1963, sep).
One-movement rhapsodic piece with contrasting sections:
Allegro moderato, Andante energico e nobile, Poco piu ani-
mato, Flessible, Tempo di marcia gaietta, and Allegro moderato. Mildly dissonant, with no key signatures. Technical

facility needed for skips and rapid broken-chord passages.
An organist-composer, DL belongs to a group known as La
Jeune France, the other members being Messiaen, Baudrier,
and Jolivet.   28 pages, 7 min. 12 sec.   Dif.

LIPATTI, DINU   (Rou 1917-1950)
        Danses roumaines, for two pianos, or piano and or-
chestra (1943-45) (SE, 1954, set).   Two-piano version of this
three-movement work by the legendary Roumanian pianist.
I. Vif, in 7/8 (2/8 + 2/8 + 3/8); II. Andantino, in 2/4;
III. Allegro vivace, in 2/4.   Rhythmic and energetic piece.
Simple folk melodies treated with dissonant harmony and fast
pianistic figurations.   Technically demanding.   44 pages. Vir.

LISZT, FRANZ   (Hun 1811-1886)
        Concerto Pathetique for Two Pianos (GS, Br&H, sep).
Liszt's one work for two pianos occupied him for over twenty
years, before he found its ideal form.   Since then misguided
pianists have turned it back into a solo concerto with orchestra, and into a Concerto for two pianos with orchestra.   It
is a bold and dramatic work in one movement, comparable
to the great Sonata in B minor, though less inspired.   A
family of three related themes in E minor are introduced in
the Allegro energico, linked and expanded with passages of
interlocking octaves, chromatic triplet figures, cadenzas.
The Patetico theme has the martial rhythm of Wagner's
wedding march, developed with clapped chords, and a martellato crescendo to the Grandioso second subject in E.   An
Andante sostenuto replaces second movement and moves from
Dolcissimo in E to Con maesta in D-flat, with cadenzas,
chord trills, timpani bass rolls.   An Allegro trionfante with
soaring octave scales in Piano I and a broad chordal melody
in E Major in Piano II closes.   The bag of tricks is all here,
but employed in a mature musicianly way.   Dif.

        Spanish Rhapsody, Rumanian Rhapsody, Rhapsody on
Hungarian Songs in A Minor.   These were all arranged for
two pianos by FL, late in his career, from earlier solo or
concerted works.   The first two are brilliant large-scale
virtuoso works (about fifteen minutes each); the last, a
simpler and more melodic piece (about ten minutes).
                                              Mod. to Dif.

        Operas and Symphonic poems.   FL himself transcribed
his solo pieces on the operas, I Puritani and Don Juan, for
two pianos.   But this is cheating, since the fun of the paraphrases is in seeing an entire opera reduced to a single key-

board.   One might as well call in a quartet of singers, along
with the second piano.   The transcriptions of the twelve symphonic poems vary in quality, as do the originals.   Since FL
treated the orchestra like a giant keyboard and the piano like
a miniature orchestra, two frustrated conductors, with enormous technic, may enjoy performing them.   All are available
in Liszt's own arrangements.   They are:

1. Ce qu'on entend sur la   7. Festklange
      montagne   8. Heroide funebre
2. Tasso   9. Hungaria
3. Les Preludes   10. Hamlet
4. Orpheus   11. Hunnenschlacht
5. Prometheus   12. The Ideals
6. Mazeppa

LOTHAR, MARK (Ger 1902-)
      Danza delle palle, Op. 79, No. 3 (B&B, 1973, set).
Brilliant salon duet in the style of the nineties with measures
of 2/4 interspersed in the waltz figures.   15 pages.   Mod.

LOUVIER, ALAIN (Fr)
      Etudes pour agresseurs (ALe, sep).   Avant-gardist,
who calls his innovative studies Etudes for Aggressors, a-
dopts two-piano for the second book.   Though the ultra avant-
garde style has almost nothing in common with traditional two-
piano playing, the medium provides the composer with a wide
screen on which to splash his abstract patterns.   True to
etude form, each of the four pieces seems to concentrate on
a specific approach, No. 1 opposing kaleidoscopic dynamic
contrasts like machine gun fire; others attempting keyboard
effects, running figures in distorted patterns, etc.   A third
piano may be added for Etude No. 3, though it means a
third copy of the music at ten-fifty.   Pianists attempting the
highly complex work need not so much an aggressive spirit
as infinite patience and strong discipline to reify the highly
abstruse pages and coordinate the two parts.   Vir.

LUBOSHUTZ, PIERRE (Rus 1894-)
      The Bat; a Fantasy on Themes from Johann Strauss'
Die Fledermaus (JF, 1951, set).   Brilliant and pianistic concert piece by this member of a well-known team.   Simple
traditional harmony.   34 pages.   Dif.

LUENING, OTTO, and ERNEST BACON
      Coal Scuttle Blues.   See BACON, ERNEST.

LUTOSLAWSKI, WITOLD (Pol 1913-)

Variations on a Theme by Paganini (1941) (PWM, 1949,
sep). Now a leader in avant-garde experimental writing, WL's
earlier music was key oriented but boldly dissonant. Written
to play with composer Panufnik during the occupation of Po-
land, this brilliant work uses the familiar violin caprice in
A minor. It is surprising that this naive theme with its five-
note tonic-dominant motif, already worked over by Liszt,
Schumann, Brahms and Rachmaninoff, could yield yet another
set of variations. WL exploits the two-piano idiom for sparkling bitonal effects, with much use of the tritone, ninth and
eleventh chords. The virtuoso writing for both players owes
much to Brahms' great solo set, but with its surprising harmonies, is invigorating. 17 pages, 6 minutes.   Dif.

McPHEE, COLIN (Can-USA 1901-1964)
     Balinese Ceremonial Music (GS, 3 sets). These tran-
scriptions by the leading authority on the gamelan are of
more interest to ethnologists than to pianists or general audiences, though one of the three (each is about five minutes)
might liven an Asian program. They are as authentic a
transfer as is possible from one percussion ensemble to another so different; McPhee knew both intimately. The per-
sistent duple rhythm and limited scale make for monotony,
without the subtle variations of metallic timbre.

     1. Pemoengkah: This opens with the same fierce
surprise as a gamelan orchestra attacking its metalophones,
then drops to a pp, with a high steady rocking minor third
chime over more varied patterns. Balinese music builds no
emotional climaxes, and seems to end as abruptly as it begins. CMcP's pieces vary in dynamics but retain the mesmeric monotony.   Dif.

     2. Gambangan: Shorter and more varied, and per-
haps most attractive on a program. Using only four or five
scale tones, the piece unfolds from a slow single-note cadenza to a complex polyphony of melo-rhythmic figures on
four or five levels. In six sharps, it is unpianistic, but
worth the trouble to learn.   Dif.

     3. Taboeh Teloe: Usually an instrumental overture,
it is placed last by CMcP, perhaps for its greater variety.
The composer suggests that it should project a mood of noble
tranquility, and advises plenty of pedal.   Dif.

MALIPIERO, GIAN FRANCESCO (It 1882-   )
     Dialoghi II, fra due pianoforti (GR, 1957). The second

of eight "dialogues" for combinations of various instruments
by this prolific composer. 29 pages, 8 minutes. Dialoghi
I, originally for chamber orchestra, is also available in a
version for two pianos, transcribed by the composer. See
Part 5.

MAMIYA, MICHIO (Jap 1919-)
    Three Movements for Two Pianos (ONT, 1952, set).
Popular and prolific composer experimented with textures
and rhythms suggested by Messiaen and Bartók.   Dif.

MANENTI, LUIGI (It 1899-)
    Fantasia, per due pianoforti (EC, 1962, sep). Large
one-movement atonal work with legato melodic lines weaving
in and out of a contrapuntal texture. Starting with Con spirito, it moves through sections marked Con movimento giocoso, Vivo e giocoso, Andantino sostenuto assorto. 34
pages.   Dif.

    Moto perpetuo, per due pianoforti (EC, 1959, sep).
Dissonant work, sonorous and driving. Lots of activity
spread between two pianos. 16 pages.   Mod. Dif.

MANNINO, FRANCO (It 1924-)
    Serie, per due pianoforte (1964) (GR, 1965). Twelve-
tone work, dense and thick-textured. Long successions of
continuous octaves, chords and double-notes of changing intervals, moving in eighths and sixteenths. Sustained "drone"
achieved by extensive use of repeated octaves and octave
tremolos. Introduced by a three-page Lento (Misterioso con
suono profondo), the rest of the piece is energetic and fast-
moving (Moderatomente mosso). 18 pages, 6 min. 30 sec.
                                                 Mod. Dif.

MARCEL, LUC-ANDRE (Fr 1919-)
    Concert pour deux pianos (1964) (EMT, 1964, sep).
This bulky book (71 pages) is a printed facsimile from a
neat manuscript, carefully annotated. The three movements
all relate to a tight B-A-C-H-like motif, mirrored and inverted, but unable to bear the weight of so massive a structure. Eminently playable in conventional keyboard figures,
overworked and overextended. Basically tonal, though without key, the music is peppered with accidentals and laced
with polytonal passages. An Andante, sustained and melodic,
separates a nervous Allegro and a propulsive Presto with
many dynamic and tempo climaxes. 24 minutes.   Dif.

MAREZ OYENS, TERA DE
       Sonatina for Two Pianos, 1961 (Don, 1962, set).
Three-movement dissonant work with a rhythmic and playful
Allegro, a quiet, nocturne-like Andante, and an Allegro de-
ciso third movement.   Extensive use of fourths and fifths.
Facsimile score.   25 pages.   Mod. Dif.

MARGOLA, FRANCO   (It 1908-   )
       La Ginevrina; fantasia in tre tempi per due pianoforti
(1951) (Bon, 1953).   FM studied at the Parma Conservatory
and his writing shows the influence of Pizzeti.   La Ginevrina
is a lengthy three-movement atonal work: Andante svero,
Adagio assai, and Allegro.   Contrapuntal, with long, angular
melodies (most of the time doubled two octaves apart) moving
continuously either in Piano I or Piano II.   40 pages, 16
min. 30 sec.   Dif.

       Notturni e danze, per due pianoforti (Car, 1958, set).
Light-textured work in six sections: Moderato alla danza,
Larghetto, Adagio, Allegretto alla danza, Calmo, Danza
finale.   15 pages.   Mod.

MARTINŮ, BOHUSLAV   (Czech-USA 1890-1959)
       La Fantaisie (MEE, 1969, set).   Brilliant single neo-
classic movement in toccata style and rondo form, exploiting
to the full the percussive and melodic capacities of two keyboards.   Much pungent dissonance, with the two pianos playing octaves, arpeggios and scales a semi-tone apart.   Demands drive, endurance and full technic.   29 pages.   Dif.

       Trois Dances Tchèques, for Two Pianos (MEE, 1966,
set).   53 pages, 16 minutes.

MASON, DANIEL GREGORY   (USA 1873-1953)
       Scherzo for Two Pianos, Four Hands, Op. 22b (CF,
1931, set).   Extended and propulsive work in one movement
by the distinguished educator and writer.   Chromatic, with
frequent shifting of tonal centers.   27 pages.   Mod. Dif.

       Prelude and Fugue, Op. 20 (JF).

MATSUDAIRA, YORITSUNE   (Jap 1907-   )
       Portrait a, per 2 pianoforti (1968) (SZ, 1969, sep).
Giant-sized loose-leaf score published in a portfolio.   There
are five sections, 20 pages each for I-IV, and 22 pages for
Section V.   Notations are enclosed in boxes of assorted sizes.
They may be played in various sequences according to the

choice of the performers.   The order of the five sections is
also up to the performers to decide.

MATTHESON, JOHANN   (Ger 1681-1764)
    Sonata for Two Cembali (HE, 1960, set).   Friend and
rival of Handel left many keyboard works, among which two
for two harpsichords have recently been republished.   Written
for Cyrill Wich, the son of the English legate in Hamburg,
who was later to become JM's employer, these belong to the
group of pieces that grew out of a teacher-pupil partnership--
Soler, Arensky.   The Sonata is in G minor, a Largo maestoso movement suggesting a French overture, with a square
eight-to-the-bar rhythm.   Rapid diatonic scales and tremolo
figures recall early English virginal music.   Effective, but
lacking the spark of originality to lift it to the level of JM's
great contemporaries.   13 pages.   Mod.

    Suite for Two Cembali (HE, 1960, set).   Four basic
dances of the classical suite, Allemande, Courante, Sarabande,
Gigue, well conceived.   The Courante uses the sort of canonic imitation that Handel favored.   The Sarabande is stately
and clean-cut.   There is little or no ornamentation, though
parts flower into 16th- and 32nd-note passages throughout.
The Sonata could be played as a prelude to the Suite.   10
pages.   Mod.

MEDTNER, NICOLAS   (Rus-GB 1880-1951)
    Knight Errant, Op. 58, No. 2 (Aug, 1946, sep).   A
composer-pianist who studied with Arensky, Taneieff and Sa-
fonoff, NM wrote mostly for piano, and was a champion of
tonal harmony.   This is a lengthy one-movement work with
sections in different tempos, in late nineteenth-century romantic style.   Technically demanding, but effective.   Dedicated to Vronsky and Babin.   44 pages.   Dif.

MESSIAEN, OLIVIER   (Fr 1908-)
    Visions de l'amen (Dur, set).   This monumental work
in seven movements (forty-five minutes) was written in 1942
for OM and his wife, Yvonne Loriod, who performed it
throughout Europe and recorded it in the early days of LP
recording.   (Recently recorded by two other teams.)   Like
the great solo set, Twenty Views of the Infant Jesus (see
AF-CPR), written two years later, this attempts an expression of mystical agony and ecstasy beyond the powers of the
piano, or of two pianos.   Organ or orchestra better convey
the complex musical thought of OM, a distinctive meld of Impressionist harmonies, row-like melodic motifs mathematically

developed, Indian Ragas and bird song. The mystical subject
is outlined in a series of symbolic leitmotifs, many of which
appear later in the solo set (in fact entire passages). OM
intended Piano I to be the intellectual partner, Piano II the
emotional; however, the two share equally the musical and
technical complexities. Players willing to master the enormously difficult keyboard idiom, here magnified by the problem of ensemble, will find the music absorbing and satisfying.
Separate numbers might be selected for concert use, as was
done in the case of the solo work. No. II, The Amen of the
Stars, is a brilliant barbaric dance; No. V introduces OM's
unique bird-song idiom; No. VI is short and brilliant.   Vir.

MEYEROWITZ, JAN   (Ger-USA 1913-   )
       Homage to Hieronymus Bosch (RoM, 1944).   A com-
poser who retains a nineteenth-century melodramatic operatic
style in a modern dissonant texture.   This large triptych
after three paintings by the fifteenth-century Dutch surrealist
was staged as a ballet in Marseilles in 1961.   It cries out
for visual representation, though there is more of the Baroque opulence of Rubens than of the fey wry humor and delicate imagery of Bosch.   Lento con elevazione is the marking
for Saint John on Patmos.   A stately 3/4 passacaglia-like
theme unifies the large movement, which grows progressively
denser in texture as rhythmic, melodic and chordal tendrils
sprout and mesh into an intricate web of sound, ending pppp
Estatico, molto tranquillo.   A similar procedure is followed
in the even more complex Prodigal Son, where the single
theme becomes impacted in opaque masses of sound.   Ecce
homo contrasts extreme dynamics and alternates jagged rhythmic sections with zigzag scale passages.   Unique work requiring full technical mastery and enormous brio.   23 1/2
minutes.   Vir.

MIHALOVICI, MARCEL   (Rou-Fr 1898-   )
       Cantus Firmus, Op. 97 (Heu, 1971, sep).   Recent
work (1970) by a senior composer trained in the French neo-
classic school of d'Indy.   An eight-measure bass moving in
half steps and thirds is developed into an elegy of grand proportions, enriched by murmuring counter-themes, rolled
chords, rapping figures, echoed canons; at the same time
pianistically effective and musically expressive.   9 pages,
4 min. 15 sec.   Dif.

MILFORD, ROBIN   (GB 1903-1959)
       Fishing by Moonlight (CFP, sep).   Originally for piano
and strings, the composer has made an effective setting for

two pianos of a movement inspired by a Dutch painting of
the same name.   The two-part work moves from an Andante
espressivo in slow barcarolle or siciliano rhythm to a Doppio
movimento, and back to the opening seascape.   Mod.

MILHAUD, DARIUS   (Fr 1892-1974)
        Scaramouche, Suite for Two Pianos (SE, set).   De-
servedly the best-known piano music by the prolific DM,
this is also one of the most durable works in the two-piano
repertoire.   Basically neo-classic, it has a quirky wrong-
note harmony, rich variety of melodic and rhythmic material,
well deployed for two players.   The three moods of the clown
are a bumptious Vif, followed by an expressive Moderé with
an attractive trio.   Best is the bouncing Brazilera, a bitonal
samba that requires careful fingering and an unflagging
tempo.   Dif.

        Le Bal Martiniquais (LPC, set).   The much-traveled
DM finds musical matter in all ports and leaves a musical
apotheosis, some more memorable than others.   The orchestra version of his visit to Martinique is better than this unpianistic, repetitious two-movement suite: A Chanson creole
and Beguine.

        Carnival a Nouvelle Orleans (LPC, 1945, set).   Not
to be confused with a 1968 composition called Musique pour
Nouvelle Orleans, this is also better in the orchestral form.

        Six Danses en trois mouvements (MEE, 1970, set).
This curious work by the distinguished septuagenarian makes
one think of the late Grieg, trying in vain to match the masterpieces of his youth; or of the late Beethoven, completely
out of touch with practical performance.   In the first movement Piano I plays a 6/8 Tarantelle over a 2/4 Bourree in
Piano II.   In the second movement, the two dances are a
Sarabande in 12/8, parenthetically marked 4 3/8, and a
Pavane, marked 6/4 or 3 4/8.   The last combines a Rumba
and a Gigue.   A note states that the parts may be played
separately, forming a Suite of Six Dances.   The duet form
is preferred, as the solo version drags out the unpleasant-
ness twice as long.   In spite of well-shaped melodic motifs,
and dance rhythms which are possible if improbable, the
total effect is maundering and meandering, amorphous and
drearily monotonous, totally devoid of euphony; and the keyboard writing is gauche and unpianistic, as if reduced from
a score, or conceived on shipboard.   Dif.

Kentuckiana; Divertissement on Twenty Kentucky Airs
for Two Pianos, Four Hands (1948) (EV, 1949, set). One-
movement rhythmic work with frequent shifting of meters:
2/2 to 3/4 to 5/4 etc. Begins and ends on G, though there
is no key signature. 22 pages.   Mod. Dif.

MOSCHELES, IGNAZ (Czech-Ger-GB 1794-1870)
Hommage à Handel, Op. 92 (SV, set). Fast, energetic piece with a broad opening. 29 pages. See also Two
at One.   Mod. Dif.

MOZART, WOLFGANG AMADEUS (Aus 1756-1791)
Sonata in D, K. 448 (GS, set; CFP, sep; IMC, set).
The ideal two-piano sonata, this has been the model for many
others. Three very Mozartean themes are aligned, tossed
back and forth, broken up, overlaid with scales in a fine exposition. An entirely new theme provides all the material
for the dramatic development. It later serves as coda and
is again introduced in the Andante. A slow tempo is best
for the second movement, whose stately sarabande theme is
later laced with scales in 32nd notes; a duet in thirds, suggesting clarinet, forms a midsection trio. The Rondo, on
the other hand, must be played as fast as possible, and if
done with both delicacy and verve, is one of WAM's most
delightful movements.   Dif.

Fugue in C Minor, K. 426. Usually published in the
same volume as the above, this is fun to play, and stirring
to hear, if well played. Fugal writing had died out in WAM's
day and the counterpoint of Beethoven is seldom inspired,
and often labored. The availability of four hands and two
keyboards for the four voices of a fugue makes possible a
welcome division of labor and a broad layout, though WAM
resists the temptation to pad with unisons and octaves. The
rococo takes over again in the coda with a rocking Alberti
bass under the fugue theme. A new edition of this (GS, set)
edited by Paul Badura-Skoda, adds an introductory Adagio,
arranged from the beautiful work for string orchestra (K. 546).
It makes a majestic opening, in French overture style, to
what Badura-Skoda considers "perhaps the greatest fugue that
has been written after Bach. "   Dif.

Concerto for Two Pianos in E-flat, K. 365 (GS, CFP,
sep; IMC, set). The orchestra is dispensable, if all tuttis
are played by all pianists. Not as original as the Sonata,
this weaves a rich tapestry of themes, and contrasts three
solid movements.   Dif.

<u>Larghetto and Allegro in E-flat</u> (GS, 1966, set). That
devoted Mozartist, Badura-Skoda, who has done so much to
vitalize ensemble piano music, has given us yet another "new"
work by the master. The manuscript of this unpublished
work for two pianos contained the complete introductory
Larghetto, and the exposition of a fine Allegro, from the
period and in the style of the great two-piano Sonata and
Concerto. A skillful, stylish and authentic-sounding development has been added, with a "new" Mozart contrasting theme,
rounded off with the traditional recapitulation. Though less
fresh and inspired than the two-piano concerto in the same
key, it is a bold, pianistic work, that will reward any team
that tackles it. A good program opener. 21 pages.
                                                              Mod. Dif.

Another version of this, the Allegro being completed
and composed in part by M. Stadler, was published by Bären-
reiter in 1964.

MURRILL, HERBERT HENRY J.   (GB 1909-1952)
      <u>Dance on Portuguese Folk Tunes</u> (JWi, 1951, set).
English organist, educator and composer who studied under
York Bowen and Stanley Marchant wrote this short work in
G minor, with a recurring melancholy melody, and a fast
middle section in G major. 10 pages.   Mod.

NEWELL, GEORGE
      <u>Mexico</u> (ECS, 1932, sep). Written in the days when
Mexico was exotic and two-piano playing a novelty, this draws
heavily on Albeniz and deFalla. Well laid out, requiring fire
and large agile hands. 21 pages.   Mod.

NEWMAN, FRANK (GB)
      <u>A Frolic</u> (Aug, 1961, set). Well-named fun piece
based on the English traditional tune "Lincolnshire Poacher."
Mildly chromatic harmonies accompany melody in unison and
octaves. Introduces two other folk songs and ends with a
three-voice fugue. 11 pages.   Mod. Dif.

NIELSEN, RICCARDO (It 1908-)
      <u>Musica a due pianoforti</u> (SZ, 1940, sep). A sonorous
and dissonant work with many fast sixteenth-note and re-
peated-chord passages. The energetic first movement with
a presto middle section is introduced by a one-page Molto
lento. Second movement is a Passacaglia with a Fugato.
35 pages, 18 minutes.   Dif.

Sonata for Two Pianos (Bon, 1954, sep). This twelve-tone work by the neo-classicist opens with a complex, contrapuntal Allegretto pastorale, followed by a Theme with three variations (cancricans, inversus, and inversus cancricans). Closes with a spirited and fast-moving Giga.   28 pages. Dif.

OGURA, ROH   (Jap 1916-   )
Dance Suite for Two Pianos (ONT, 1953, sep).   Neo-classic work in French manner, lyrical and improvisatory in effect.   Mod. Dif.

OHANA, MAURICE   (Fr 1914-   )
Sorôn-ngô (SE, 1971, sep). Successful French pianist-composer offers an avant-garde piece of great complexity, using tone rows, chord clusters, aleatoric effects.   Directions in French.   For two advanced explorers.   24 pages. 12 1/2 to 14 minutes.   Facsimile score.   Vir.

O'NEILL, NORMAN   (GB 1875-1934)
Variations and Fugue on an Irish Theme, for Two Pianos, Op. 17 (Scho, 1905, sep).   Nine variations and a fugue. Traditional harmony and keyboard figurations.   O'Neill was music director of the Haymarket Theatre and taught harmony and composition at the Royal Academy of Music.   27 pages.
                                                                    Mod. Dif.

OTAKA, HISATADA   (Jap 1911-1951)
Midare, Capriccio for Two Pianos (ONT, 1939).   Symphony conductor trained in Vienna.   "Midare" is the name of a famous seventeenth-century koto piece, and the piano duet incorporates elements of Japanese harmony and koto figuration in a post-Romantic texture.   Though HO was not a pianist, the ten-minute work, which had its premier in Vienna, is well laid out for the two instruments.   Dif.

PAGANUCCI, A.
Valse Debonnaire (GS, 1936, set).   If you can never get enough of salon valses, here is yet another.   Chabrier, who should have said the last word in his Trois Valse Romantiques, only spawned another large family.   Graceful, melodious and soporific.   7 pages.   Mod.

PALESTER, ROMAN   (Pol 1907-   )
Varianti, per due pianoforti (SZ, 1967, set).   Twelve-tone avant-garde work with formidable rhythmic patterns. Theme, Interlude, and Coda, followed by four variations. 11-12 minutes.   Dif.

PALMER, ROBERT (USA 1915-)
  Sonata for Two Pianos (1944) (PIC, 1959, set). Brilliant neo-classic work which deserves to be heard. Long
Allegro energico first movement, shorter Andante sostenuto
and Allegro giusto. The writing is almost calligraphic in its
linear emphasis, but thickened with octaves and chords for
focal points. A free-ranging chromaticism which sounds
tonal, though without key signatures, is matched by fluid
polymetric rhythm. The two players at times have different
time signatures, but the bold shape of the figures and the
helpful editing facilitate performance. 32 pages.   Dif.

PARROTT, IAN (GB 1916-)
  Fantasy and Allegro for Two Pianos, Four Hands
(1946) (ALen, 1947, sep). Though written with no key signature, this mildly dissonant work by the British composer,
educator and writer begins and ends in D. Clearly defined
themes in a transparent tissue are often imitated between
pianos. 27 pages.   Mod.

PASQUINI, BERNARDO (It 1637-1710)
  Sonatas for Two Cembalos. This early Italian composer, noted for his brilliant organ and harpsichord playing,
left some little-known music for one and two cembalos. The
manuscripts, in the British Museum, contain fourteen Sonatas
or Suites, many of which appear to be for two keyboard instruments. They seem to have been written to play with a devoted nephew, Ricordati, who copied and preserved them, and
also honored BP with a fine tomb. In the manner of the day,
they consist in a single line for each instrument. On this
part, which contained only the bass line and figures for the
harmony, each player "realized" a treble part, with melodies,
chords, counter-melodies, rhythmic motifs and ornaments.
Thus the earliest of all two-keyboard works anticipate some
of the aleatoric music of our day, as each player improvised
a part that was never twice the same. Three of the Sonatas
have been published in two piano settings. They are all in
three movements in the same key, with graceful melodic lines
and concise structure, often binary. Sonata in G minor and
Sonata in F are edited by the distinguished Italian, F. Boghen,
published by Durand. Sonata in D minor has been published
twice, and a comparison will show that wide variation was
possible in realizing a figured bass. The edition by W.
Danckert is published by Barenreiter; that by J. S. Shedlock,
by Novello.   Mod.

PATTISON, LEE MARION (USA 1890-1966)

The Arkansas Traveller (GS, 1925, set). Both partners of the team Mayer and Pattison made numerous arrangements for two pianos. This original composition on the old
fiddler's tune is a good encore number, boisterous and un-
inhibited with amusing harmonization and surprising counter-
themes. 11 pages.   Mod. Dif.

Coronation Scene from Mussorgsky's "Boris Godounov"
(GS, set). The nineteenth-century custom of two-piano arrangements of operas serves well with this composer whose
brilliant music was neither pianistic nor instrumental but
ideal. Large hands and skillful pedaling needed to evoke the
scene.   Dif.

PERSICHETTI, VINCENT (USA 1915-)
Sonata, Op. 13 (LPC, 1940). Distinguished and prolific composer wrote this early work to play with his wife.
VP has developed a distinctive personal idiom that finds expression in numerous piano and chamber works in classical
Sonata form. This form subsumes a recognizable system of
tonal progressions, and in the later works is often vitiated
by a highly arcane harmony. Here tonality is freely treated,
without key signatures, but is always present. Outer movements in E-flat minor; the four movements are unified by
common motifs ingeniously treated. The first movement is
rhapsodic in character, with contrapuntal episodes, building
to an ecstatic close. A lilting waltz-like Allegretto is closer
to Ravel than to Hindemith, harmonized with sevenths and
augmented and diminished fifths. The Largo is a two-page
gem, grown from the same seed. The rhythmic Vivace finale
makes further exciting uses of the material. Recommended
for teams looking for a major work that is modern yet euphonious.   Mod. Dif.

PETERS, J. V.
Prelude and Chorale for Two Pianos (OxU, 1950, set).
Both Prelude (Alla marcia) and Chorale (Andante con moto)
move in leisurely quarter and eighth notes. Contrapuntal,
free flowing, harmonized with seventh and ninth chords. The
chorale is based on "Wie schön Leuchtet die Morgenstern,"
1599. 10 pages.   Mod.

PETYREK, FELIX (Czech 1892-)
Six Concert Etudes for Two Pianos, Four Hands (1934)
(UE, 1935). Pianist-composer, pupil of Godowsky and Sauer,
wrote these studies in rapid sixteenth notes, scales, arpeggios, double thirds and sixths, chord trills, etc. Reminiscent

of Czerny studies, except the drills here are to be played
by two people together, which makes it twice as difficult.
48 pages.   Dif.

Toccata and Fugue in the Mixolydian Mode for Two
Pianos, Four Hands (1934) (UE, 1935). The Toccata has a
calm beginning, moving into passages of contrasting dynamics
and texture, of broken chords, octaves, double fourths and
fifths. The second part starts with a quiet Fuge I, followed
by a short Arioso, and then Fuge II, a brisk mirror fugue.
24 pages.   Mod. Dif.

PHILIPP, ISIDOR   (Fr 1863-1958)
        Feux-Follets (Jack o'Lanterns), Op. 24, No. 3 (GS,
1953, set). Distinguished French pianist and pedagogue
whose exercises are still played had one solo piece which became a cheval de guerre for many pianists. Seldom heard
today, the two-piano arrangement by the composer would
make a brilliant encore number for two players with a fleet
sure-fingered technic. 13 pages.   Mod. Dif.

PIJPER, WILLEM   (Neth 1894-1947)
        Sonata (1935) (Don, 1948, set). Large work, well-
conceived and boldly executed. First movement has a spon-
taneous 5/4 melody and occasionally superimposes a waltz
rhythm for one piano over the five beats in the other. Chromatic pantonality is used in original but pianistic figures.
Adagio second movement keeps hands busy ranging the keyboard in vivid patterns. The score is a manuscript facsimile,
not always clear. 33 pages.   Dif.

PINTO, OCTAVIO   (Bra 1890-1950)
        Scenas infantis (GS, 1934, sep). The solo version of
this is so demure and winsome that playing it on two pianos
seems like gilding the lily. Though the subdivision and
doubling of parts is artistically done, and counter-themes
have been cleverly added, it becomes an entirely different
work. A four-hand arrangement might have retained the
simplicity of the original miniatures, which here become
sparkling showpieces. 25 pages.   Mod.

PIRANI, EUGENIO   (It-Ger 1852-1939)
        Gavotte, Op. 36 (CF, 1908, set). Each player here
must guess what the other will do next as only one part is
printed in each score. Fortunately there are no surprises,
and the rococo dance is given a standard nineteenth-century
workout, with up-down chordal accompaniment, broken chords,
arpeggios and one change of key. 6 pages.   Mod. E.

PISK, PAUL AMADEUS (Aus-USA 1893-)
     My Pretty Little Pink; a Merry Fugue on a Southern
Folk Tune for Two Pianos (LPC, 1945, set). Fast and gay.
Simple textured fugue, traditional harmony. 7 pages. Mod.

PLESKOW, RAOUL (USA 1931-)
     Music for Two Pianos (1965) (SMC, 1968). Three
movements. Tempos indicated by metronome marks. Complex rhythm. Arm clusters and plucking of piano strings.
Dedicated to Stefan Wolpe (quotation of Wolpe's Trio used in
second movement). Facsimile score. 29 pages.   Dif.

PONCE, MANUEL (Mex 1882-1948)
     Idilio Mexicano (1939) (SMP, 1952, sep). Honored as
the father of modern classical music in Mexico, MP is known
to the rest of the world by his song, Estrellita, the only one
of his many compositions with enduring inspiration. This
duo, published after his death, is neatly laid out for the two
players, contrasting flowing scales and a tamboura beat with
a lilting 6/8 tune of little distinction. 8 pages.   Mod.

POOT, MARCEL (Bel 1901-)
     Rhapsodie, pour deux pianos (1947) (CBDM, 1956,
sep). Critic, educator, as well as composer, MP was one
of the founders of Synthésistes, a group of Belgian composers
who championed new ideas. This is a one-movement work
with several tempo changes. Dissonant but tonal. 20 pages.
Facsimile score.   Mod. Dif.

POULENC, FRANCIS (Fr 1899-1963)
     Sonate pour deux pianos (ME, 1953, set). Seeking to
repeat the success of his very popular Concerto for Two Pianos, FP wrote this four-movement work for the same team
(Poulenc and his old friend Jacques Février) to perform.
Though well deployed for the two players, it falls flat, tripped
on its own devices, overblown and pompous. FP's muse was
not tragedy but comedy, and this is too solemn. A Prologue
is marked "extremely slow" and ends "even slower." The
dynamics range from fff to ppp; the tocsin-like octaves are
striking, but the FP melody does not lend itself to slow-mo-
tion. The Allegro molto repeats many pianistic devices better used elsewhere. The third movement is the only one
with a key signature. The Epilogue abounds in typical Poulenc idioms at a dashing speed, broken by quotes from the
slow Prologue and Andante.   Dif.

     L'embarquement pour Cythere, valse-musette (1951)

(MEE, 1952, sep).   A lyrical pastorale on the subject of
Watteau's painting, which also inspired Debussy's L'Isle
joyeuse.   11 pages.   Mod.

Elegie, pour deux pianos (1959) (MEE, 1960, set).
A slow, quiet, melancholy piece with syncopated chords between two pianos.   According to the composer's note, it
should be played in an improvisatory manner with lots of
pedal.   11 pages.   Mod.

POUSSEUR, HENRI (Bel 1929-)
      Mobile (SZ, 1961, set).   The use of the element of
chance in music seldom produces the beauty captured by
Alexander Calder in his airy, fluid mobiles.   Avant-gardist
HP writes in a post-Webern pointillistic style, providing each
of the two pianists with three optional "mobiles" on inserted
sheets, mercifully printed in clear, normal-sized notes.
Players must know French to follow the cues; and there is
another insert containing ten pages of interpretation of the
notation (in four languages).   Mastering the new notation is
not a simple matter, requiring the player to remember,
among other things, that whole notes do not mean whole
notes but flatted notes.   If the music sounds like the explica-
tion, it is totally devoid of humor, poetry, or euphony.   Dif.

POWELL, JOHN (USA 1882-1963)
      Dirge: Natches-on-the-Hill: Three Virginia Country
Dances, Op. 30 (GS, set).   This Leschetizsky pupil who won
fame as a pianist first in Europe, then in America, wrote
several amiable works for two pianists.   American folk
rhythms and a bucolic atmosphere are combined with vigorous piano writing in a derivative style.   His most famous
work, a concerto using Afro-American themes called Rhapsodie Negre, was inspired by Joseph Conrad's Heart of Dark-
ness.   It has been arranged for two pianos.   Mod. to Dif.

RACHMANINOFF, SERGEI (Rus-USA 1873-1943)
      Suite No. 1 (Fantasy), Op. 5 (IMC, set).   This pian-
ist-composer, who found time to write numerous preludes,
etudes and pieces for piano, of which many are staples of
the solo repertoire, and two of whose five concertos are
standard works, also wrote two suites for two pianos.
Though both have been recorded by several teams and are
occasionally programmed, neither is very satisfactory.   The
writing is complex, dense and opaque, and all movements
are overextended and under-inspired.   The four pieces in Op.
5 are Barcarolle, O Night of Love, Tears, and Easter, and

the music is almost as embarrassing as the titles.   The last
number is shorter and makes a resonant climax, imitating
the clangorous chiming of church bells and enriched by a
Russian liturgical chant.   Dif.

   Suite No. 2, Op. 17 (IMC, 1953, set).   Indefatigable
devotees of duo-piano playing may wish to tackle this ex-
hausting work.   The Introduction begins boldly, but has little
distinction.   The Valse is graceful, but the dance form is
vitiated by incessantly chattering figures in one piano or the
other.   A slow Romance and a fast Tarantelle extend the
work to twenty-five minutes.   This is the composition which
broke the silence of the depression of SR's early years and
paved the way for the great second concerto.   However, the
luxuriant harmony that distinguishes that work is heard here
only fleetingly in bridge passages.   The rest might have been
written by any late romantic composer of the Germano-Russian
tradition.   There is an obsessive need to keep one part always moving, and throughout all four movements a triplet figure natters away, at first chiming euphoniously, then murmuring gently, occasionally building a hammered climax, but in
the end vitiating the rather pedestrian melodies and common-
place harmonies and stupefying both players and listeners.
55 pages.   Dif.

   Russian Rhapsody (LPC, set).   Published in 1955,
this work, now out of print, dates from SR's student years.
Less promising than Scriabin's two-piano Fantasia of about
the same time, this suffers from a rather banal theme which
palls in the course of the thirty-five pages.   The variations
at which the two players take turns grow progressively more
elaborate, but, though well-deployed for the twenty fingers,
they are monotonously unimaginative.   There is one brief
hint of the rich sliding chromaticism in anchored chords, which
were to become such a hallmark of SR's music; and the Andante has a pale wistfulness.   Mod. Dif.

   Symphonic Dances, Op. 45 (CFo, 1942, sep).   SR's
last composition, written in 1940, concurrently with the orchestral version.   I. Non allegro.   II. Andante con moto.
III. Lento assai -- Allegro vivace.   Large-scale work requiring virtuosity of both players.   102 pages.   26 minutes.
                                                                 Vir.

RANDS, BERNARD (GB 1935-)
   Espressione IV (UE, 1965).   Avant-garde work using
notations with crossbars, arrows, dots, and inside boxes

where "the instrumentalists may freely distribute the tones, the groups of tones, and clusters, within the time limits suggested by the size of the squares and rectangles." Some of the tones are to be tapped with fingernails or knuckles on the keyboard without depressing the keys. Other notes are to be depressed silently to produce harmonics. Requires careful study and rehearsal. 19 pages.   Dif.

RAPOPORT, EDA
    Suite for Two Pianos (IMP, 1941, set). 1. Out for a Stroll (In brisk march tempo). 2. By the Sea (Allegro, in undulating sixteenth notes). 3. Sunset (Moderato con moto, legato and expressive). 4. Dance of the Fireflies (Rhythmic, light, staccato, fast). Much use of fourths and fifths. 18 pages.   Mod.

RAVEL, MAURICE (Fr 1875-1937)
    Rhapsodie espagnole (Dur, set). The third piece in this four-piece suite is a Habanera, originally written for two pianos, and intended to be paired with Entre Cloche. Later MR incorporated it into the Spanish Rhapsody, adding Prelude à la nuit, Malaguena and Feria, for a dashing orchestral number. Still later he transcribed the set for two pianos, in which form it is also attractive and playable.
                                                      Mod. Dif.

    Bolero (Dur). MR had a very limited output, and spent much of his time rewriting his own music, for different combinations. This orchestral tour de force, with its single rhythm and single varied theme using all the brass and wind of the orchestra, would hardly seem suitable for piano. It is fun to play, if somewhat boring for the listener familiar with the colorful orchestration. Also arranged for four hands by MR.   Dif.

    Les Sites auriculaires. Early sketch for a two-piano suite, containing the Habanera, later used in Rhapsodie espagnol, and Entre Cloche. Unpublished, but available on records.

REGER, MAX (Ger 1873-1916)
    Variations and Fugue on a Theme by Beethoven, Op. 86 (B&B, set). Teutonic scholarship and prolixity quite bury the simple Bagatelle tune under masses of opaque murky harmony and counterpoint.   Dif.

    Introduction, Passacaglia and Fugue, Op. 96 (B&B,

set).   Another horrendous work for two Brobdingnagian pianists.   Useful for study and analysis of modern contrapuntal
technics, and for advanced sight-reading.   Dif.

REINECKE, CARL   (Ger 1824-1910)
        Andante and Variations, Op. 6 (FH, set); Impromptu
on a Motif from Schumann's Manfred, Op. 66 (AMP, set);
Variations on a Sarabande by Bach Op. 24b (ES, set); Improvi-
sations on a French Folk Song, Op. 94 (Br&H, set); Improvi-
sations on a Gavotte by Gluck, Op. 125 (CFP, set); Variations on A Mighty Fortress is our God, Op. 191 (RF, set);
Four Pieces, Op. 241 (CFP, set); Three Sonatas, etc.   Prolific composer whose many two-piano works await revival by
some devoted team.   Thoroughly professional work, refined
and balanced, in the nineteenth-century romantic-classic tradition, rather low-key emotionally.   Mod.

RIEGGER, WALLINGFORD   (USA 1884-1961)
        Scherzo, Op. 13a (PIC, 1954, set).   From the point
of view of 1954 this was an important work, a large-scale
concert piece entirely derived from a twelve-tone row.   After
a brief fanfare introduction, the row is set forth in all four
forms, unadorned, like a fugue theme, then skillfully developed in a bold toccata style.   In the intervening twenty
years since this was written, serial music has failed to gain
an audience, and has lost most of its adherents among performers and composers.   Compare this with the earlier four-
hand music of WR, whose dissonant tonality is still powerful
and appealing.   22 pages.   Mod. Dif.

        Canon and Fugue, Op. 33c (HF, 1954, set).   Here the
dedicated serialist surprises us with a small masterpiece in
a strict classical form, chaste and tonal.   The sostenuto
Canon serves both as introduction and as da capo ending.   It
begins amiably and builds to an imposing D major close.
The three-voice fugue in a clear, if highly chromatic D min-
or, is brilliantly developed with a broad chordal countersubject.   Requires musical maturity as well as a good octave
technic for the fugue climax.   7 pages.   Mod. Dif.

        Evocation (1933), The Cry (1935), New Dance (1935)
(PIC, 3 sets).   Written as Gebrauch Musick for Martha
Graham and her exponents of modern dance, any of the three
would make a good concert duet, though the three together
lack contrast.   All are Expressionistic, with a wide dynamic
range, broken phrases in strong but irregular rhythms with
much pseudo-orchestral tremolo and trill.   Though not strictly

serial, they are often twelve-tonal, the unrelieved dissonance
mitigated by the clearly defined rhythmic and melodic motifs.
The titles seem arbitrary without the dance movements, and
though the composer tells us that the first expresses the
spirit of tragedy, the second that of romanticism, the third
joyous affirmation, they are much of a piece.   Pianistic
writing with good division of keyboard labor.   Mod. to Dif.

RIETI, VITTORIO   (It-USA 1898-)
       Second Avenue Waltzes (1942) (AMP, 1950, set).
More of those always popular program items, concert waltzes.
These six are lightweight, with flashes of brilliance, puddles
of sentiment, moments of humor from bitonal, polytonal
wrong-note oppositions.   49 pages.   Mod. Dif.

       Chess Serenade (1945) (AMP, 1951, set).   Sophisti-
cated and sparkling set of five pieces, including yet another
waltz (the easiest).   Good show, if done by two well-matched,
well-oiled players.   Why "Chess" for such fast-moving non-
cerebral activity?   48 pages.   Mod. Dif.

       Suite Champêtre (1948) (AMP, 1952, set).   Written for
Gold and Fizdale in their salad days, this is a large work of
moderate difficulty, containing a lengthy Bourree (20 pages),
Aria and ecossaise, and a Gigue.   The Bourree is an extended rondo, cheeky and dashing, energico e spiccato throughout
with humorous surprise cadences and altered chords in a
firmly tonal harmony.   In the Aria, the dissonances grate un-
pleasantly, as if arbitrarily wedged into the otherwise euphonious texture.   The Gigue alternates staccato and legato
in its racing eight-note figures, with more wrong-note harmony in a B-flat major tonality.   39 pages.   Mod. Dif.

       Three Vaudeville Marches (1969) (GMP, 1971, set),
20 pages; Valse Fugitive (1970) (GMP, 1971, set), 7 pages.
VR continues to add to the two-piano library, though his recent pieces sound like more verses to the same song.   In
fact the nineteen-twenties cabaret style of the Marches and
the Valse makes one wonder if the music was not actually
written then, and just dug out from the bottom of the barrel,
to keep the pot boiling.   They offer little to today's pianists.
                                                         Mod.

       Chorale, Variations and Finale (1969) (GMP, 1971,
sep).   Again dedicated to Gold and Fizdale, this has been
dutifully recorded by them.   It completely eschews the music-
hall gaiety and the pseudo-modernism of the early works, for

a chromaticism harmonized with augmented triads and ninth
chords. The attractive Tema Corale is treated in nine variations and a Coda, with imaginative keyboard figures, alternating brilliance and expressiveness. Excessively long. 36
pages.   Mod. Dif.

New Waltzes for Two Pianos (AMP, set). Six more
waltzes of moderate difficulty. 1. Belinda waltz. 2. Valse
caprice. 3. Valse champêtre. 4. Valse Légère. 5. Valse
Lente. 6. Rondo Waltz. 73 pages.

RIVIER, JEAN (Fr 1896-)
Quatre Sequences dialogues (GBil, sep). Once popular French composer who blended neo-classic and impressionistic technics, here attempts to please all, by updating
his style in a way that may end by pleasing no one. Standard keyboard figures of chords, octaves, thirds, sixths, arpeggios and glissandi give a comfortable texture to the work.
Though the first movement is clearly tonal, hovering around
D minor and ending in F-sharp major, it has an irritating
overlay of polytonality, and an arbitrary and unconvincing use
of dissonance, like a student work souped-up with a generous
sprinkling of accidentals for a mod comp class. A Presto
jocando is built on a melodic interval of the seventh, with a
harmony of augmented fourths incongruously linked with diatonic scales. A Quasi notturno uses a twelve-tone row for
a theme, but suddenly reverts to parallel thirds over tonic
triads. The closing Allegro ruvido keeps the serial sound
in a large movement that alternates the popular, the tender
and the strident. 45 pages, 19 minutes.   Dif.

ROCHBERG, GEORGE (USA 1918-)
Prelude on "Happy birthday" for Almost Two Pianos
(1969) (TP, 1971). Piano I starts with the altered but
recognizable happy birthday theme, at first quietly, then
builds up to fff, to resemble great pealing of bells. It is
joined by the second pianist, who is advised to improvise
atonally or play another composer's music. And, "to in-
crease the effect," a radio may be turned on loud at the
same time. Piano I and Piano II gradually fade out at the
end. 4 pages.

ROPARTZ, J. GUY (Fr 1864-1955)
Piece in B Minor (Dur, 1899, set). Lyric and ro-
mantic piece written in 1898. 24 pages.   Mod. Dif.

ROREM, NED (USA 1923-)

Sicilienne (1950) (SMP, 1955, set).   This is off the
same spool as the solo piano music of NR, which is, unfortunately, not the same spool as that from which the lilting
songs were wound.   For comments on NR's piano style, see
AF-CPR, p. 254.   In three sections (each repeated).   8
pages.   Mod.

ROSENTHAL, MANUEL (Fr 1904-)
La Belle Zélie (New York, 1948) (JJ, 1959, set).
Curious suite by the French conductor-composer (not to be
confused with the pianist, Moriz), evidently intended as light
entertainment, but extended for sixty-four pages in a heavy-
handed unpianistic style.   The six movements are: I. Pastorale en rondeau; II. Le valet malicieux et la soubrette
mélancolique; III. Minuet burlesque; IV. Ballabile; V. L'Es-
carpolette; VI. Final (French can-can).   Dif.

RUBINSTEIN, BERYL (USA 1898-1952)
Suite for Two Pianos (GS, set).   Written during BR's
partnership with Arthur Loesser, this neo-classic set of
four numbers is a brilliant solution of the problem of dis-
position of parts at two pianos.   The Prelude is genial and
sparkling, in rondo form; Canzonetta has a broad melody,
leading to a second which mounts to a climax.   Jig is a
spirited Celtic dance.   The closing Masks is bold and primi-
tive, suggesting barbaric spirit rites.   Dif.

SAINT-SAËNS, CAMILLE (Fr 1835-1921)
Variations on a Theme by Beethoven, Op. 35 (GS,
1922, sep; EV, set).   Because of the dearth of good two-
piano music, this is often rated higher than its intrinsic
worth merits.   Beethoven said about all his simple Minuet
trio had to say, in sixteen measures (Op. 32, No. 2).   CSS
extracts an introduction, a fugue, a Presto orchestral coda
from it, and spends the remaining pages tossing the ante-
cedent and consequent of the eight-measure phrase back and
forth between the pianos, as chords, trills, scale figures,
zigzag broken chords, xylophone effects (lifted from Samson
and Dalila).   49 pages (GS).   Mod.

Carnival of Animals (Dur, 1947, set; EV, set).   This
unique work, called a "Grande Fantasie Zoologique," was
withheld from publication during the composer's life, but is
now rated as his finest work.   Though written for two pianos
and a small orchestra of strings, flute, clarinet, harmonica
and xylophone, most of it can be effectively played on two
keyboards.   The entire suite of fourteen numbers takes forty

minutes, but separate numbers or a selection can be played. The Grand Royal March of the Lions is a pompous circus fanfare. Hens and Cocks has the pianos' crowing answered by pizzicato strings. Wild Asses is a scale study with the pianos playing unison two octaves apart. In No. 4, Piano I plays octave triplet chords over a creeping theme for the Tortoise, played unison by the orchestra (or Piano II). For The Elephant, one piano plays the om-pa-pa of a waltz, and the other a theme from a Berlioz ballet, lumbering in the bass. Leaping chords suggest Kangaroos. In Aquarium a shimmering aqueous sound results from chord-arpeggio patterns accompanied by muted strings, flute and glass harmonica (possible on two pianos, but impoverished). Personages with Long Ears might better be omitted in the piano version; it is only twenty-six measures, and the braying mules are suggested by string glissandos. For The Cuckoo in the Woods, the clarinet is instructed to hide in the wings. No. 10, Birds, might also be omitted by duo-pianists, as it is for flute and strings. The next is a must; "Pianistes" (with a feminine ending) must "imitate the gaucheries of a debutante" in inane Hanonic passages through the keys of C, D-flat, D, E-flat. Fossils is a "Ridiculous Allegro" gavotte, quoting from various antiquated composers (CSS included his own famous Danse Macabre). The familiar Swan was originally a cello solo accompanied by both pianos. The Finale is a reprise with the duettists chasing scales and glissandi over martial chords.   Mod. Dif.

          Caprice arabe pour deux pianos, quatre mains, op. 96 (Dur, 1894, set). One-movement brilliant pianistic showpiece with fast running passages, skips, octaves, broken octaves, etc. Piano I and Piano II each has its own score, with the other piano represented only in abbreviated form on a single staff for reference. 17 pages.   Dif.

          Scherzo, Op. 87, for Two Pianos, Four hands (IMC, 1944, 1970, set). Written in 1889 and published in the following year, the Scherzo was described as "a wildly exhilarating and fanciful composition" by Arthur Hervey, one of CSS' biographers. Requires agility and facility at the keyboard. 30 pages.   Dif.

SALMON, KAREL (Ger-Isr 1897-   )
          Suite on Greek Themes (1943) (IMI, 1966, sep). Composer's adaptation of a symphonic work, this four-movement, eighteen-minute suite is impressive and exciting. Each movement is based on a song or dance rhythm, occasionally with

a second tune which provides a welcome relief from the many
repetitions.   Except for a few quasi-instrumental effects, the
keyboard writing is pianistic, and builds climactically in each
movement.   Greek and Hebrew elements combine and the use
of modal alterations, parallel thirds, irregular meters (5/8,
7/8) give an authentic and poignant flavor to the writing.
The work has been associated with several distinguished
teams; dedicated to Vronsky and Babin, who played frequently
in Israel, it was premiered by Menahem Pressler and Elia-
hu Rudiakow, and has been recorded by the Israeli Duo-Pianists, Eden and Tamir.   68 pages, 18 minutes.   Dif.

SANUCCI, FRANK (Arg-USA)
        Argentinian Rhapsody (MAP, 1965, sep).   A showy
duet in what might be called standard Latin.   Piano I plays
broad melodies in chords and octaves while Piano II taps
out drum and castanet rhythms with bits of counter-theme.
Music urges to a Vivo climax, then folds in an Adagio maestoso coda.   15 pages.   Mod.

SAUGUET, HENRI (Fr 1901-)
        Valse brève, pour deux pianos (1949) (MEE, 1955,
set).   A concert waltz written for Gold and Fizdale, this is
graceful and effective, with materials well-deployed between
the two players.   Best known for his ballet and film music,
HS studied with Canteloube and Koechlin, and was associated
with Satie.   12 pages.   Mod.

SCHLEGEL, LEANDER (1844-1913)
        Passacaglia for Two Pianos on Rising and falling
scales, Op. 31 (Bos, sep).   Rising and falling scale tones are
harmonized in fourteen short episodes, followed by a Fugato
e Finale and an Epilog.   Most of these are in G, and in
leisurely tempo.   Traditional progressions and modulations.
Good study for keyboard harmony.   31 pages.   Mod.

SCHMITT, FLORENT (Fr 1870-1958)
        Three Rhapsodies, Op. 53 (Dur, set).   For lovers of
the two-piano waltz, here are three more large ones.   The
first is Francaise, the last, Viennoise, and the second Polonaise.   All are pianistic and brilliant, the second also lyrical
and melodious.   Mod. Dif.

SCHOEMAKER, MAURICE (Bel 1890-)
        Tombeau de Chopin; variations sur le prélude no. 20
pour deux pianos (CBDM, 1963).   Both Busoni and Rachmaninoff have written sets of variations on the Chopin C minor

prelude. Here is another set, for two pianos. Although MS
was one of the founders of a group devoted to modern music,
known as the Synthésistes, these variations are mostly traditional, except portions which are oddly complex and difficult.
The score is a facsimile of a carelessly copied manuscript
with obvious mistakes and omissions. 26 pages, 13 min.
30 sec.   Dif.

SCHÜTT, EDUARD (Rus-Aus 1856-1933)

Impromptu-rococco, op. 58, no. 2 (Sim, 1899). Rus-
sian-born pianist-composer who studied with Reinecke and
Leschetizky wrote this pianistic piece in nineteenth-century
traditional style, with conventional figuration: octaves and
chords, rolled chords, arpeggiated sixteenth notes. Big ending. 15 pages.   Mod. Dif.

SCHUMANN, ROBERT (Ger 1810-1856)

Andante and Variations, Op. 46 (GS, sep; CFP, set).
This gentle, lyrical duet is the dual-natured RS having a
dialogue with himself. The two parts alternate, answer and
punctuate each other, rather than amplify or challenge. The
persistence of the triple meter with only piu and meno mosso
changes, and only two key shifts, makes for a rather demure
and unexciting piece. The keyboard figures are always felicitous, though they require a good technic, and the melody
is fluent and quietly joyous. 33 pages.   Mod. Dif.

SCOTT, CYRIL (GB 1879-1971)

Theme and Variations (Elk, set). Lengthy set of ten
variations in CS' later style, quartal harmony and melodies
in fourths. Complex and dense, they build to a fugal climax.
                                                             Dif.

SCRIABIN, ALEXANDER (Rus 1872-1915)

Fantasy, Op. Posthumous (OxU, sep). Like Chopin,
this pianist-composer who so greatly enriched the solo repertoire, rejected the duet idiom after youthful experiments.
AS was twenty-one and just out of the Moscow Conservatory
when he wrote Fantasy, first published in 1940. It seems
to have been conceived as a piano solo with second-piano accompaniment, but the editor has balanced the parts in duet
style. There are only fleeting wisps of the delicious piano
texture that was to emerge in the Piano Concerto, Op. 20,
the Preludes, Etudes and Sonatas. Of historical interest,
it is recommended for two young students, for whom the
world of music is their oyster, still waiting to be opened.
6 minutes.   Mod.

SHAW, CLIFFORD (USA 1911-)
    Third Street Rhumba (OD; TR, 1951, set). To be
played "buoyantly with abandon," this is fun and games for
pianists, with one player or the other beating out mashed
seconds under and around the typical rising-falling arc of
rhumba melody. 7 pages.   Mod.

SHOSTAKOVICH, DMITRI (USSR 1906-1975)
    Concertino, Op. 94 (IMC, 1966, set). It is hoped
that this work satisfied the Politburo. It cannot have served
any other important purpose as it is totally devoid of musical
character. Piano I announces a farrago of banal cliches
linked by C major scales, the left hand doubling the right
hand an octave lower throughout, while Piano II supplies the
requisite bass beats and chords in a tired predictable pattern. 32 pages.   Mod. E.

    Festive Overture, Op. 96 (1954) (EFK, sep). Another
functional piece for two indifferent players. It differs from
the above only in the use of 3/4 instead of 4/4 time. 32
pages.   Mod. E.

SINDING, CHRISTIAN (Nor 1856-1941)
    Variations in E-flat Minor, Op. 2 (WH, set). Early
work in nineteenth-century Lisztian style, on a somber theme.
Spring had not yet begun to rustle.   Dif.

SMITH, JULIA FRANCES (USA 1911-)
    American Dance Suite (TP, 1968, set). Four pieces
on cowboy, old-fiddler, square-dance tunes and an Afro-
American Lullaby. Well-written in a traditional idiom with
few surprises. 21 pages. 9 1/2 minutes.   Mod.

SOLER, PADRE ANTONIO (Sp 1729-1783)
    Six Concertos for Two Keyboards (UME, sep). These
must rank among the earliest and the most extensive sets
of pieces for two keyboards. Written by the Spanish Padre
who during his thirty years at the Spanish court turned out
over five hundred compositions, including many solo sonatas
now finding a place on piano and harpsichord programs (see
AF-CPR). These six were for "two obligato organs" and
were written for the Padre's royal pupil, the Infanta Gabriel.
Most authorities agree that two chamber organs were intended,
as the brilliance of the writing and the dance movements pre-
clude their use in the Royal chapel, where Fr. AS was the
resident organist. The gifted royal pupil and the Padre must
have found the gay, playful music a welcome escape from the

austere monastic life of the winter palace. They sound well
on two pianos and are a welcome addition to the literature.
There is another edition by Musica Hispana; both are difficult
to obtain from Spain. They are published separately, and
the following is a guide to selection.

Concierto I in C: All have two movements except
No. II. Here a well-organized Andante in binary form contrasts themes and keys in sonata style (they might better
have been called Sonatas). All closing movements are
minuets with sets of ornamental variations and a da capo.
5 1/2 minutes.   Mod.

Concierto II in A Minor: Here the opening Andante
is 3/4 and has the stately character of a chaconne. An
added second movement is Allegro in a spirited gigue style,
followed by the usual Minuet. The longest, 11 min. 40
sec.   Mod. Dif.

Concierto III is eupeptic, with sprightly rhythms, developed in a Musette over a pedal point. The Minuet is
elaborate, with a trio, echo and imitation effects over a
rumbling bass.   Mod. Dif.

Concierto IV is more formal and stately. The Minuet
is a simple country dance, each successive variation doubling
the number of notes per beat for climactic effect.   Mod.

Concierto V is in similar style, but somewhat larger
scaled, and with an enigmatic registration. 8 min. 45 sec.
                                                             Mod. Dif.

Concierto VI is a big work, imaginative and attractive.
7 or 8 minutes.   Mod. Dif.

SPINKS, CHARLES (USA 1915-   )
Variations on a Greek Folk Song (HE, 1951, set). A
large-scale work, fresh and original, in the manner of the
great nineteenth-century sets. The naive folk theme is retained throughout a series of seven transformations, which
present it as a scherzo, a lively dance, a solo for Middle
Eastern dulcimer, with bell and harp effects, with a 5/8
ostinato cam-figure, as a broad exultant song, and in a
swirling finale.   Dif.

STARER, ROBERT (Aus-USA-Isr 1924-   )
The Fringes of a Ball (TP, 1962, set). Subtitled

Waltz Variations on a Theme by William Schuman, the music prints the tone row and WS' Waltz theme derived from
it.   The two pianists take turns with the theme, presto
leggiero, while the other part blurs the sound for an effect
of remoteness and nostalgia, with counter-themes and chord
trills, pressing to an acme, grandioso fff.   15 pages.   Dif.

STEHMAN, JACQUES   (Bel 1912-   )
       Colloque, à deux pianos (CBDM, 1960).   Very fast
piece with climactic ending.   One movement.   Dissonant but
tonal.   Facsimile score.   21 pages, 5 minutes.   Dif.

STERNKLAR, AVRAHAM   (It-Isr-USA 1930-   )
       Andante (AS, 1972, set).   Unpretentious short work
(five pages).   The players take turns with the folkloric melody in Dorian mode, ornamenting it with spare fifths and
broken octaves, later expanded and spread over the keyboard
for a brief climax, breaking into a barless cadenza (actually
4/4) retaining the folk theme.   Unusual.   Mod.

STONE, GREGORY   (USA 1900-   )
       Burlesque Tzigane (EBM, 1936, set).   This occasional
piece, called a Musical Caricature On a Celebrated Gypsy
Theme, was written for the celebrated team of Josef and
Rosina Lhevinne.   Other teams of advanced players may enjoy its antics with Black Eyes, lavishly tricked out à la
Liszt, Chopin, Sarasate, Tchaikovsky and Wagner.   For one
caricature, The Chopin Revolutionary Etude is played in toto
by Piano II, while Piano I lays on Black Eyes in full chords.
There are several more of these elaborate musical pranks
using other well-known tunes.   22 pages.   Dif.

       Boogie Woogie Etude for Two Pianos, Four Hands (Ch,
1947, set).   Brilliant rhythmical piece in A-flat.   The boogie
woogie figure is carried out by the left hand of Piano II,
while the other three hands add chords, running figures,
etc.   Effective.   15 pages.   Mod. Dif.

STRAVINSKY, IGOR   (Rus-USA 1882-1971)
       Sonata for Two Pianos (1943-4) (Ch, AMP, BMI, set).
One of IS' few ingratiating piano works, this is a big im-
provement over the solo sonata of twenty years earlier.   The
twenty-minute, three-movement piece opens with a hypnotic
Moderato that evokes the sound of a gamelan, with its in-
sistence on the fourth and seventh scale tones.   Theme with
Variations is a spacious chorale varied with two dance-like
passages, a rapid-note toccata, and a broad resonant conclu-

sion. The closing movement is in simple three-part song
form, with an almost Bartokian folk tune for mid-theme between repetitions of a flowing passage in the opening modal
style. The parts reveal IS' struggle with a new medium, and
are almost four-hand music, with piano II playing an accom-
panying role, often in the bass clef.   Mod. Dif.

        Concerto per due pianoforti soli (1935) (ES, 1936,
sep). Written for the composer to perform with his pianist
son, Soulima, "in cities without an orchestra," this Concerto has symphonic proportions. Though formidably difficult, it is the most successful of IS' keyboard works, and
deserves to be heard more often. Laid out in four movements, it is serious and weighty, brightened with salient
themes and striking rhythms, though it does not entirely escape the unpianistic, unimaginative keyboard figuration that
mars so much of the passage work in this composer's piano
music. The opening Con moto is an Allegro in square duple
rhythms, much martellato, marziale, marcatissimo, but with
a soft thrumming second theme. The Notturno second movement is not the sentimental or ghostly night music of Chopin
or Bartok, but "after dinner music" to link the heavy first
with the big lively third, a set of Four Variations with textures and themes similar to the Allegro. Preludio e fuga
opens and closes with tolling chords introducing the fugue
theme, derived from the variations, and given a contrapuntal
workout, building climactically. In spite of the special two-
manual instrument he had built to compose this, IS never entirely escapes from the one-piano primo-secondo relationship
of parts, and Piano II is definitely in a bass supporting role
throughout. Challenging, both technically and musically. 20
minutes.   Vir.

STRONG, GEORGE TEMPLETON   (USA 1856-1948)
        Trois Morceaux (Hen, 1924, set). Intrada (Prelude,
Moto adagio), Sarabande (Lento), Babillage (Twaddle, Allegro molto). 11 pages.

        Trois Idylles, Op. 29 (Hen, 1887). Lengthy suite
dedicated to Edward MacDowell.

        Cortege oriental and March militaire, Op. 39, No.
1 and 2 (APS, 1892).

        An American composer who lived most of his life in
Europe, GTS was a member of the Liszt Circle which included Siloti, Friedheim, Dayas and Krause. These pieces

are all in nineteenth-century traditional style, and are moderate in technical demands.

SURINACH, CARLOS (Sp-USA 1915-)
    Flamenquerias (AMP, 1952, set). Three pieces, a
fast light Moorish dance, a Romance, a dance from Seville.
Brilliant large-scale suite capturing in a modern idiom spiced
with dissonance, the ardor and languor of flamenco dancing,
singing and guitar. The latter does not transfer well to the
keyboard, and the parts, while well deployed, are often unpianistic. 27 pages.   Dif.

SZAJNA-LEWANDOWSKA, JADWIGA
    Funerailles, per 2 pianoforti (1970) (PWM, 1973, sep).
Dissonant piece in four sections: Adagietto, Andante con
moto, Allegro drammatico, Andante quasi marcia. 15 pages,
7 min. 30 sec.   Mod.

TAILLEFERRE, GERMAINE (Fr 1892-)
    Jeux de plein air (Dur, 1919, set). By the female
member of Les Six, this well-wrought and imaginative piece
deserves to be heard. The two movements of the "Outdoor
Games" are both based on French folksongs. Harmonized in
the late Impressionist manner with many ninths and parallel
sevenths, the piece has a lilting alfresco quality. Though
modest in demands and lean and transparent in texture, the
sound is rich, suggesting a chamber ensemble. 19 pages.
                                                        Mod.

    Deux Valses pour deux pianos (EHL, 1962, set). A
three-page Valse lente in E, dedicated to Henry Sauguet, and
an eight-page Valse brillante in G minor, dedicated to Vittorio
Rietti. Light and pleasing. Use of ninth and eleventh chords,
and parallel fifths.   Mod.

TALMA, LOUISE (USA 1906-)
    Four-handed Fun, for Two Pianos (CF, 1949, set).
Not a children's piece, as the title might suggest, this is a
spirited scherzo with dashing scale passages and dancing
staccato figures tossed back and forth between the two players. In one movement, the central section moves to minor,
building from fragmentary phrases a cumulative crescendo
and returns to the opening theme.   Mod.

TANSMAN, ALEXANDRE (Pol-Fr 1897-)
    Fantaisie sur les valses de Johann Strauss, pour deux
pianos (MEE, 1964, set). An impressionistic concert waltz

in which the familiar Strauss melodies appear one after the
other in quick succession.   Mod. Dif.

TCHEREPNIN, ALEXANDER (Rus-USA 1899-)
     Rondo, Op. 87a (CFP, 1957, set).   Effective recital
number for two advanced students.   Straightforward harmonic
writing, the episodes derived from the Rondo theme, but
contrasting octave and chord passages with linear and passage
work.   12 pages.   Mod. Dif.

TERZIAN, ALICIA (Arg)
     Atmosferas para 2 pianos (1969) (RA, 1972, sep).
Fourteen short episodes (mostly one or two pages) by the
young Argentine pianist, composer and educator.   Atonal,
with occasional use of tone clusters and glissandi.   Light and
airy in texture, most of the pieces are quiet and expressive.
23 pages.   Mod. Dif.

THOMSON, VIRGIL (USA 1896-)
     Synthetic Waltzes (1925) (EV, 1948, set).   A chain of
waltzes, linked in the Viennese style, amiable, sentimental,
fluent and well-structured.   VT has never adopted a very advanced idiom, and these early duets are very traditional.
18 pages.   Mod. Dif.

TIPPETT, MICHAEL (GB 1905-)
     Fantasia on a Theme of Handel (AMP, set).   Important
work by an eclectic composer who blends Sibelius-modern with
romantic elements in traditional keyboard figures, pianistic
and euphonious.   Mod. Dif.

TOEBOSCH, LOUIS (Neth 1916-)
     Suite polyphonica, per due pianoforte, op. 30b (Don,
1962, set).   Linear and contrapuntal, in three movements.
A short maestoso Intrada is followed by Passacaglia and
Ricercare, both in leisurely tempo.   Ends with a fast, staccato Fuga.   Extensive use of parallel fourths and fifths, and
open triads.   33 pages.   Facsimile score.   Mod. Dif.

TRIGGS, HAROLD (USA 1900-)
     Spiritual: Death, Ain't yuh got no Shame (GS, set).
HT formed a team with the pianist and writer, Vera Brodsky,
for whom he arranged and composed several two-piano pieces.
                                                         Mod.

     Valse (GS, set); Autumn Legend (JF, set); Tyrollienne
(JF, set).

Danza Brasiliana (CF, 1947, set).   Encore number in the style of Arthur Benjamin's Jamaica Rhumba.   13 pages, 3 minutes.   Mod.

TRIMBLE, JOAN (GB 1915-   )
The Green Bough, for Two Pianos, Four Hands (B&H, 1951, set).   Irish pianist and composer-arranger of two-piano music wrote this modal, lyric piece, to be played "slow --with feeling and freedom." As duo-pianists, JT and her sister Valerie often appeared together.   10 pages.   Mod.

VAUGHAN WILLIAMS, RALPH   (GB 1872-1958)
Introduction and Fugue for Two Pianofortes (OxU, 1947, sep).   A sonorous four-page Introduction leads quickly into the Fugue.   Modal, tuneful, with thick, rich sound.   44 pages.   Mod. Dif.

VELDEN, RENIER VAN DER   (Bel 1910-   )
Beweging, voor twee klavieren (Movement for Two Pianos) (1965) (CBDM, 1967, set).   One movement, extended, atonal.   Much use of trills and running figures in high register.   Octaves are used as melody and as accompaniment in the low register.   23 pages.   Facsimile score.   Dif.

WALKER, ERNEST   (GB 1870-1949)
West Africa Fantasy, Op. 53; Waltz Suite, Op. 60 (OxU, set).   Oxford don and editor of OxU Press published two competent suites for two pianos, attractive if not in-spired.   Mod.

WEINER, LEO   (Hun 1885-1960)
Variations on a Hungarian Folk-song, for Two Pianos (EM, 1969, sep).   Theme and seven variations in traditional style.   LW studied and taught at Landesakademie in Budapest. 23 pages.   Mod.

WEISGALL, HUGO   (Czech-USA 1912-   )
Fugue and Romance, Op. 2, No. 1 (MW, 1940, set). Early work by a prolific composer of opera and ballet scores, this is taken from his first ballet, "One Thing is Certain." Fugues lend themselves well to two-piano writing, and this is pianistic, with flowing scales for countersubjects, octaves and chords accruing for a climactic ending.   The short Ro-mance, sempre una corda, is rather insipid.   12 pages.
Mod.

WIGHAM, MARGARET

Concerto for Two Pianos (RDR, 1969, set).   Useful
new work for two matched players of only moderate skill
familiar with standard repertoire.   Though no new ground is
broken, and the facile keyboard figures verge on the cliche,
the three balanced movements make a satisfying work, with
the best saved for the jazzy close.   24 pages.   Mod. E.

WILLIAMSON, ESTHER   (USA 1915-   )
        Sonata (MMC, set).   Neo-classic three-movement
work, traditional but fresh and attractive.   Mod.

WILLIAMSON, MALCOLM   (Aus-GB 1931-   )
        Sonata for Two Pianos (JW, 1967, sep).   Successful
British composer of opera and symphonic works, after ex-
perimentation with serial composition, returned to a freely
chromatic tonal style.   Written for the team of Ogdon and
Lewis, this requires full mastery of the keyboard.   Single
rhapsodic movement with programmatic suggestions.   Rolling
arpeggio figures pass from one end of the keyboard to the
other, and from one piano to the other, offsetting staccato
chordal melodies, and alternating with driving, thrusting octave passages.   Challenging.   31 pages.   Dif.

WISSE, JAN   (Neth 1921-   )
        Cristalli (Don, 1959, sep).   For devotees of the
pointillistic, serialistic style, three short pieces.   Good eye-
sight is needed for the blurry facsimile score.   The arbitrary
dynamics marked for each note vitiate any sense of cohesion
or mood the music might generate, though an occasional frag-
ment is outlined by a conventional crescendo.   Pedals are
indicated, and the third crystal is slow and soft, studded with
only a few ffff sequins.   9 pages.   Mod. Dif.

WOLFF, CHRISTIAN   (Fr-USA 1934-   )
        Duo for Pianists I; and II (CFP, 1962, set).   This
doctor of comparative literature, professor of Greek at Har-
vard, studied composition with Cage, who acclaimed his odd
compositions, using only three or four notes or pitches.
Time values and duration of rests are arithmetically progressive.   A purist who has shunned all contact with traditional and classical music, his music is described as "pieces,
quiet, short and very beautiful."   (V. Thomson, American
Music Since 1910.)

WYTTENBACH, JURG   (Swi 1935-   )
        Nachspiel in drei Teilen (1966) (AVV, 1969, sep).
Swiss pianist, composer, educator writes in an avant-garde

style. Three-part Postlude in post-Webern pointillism, beginning with both pianos in the bass, it spreads out to the
limits of the keyboard. Uses chord clusters, glissandi and
numerous trills. In Part II, sempre ff, the dispersed groups
become ninth chords; Part III is ppp, with frequent long
fermata over both notes and pauses. 15 pages, 8 minutes.
Dif.

ZIMMERMANN, BERND A. (Ger 1918-)
    Perspektiven; Musik zu einem imaginären Ballet für
zwei Klaviere (BSS, 1956, sep). One movement, atonal,
with complex rhythm, clusters, skips, glissandi, trills. 27
pages.   Dif.

PART 3

THREE OR FOUR AT TWO

Music for two pianos,
three or four players,
six or eight hands

THREE OR FOUR AT TWO

Three at Two

GRAINGER, PERCY ALDRIDGE (Aus-USA 1882-1961)
    Green Bushes (Passacaglia) (GS, set). In this tran-
scription of an orchestra work based on an old English folk
song, Piano I is played by one pianist, while two players
share the music for Piano II.   PG states that he chose Passacaglia form to suggest the "keeping-on'ness" of dance-folk-
songs, which often have from twenty to a hundred verses.
He preferred this form to variations, as the melody is always clearly stated, each repetition being enhanced by a different counter-theme, counter-rhythm, harmony or keyboard
figuration.   Fun for all.   See also PG under Two at Two.
                                                       Mod. E.

Four at Two

DAHL, INGOLF (Ger-USA 1912-1970)
    Quodlibet on American Folk Tunes (CFP, 1957, set).
Subtitled "The Fancy Blue Devil's Breakdown" (an incipit
based on the titles of the six tunes), this unique revival of
a Baroque form of medley is such a good idea that it is a
pity that it is ultimately so disappointing.   The four old-
fiddler's tunes, one hill-billy song, and one cowboy tune are
too similar (largely pentatonic) to provide the needed contrast; the fiddle figuration, as well as the counter melodies
are unpianistic; the attempt at canonic writing is dull.   There
remains the excitement of four people trying to keep together
at a dashing speed.   22 pages.   5 min. 40 sec.   Dif.

POWELL, JOHN (USA 1882-1963)
    In a Hammock, Op. 19 (GS, set).   Called a "scene
sentimental," this unusual work floats a cantabile theme on
undulating figures, dispersed among the four players.   Should
be revived.   Mod.

112

SMETANA, BEDRICH (Czech 1824-1884)
     Sonata in One Movement for Two Pianos Eight Hands
(1849) (HE, 1938 set; CFP, set). Unusual large-scale work
modeled on the B Minor Sonata of Liszt, who was a patron
of BS' new conservatory in Prague. Though the themes are
rather undistinguished, the work has a joyful verve, relating
perhaps to the successes of the composer's private and public
life at the time. In the absence of any of the polkas or program music which BS wrote so well, we must be grateful for
this number for the rare combination of two pianos, eight
hands.   Mod.

     Rondo in C (CFP, set). The headmaster knew how
to keep the students busy. Another piece for four players at
two pianos, shorter and simpler than the Sonata, this has
some of the sprightliness of the polkas. 13 pages. Mod. E.

PART 4

THREE AT THREE
AND FOUR AT FOUR

Three or four players at
three or four pianos

Three at Three

BACH, JOHANN SEBASTIAN (Ger 1685-1750)
Concerto for Three Cembalos in D minor, BWV 1063
(CFP, IMC, Br&H, set). JSB is known to have had three
harpsichords in his home, as well as several homegrown
players; but these works were probably planned for presenta-
tion at the New Collegium Musicum, which met in Mizler's
coffee room at the Swan. Recent scholarship has cast doubt
on the original authorship of all piano ensemble concertos by
Bach, but this need not bother the players. Though some of
the concertos are more hastily assembled than others, all
bear the strong stamp of JSB's inspired workmanship. Though
written with string accompaniment, the D minor is well worth
playing on three pianos alone. It is vigorous and driving, and
old Bach himself probably manned Piano I, which has a dom-
inating role. The second movement Siciliano varies the graceful theme, with all instruments taking turns. All join in the
bright finale. Mod. Dif.

Concerto for Three Cembalos in C, BWV 1064 (CFP,
IMC, Br&H, set). An imposing and grand work, with equal
distribution of parts. Three well-structured movements.
Though the orchestra is active, the parts can be assimilated
by the three keyboard players. Mod. Dif.

BROWN, EARLE (USA 1926-)
Corroboree for Three and Two Pianos (UE, 1970, set).
The title is an Australian native word meaning, according to
Webster, "a nocturnal festivity with songs and symbolic
dances by which the Australian aborigines celebrate events of
importance: a noisy festivity: tumult." Composed in 1963-
64, on commission by Radio Bremen, Germany, it was first
performed for the Bremen Festival in May, 1964, by Aloys,
Alfons and Bernhardt Kontarsky. Five kinds of piano sounds
are utilized: single notes, chords, clusters on the keyboard,

and pizzicato and muted sounds on the strings produced by
nails and fingers. All together there are twelve lines of
music; each line is marked to be played in 30, 45, 60 or
120 seconds. There are free areas where the performers
could choose to play the written material at any sequence or
tempo. All are explained in the detailed notes at the beginning of the piece. Four scores are included, a different
one for each of the three pianos, and one including all three
parts.   Dif.

DALLAPICCOLA, LUIGI (It 1904-)
        Musica per tre pianoforti (1935) (Car, 1936, sep).
LD's piano music looks profound and sounds simplistic.
These three pieces for three pianos could be read by three
students, but fine musical imagination is needed to reify
them.   All themes sound like hymns or carols, and chime
and bell effects abound in the three movements Allegro, molto
sostenuto; Funebre; Allegramente, ma solenne.   Though accidentals are sprinkled throughout, the first movement moves
from G to D, the second is E minor, the third, E.   Each is
basically a set of variations on a single theme.   The paucity
of melody demands great attention to dynamics, touch and
tempo, all clearly marked.   15 minutes, 40 pages.   Mod.

FELDMAN, MORTON (USA 1926-)
        Extensions 4 for Three Pianos (1952); Piece for Four
Pianos (1957) (CFP, set).   The principle of predetermined in-
determinacy is here written out.   The parts indicate pitch
location but not time value, so that each player is free to
establish his own rhythm or non-rhythm, within a given time
duration.   The intervals are largely thirds, sixths and sevenths, and when they happen to sound together form delicate
chords of ninths, elevenths, thirteenths.   "As we proceed to
experience the individual time-responses of the four pianists
we are moving inexorably toward the final image where the
mind can rest, which is the end of the piece." Amen.

GODOWSKY, LEOPOLD (Rus-USA 1870-1938)
        Contrapuntal Paraphrase on Weber's "Invitation to the
Dance." See Two at Two.

LUENING, OTTO (USA 1900-)
        The Bells of Bellagio (CFP, 1973, sep).   Distinguished
educator, administrator and composer, one of the first to use
tape in serious music.   Basically a canon in augmentation,
for two or three players at one, two or three pianos.   Section
one, "Hail," has player II producing bell-effects in middle

range by repeating treble part at half speed, while player III
does the same in the bass at quarter speed.   The second
part, called "Farewell," is a double canon for each player,
and spreads out over the keyboard, so that three pianos are
simpler than one (but require three scores).   Maximum effect with moderate means.   11 pages.   Mod.

MOZART, WOLFGANG AMADEUS   (Aus 1756-1791)
        Concerto for Three Pianos in F, K. 242 (EFK, set).
Though written to be played with orchestra, this can be very
effective unaccompanied, with the three pianos joining in the
tutti passages.   Written for two lady friends and a daughter,
it is a graceful lightweight work.   Three levels of skill are
apparent, the first piano taking the burden, the second some
nice solo bits, and the third following with frequent rests
that must be counted.   Attractive themes are well developed.
The Adagio is black with 32nd notes and less inspired; the
Minuet finale is charming.   All three movements have cadenzas, Piano I leading off, joined by II in imitation, or
parallel figures; Piano III is occasionally given a share.
                                        Mod. E. to Mod. Dif.

PHILIPP, ISIDORE   (Fr 1863-1958)
        Concertino sans orchestre, pour trois pianos (SE,
1931, set).   Large-scale four-movement work in traditional
style.   Prelude (Andante), Barcarolle (Allegretto malinconico),
Scherzo et intermezzo (Vivacissimo), Toccata (Allegro vivo).
Pianistic and brilliant, with materials well deployed among
three players.   Each performer has a different score which
contains his part only.   24 pages for Piano I, 23 for Piano
II, and 28 for Piano III.   Mod. Dif.

                          Four at Four

HAMPTON, CALVIN   (USA 1938-   )
        Catch-Up; for Four Pianos or Tape Recorder and Two
Pianos (CFP, 1970, set of 2).   Fun and games for avant-
gardists.   The score contains parts for first pianos, marked
♮ , and second pianos, marked ♭, which should be tuned one
quarter-tone lower, if feasible.   A conductor is recommended
for performance either on four pianos, or with two players
and a tape recording in two channel stereo, in this case the
conductor should wear earphones.   Four ideas, A, B, C and
D, each five measures long, are presented in different or-
ders in two versions, with an E section, also five measures

but mostly rests, added to version two.   The first version
may be played by two pianos or pre-recorded, and the second played in live performance against the first one.   Because of their different lengths, version one is repeated five
times and version two four times "before the two sets re-
solve their asymmetry and catch up with each other." For
a recording of this, see Part 6.   Mod.

PART 5

ARRANGEMENTS AND TRANSCRIPTIONS

1. FOR ONE PIANO, FOUR HANDS

ARENSKI, ANTON
Intermezzo for Orchestra, Op. 13.   Arr. by the composer.   PJ (1892).

ARNOLD, MALCOLM
English Dances.   Arr. by F. Reizenstein.   MMC (1958).

AURIC, GEORGES
Les Matelots.   Arr. by the composer.   Heu (1925).

BACH, J. S.
Art of Fugue.   Arr. by Bruno Seidlhofer.   Br&H (1937).

Brandenburg Concertos (2 v.).   Tr. by M. Reger.
IMC (1944-45).

Fantasia in G Major for Organ, S. 572.   Arr. by M.
Reger.   Aug.

Jesus, Joy of Man's Desiring (Chorale from Cantata
No. 147).   Arr. from piano transcription by Myra Hess.
OxU (1934).

Orchestral Suites (4).   Arr. by M. Reger.   IMC, CFP.

Organ Works Arranged for Piano, Four Hands, by
Gleichauf.   IMC.
  Vol. I: Prelude and Fugue in C, G, A, a, e, and b
             Passacaglia in C Minor
             Pastorale in F Major
             Fantasia and Fugue in G Minor
  Vol. II: Prelude and Fugue in F, c, C, E-flat
             Toccata and Fugue in F, d (The Dorian).

Sleepers Wake.   Arr. by Harriet Cohen.   OxU (1952).

BALAKIREV, MILY
            Thamar, Symphonic Poem.   Arr. by G. Glazounow.
PJ.

BARTOK, BELA
            The Miraculous Mandarin.   Arr. for piano, 4 hands.
B&H (1952).

BEETHOVEN, LUDWIG VAN
            Grand septour.   Arr. by the composer.   London,
Clementi (1817).

            Septet for Violin, Viola, Clarinet, Horn, Bassoon,
Violoncello and Contrebass, Op. 20.   Arr. by C. Czerny.
Berlin, C. Paez   (1841).

            Symphonies (Complete in 2 v.).   Arr. for piano, 4
hands.   CFP, GS.

            Symphony No. 6, Op. 68.   Arr. by C. Czerny.   Leip-
zig, H. A. Probst (1828?).

BENJAMIN, ARTHUR
            Jamaican Rumba.   Arr. by J. Trimble.   B&H.

BERLIOZ, HECTOR
            Grande ouverture de Benvenuto Cellini.   Arr. by H.
de Bülow.   Schl (186?).

            Ouverture des Francs-Juges, Op. 3.   Arr. by C.
Czerny.   Bronsvic, G. M. Meyer (18?).

            Romeo et Juliette (Selections).   Arr. by Otto Singer.
CFP.

            Symphonie fantastique, op. 14.   Arr. by Otto Singer.
CFP.

BIZET, GEORGES
            L'Arlésienne.   Suite No. 1-2.   Arr. by Otto Singer.
CEP.

BORODIN, ALEXANDER
            In the Steppes of Central Asia.   Arr. by the composer.
DR.

BOUTRY, ROGER

Le voleur d'étincelles. Tabatière a musique.   Arr.
for piano, 4 hands.   SE.

BRAHMS, JOHANNES
Piano Quartet No. 1 in G Minor, Op. 25;
Piano Quartet No. 2 in A Major, Op. 26;
Piano Quartet No. 3 in C Minor, Op. 60.   Arr. for
piano, 4 hands.   UE.

BRITTEN, BENJAMIN
Playful Pizzicato (from "Simple Symphony").   Arr. by
H. Ferguson.   OxU (1972).

Sentimental Saraband (from "Simple Symphony").   Arr.
by H. Ferguson.   OxU (1972).

BRUCKNER, A.
Symphony No. 3 in D Minor.   Arr. by Gustav Mahler.
TR.

BUSONI, FERRUCCIO
Finnländische volksweisen, Op. 27, C Major.   Arr.
for piano, 4 hands.   HE (1953).

CHAUSSON, ERNEST
Symphony, Op. 20, B-flat Major.   Arr. by the composer.   EB.

Viviane, Symphonic Poem.   Arr. by Vincent d'Indy.
OB (19?).

CLEMENTI, MUZIO
Two Duettinos for Piano, Four Hands.   Tr. by Pietro
Spada.   GS (1972).

DEBUSSY, CLAUDE
La Boîte à joujoux (Selections).   Arr. by Léon Rogues.
Dur (1914).

Cortège et air de danse (from L'Enfant prodigue).
Arr. by the composer.   Dur (1905).

Danses, pour harpe chromatique ou piano avec acct.
d'orchestre d'instruments à cordes.   Tr. by A. Benfeld.
Dur (1904).

Ibéria (from Images pour orchestre).   Tr. by Andre
Caplet.   Dur (1910).

Marche écossaise sur un thème populaire. Arr. for piano, 4-hands. JJ (1930).

La mer. Arr. by the composer. Dur (1905-07).

Pelléas et Mélisande. Tr. by Léon Rogues. Dur (1911).

Prelude de L'enfant prodigue. Arr. by the composer. Dur (1907).

Rhapsodie pour orchestre et saxophone. Arr. by L. Garban. Dur (1919).

Sonate pour flûte, alto et harpe. Arr. by L. Garban. Dur (1917).

String Quartet, Op. 10. Arr. by A. Benfeld. EV (1957).

Suite Bergamasque (Prelude, Menuet, Clair de lune, Passepied). Tr. by H. Woollett. JJ (1914).

La triomphe de Bacchus; divertissement pour orchestre. Tr. by the composer. Cho (1928).

DELIUS, FREDERICK
Dance Rhapsody No. 2. Arr. by Philip Heseltine. Aug (1922).

Eventyr. Tr. by B. J. Dale. Aug (1921).

North Country Sketches. Tr. by P. Heseltine. Aug (1922).

A Song before Sunrise. Tr. by P. Heseltine. Aug (1922).

DELLO JOIO, NORMAN
Christmas Music. Tr. for piano, 4 hands. MaM (1968).

DVOŘAK, ANTONIN
Bagatelles, for 2 Violins, Cello, Harmonium, Op. 47. Arr. by the composer. Sim (1879).

Carnival. Arr. by the composer. Sim (1894).

Golden Spinning Wheel. Arr. by J. Spengel. Sim
(1896).

The Noon Witch. Arr. by J. Spengel. Sim (1896).

String Quartet No. 10, Op. 51, E-flat Major. Arr.
by the composer. Sim (1879).

The Wild Dove. Arr. for Piano, 4 hands. Sim
(1899).

ELGAR, EDWARD
Cockaigne Overture, Op. 40. Arr. for Piano, 4
hands. B&H.

Pomp and Circumstance Military March No. 1 and 4.
Arr. for Piano, 4 hands. B&H (1901).

Sarabande and Bourrée. Arr. by R. Elkin. GMC
(1958), Elk.

FALLA, MANUEL DE
Danses espagnoles. Arr. by G. Samazeuilk. MEE
(1923).

FAURE, GABRIEL
Masques et bergamasques, Op. 112. Arr. by the
composer. Dur (1919).

FOERSTER, JOSEF
Meine Jugend, Op. 44. Arr. by the composer. UE
(1910).

FRANCK, CESAR
Sonate. Tr. by Alfred Cortot. JH (1905?).

GERMAN, EDWARD
Suite from the Music to Shakespeare's Romeo and
Juliet. Arr. by the composer. Nov (1896).

Three Dances from the Music to Henry VIII. Arr.
by the composer. Nov (1892).

GERSHWIN, GEORGE
Cuban Overture. Arr. by the composer. NWM (1933).

Preludes. Arr. by Gregory Stone. NWM.

Rhapsody in Blue. Arr. by Henry Levine. NWM (1943).

GILBERT, HENRY F.
Three American Dances. Arr. by Henry Gilbert. BMC (1919).

GLAZOUNOV, ALEXANDER
The Forest, Fantasy for Orchestra, Op. 19. Arr. by the composer. MPB (1887?).

A la mémoire de Gogol. Arr. by the composer. MPB (1912).

A la mémoire de N. Rimsky-Korssakow. Arr. by the composer. MPB (1911).

Stenka Rāzine, Symphonic Poem. Arr. by the composer. MPB.

Symphony No. 2, Op. 16; No. 4, Op. 48; No. 7, Op. 77. Arr. by the composer. MPB (1886-1902).

Symphony No. 6, Op. 58. Arr. by S. Rachmaninoff. MPB (1898).

GLINKA, MIKHAIL
Komarinskaja. Arr. by S. Liapunow. PJ (1907).

GOTTSCHALK, LOUIS MOREAU
There are many four-hand arrangements of Gottschalk's piano works, several of which, very effectively arranged by the composer himself, may be found in The Piano Works of Louis Moreau Gottschalk. Edited by Vera Brodsky Lawrence. Arno Press & the New York Times, 1969.

GOUNOD, CHARLES F.
Faust. Arr. by George Bizet. Cho (18?).

GRIEG, EDVARD
Peer Gynt Suite No. 1, Op. 46. Arr. by A. Rut-hardt. CFP.

Symphonic Dances, Op. 64. Arr. by the composer. CFP.

Symphonic Pieces, Op. 14. Arr. for piano, 4 hands. CFP.

HANDEL, GEORGE FRIDERIC
   The Arrival of the Queen of Sheba (from "Solomon").
Arr. by G. Bryan.   JMC (1955).

   Oratorios (selections).   Arr. by C. Czerny.   Sim
(1937).

   Organ Concertos (2 v.).   Tr. by H. Schenker.   IMC
(1949).

   Suite from the Water Music.   Tr. by L. Duck.   HE
(1951).   Arr. by A. Richardson.   OxU (1954).

HAYDN, JOSEPH
   Serenade, Op. 3, No. 5.   Arr. by T. A. Johnson.
HE, CFP (1966).

HEROLD, L. J. F.
   Overture to Zampa.   Arr. by the composer.   Balti-
more, G. Willig.

HERZ, HENRI
   Variations brillantes.   Arr. by the composer.   BSS
(184?).

HINDEMITH, PAUL
   Symphonic Dance for Orchestra.   Arr. for piano, 4
hands.   BSS (1939).

   Symphonie Mathis der Maler.   Arr. by the composer.
AMP (1934), SS.

HONEGGER, ARTHUR
   Le chant de Nigamon.   Arr. for piano, 4 hands.
EMS (1926).

   Pastorale d'été.   Tr. by the composer.   EMS (1921).

   Trois contrepoints pour petite flûte, hautbois (cor
anglais), violon et violoncelle.   Edition for piano, 4 hands by
the composer.   WH (1926).

INDY, VINCENT D'.
   Concert pour piano, flûte et violoncelle avec orchestre
à cordes, op. 89.   Arr. by the composer.   RL (1927).

   Poème des rivages; suite symphonique en 4 tableaux,

op. 77.   Arr. by the composer.   RL (1922).

IRELAND, JOHN
        The Forgotten Rite.   Arr. by the composer.   Aug
(1918).

        Symphonic Rhapsody.   Arr. by the composer.   Aug
(1931).

KALINNIKOV, VASSILI
        Deux intermezzo pour orchestre.   Arr. by Victor
Kalinnikov.   PJ (1901).

        Suite for Orchestra.   Arr. by the composer.   PJ
(1902).

KHACHATURIAN, ARAM
        Sabre Dance (from "Gayne Ballet").   Arr. by M.
Karpov.   MCA (1947).

LECUONA, ERNESTO
        Danza lucumi (from Danzas afro-cubanas suite).   Arr.
by L. Sugarman.   MaM (1950).

LISZT, FRANZ
        Deux Transcriptions d'après Rossini pour piano.   Arr.
by H. Cramer.   BSS

        Les Préludes (symphonic poem after Lamartine).
Arr. by the composer.   GS (1903).

        Symphonic Poems.   Arr. by the composer.   Br&H.

MACDOWELL, EDWARD
        Hamlet and Ophelia, Op. 22.   Arr. by the composer.
GS (19?), JH (1885).

        Indian Suite, Op. 48.   Arr. by Otto Taubmann.   Br&H
(1905).

        Lamia, Op. 29.   Arr. by the composer.   APS (1908).

        Lancelot and Elaine, Op. 25.   Arr. by the composer.
JH (1888).

        Poesien, Op. 20.   Arr. by the composer.   GS (19?).

Suite for Orchestra, Op. 42.   Arr. by the composer.
BSS, APS (1891).

Woodland Sketches.   Tr. by F. Fox.   APS.

MAHLER, GUSTAV
Symphony No. 2, in C Minor.   Arr. by Bruno Walter.
UE (19?).

MARTIN, FRANK
Pavane couleur du temps pour quintettes à cordes ou
petit orchestre.   Arr. by the composer.   Hen (1921).

MENDELSSOHN, FELIX
Andante and Variations, Op. 83a.   Arr. by the composer.   IMC.

Midsummer Night's Dream (Scherzo, Intermezzo, Noc-
turn and Wedding March).   Arr. by the composer.   Br&H
(184?).

Variations sérieuses, op. 54.   Arr. by C. Czerny.
Vienne, Pietro Mechetti qm. Carlo (1842).

MILHAUD, DARIUS
Le boeuf sur le toit.   Arr. by the composer.   Si
(1920).

Suite francaise.   Arr. by the composer.   LPC (1950).

MOSZKOWSKI, MORITZ
Aus aller Herren Länder.   Arr. by the composer.
JH (1879).

Joan of Arc, Symphonic Poem in Four Movements.
Arr. by the composer.   Aug

MOZART, WOLFGANG AMADEUS
Eine Kleine Nachtmusik; Serenade, K. 525.   Arr. by
O. Singer.   CFP.

String quartets (selections).   Arr. by C. Czerny.
FK (1850).

Twelve Celebrated Symphonies (2 v.).   Arr. by H.
Ulrich and A. Horn.   GS (1897-1902?).

MUSSORGSKY, MODEST
      Intermezzo.   Arr. by D. Kabalevsky.   UE (1931).

RACHMANINOFF, SERGEI
      Fantaisie pour orchestre, op. 7.   Tr. by the com-
poser.   SME (1928).

RAVEL, MAURICE
      Daphnis et Chloé, Suite no. 1.   Arr. by Leon Rogues.
Dur (1911).

      Rapsodie espagnole.   Arr. for piano, 4 hands.   Dur
(1908).

      La Valse.   Tr. by L₀ Garban.   Dur (1920).

REGER, MAX
      Variations and Fugue on a theme of Mozart, Op. 132.
Arr. for piano, 4 hands.   CFP (1915).

REINECKE, CARL
      String Quartet No. 3, Op. 132, C Major.   Arr. by
the composer.   RF (19?).

RIMSKI-KORSAKOV, NIKOLAI
      The Fairy Tale of the Czar Saltan Suite.   Arr. by
Nadeshda Rimsky-Korsakov.   SME (1927).

      The Golden Cockerel, Suite.   Arr. by A. Glazounov
and M. Steinberg.   PJ (1910).

      Scheherazade, after the "Arabian Nights" Symphonic
Suite, Op. 35.   Arr. by P. Gilson.   GS (1918).

ROSSINI, GIOACCHINO
      Largo al factotum (from The Barber of Seville).   Arr.
by A. Diabelli.   D&B (183?).

      Stabat Mater.   Arr. by C. Czerny.   BSS (184?).

      William Tell Overture.   Arr. by L. M. Gottschalk.
WmH (1864).

RUBINSTEIN, ANTON
      Romance, Op. 44, No. 11.   Arr. for piano, 4 hands.
PJ (1891).

      Tarantelle, Op. 14.   Arr. for piano, 4 hands.   PJ (187?).

SAINT-SAËNS, CAMILLE
Le Carnaval des animaux. Tr. for piano, 4 hands.
Dur, TP (1922).

Gavotte en ut mineur pour piano, op. 23. Arr. by
Jacques Charlot. Dur (1912).

Sarabande et rigaudon, Op. 93. Arr. by Jacques
Durand. Dur (1893).

SATIE, ERIK
Cinéma; entr'acte symphonique de "Relâche". Arr.
by Darius Milhaus. RL (1926).

Parade, ballet réaliste. Arr. for piano, 4 hands.
RL (1917).

SCHÖNBERG, ARNOLD
Serenade, Op. 24. Arr. by F. Greissle. WH

String Quartet No. 2, Op. 10. Arr. by F. Greissle.
UE (1923).

SCHUBERT, FRANZ
Rosamunde, Overture. Arr. by C. Burchard. GS.

SCHUMANN, ROBERT
Six études, op. 56, en forme de canon pour piano à
pédales. Tr. by Georges Bizet. Dur (190?).

Symphony No. 2, Op. 61. Arr. by the composer. FW
(1859).

SCRIABIN, ALEXANDER
Le Divin Poème, Op. 43 (Symphony No. 3). Arr. by
L. Conus. MPB (1905).

Reverie; pour orchestre, op. 24. Arr. by A. Wink-
ler. MPB (1899).

SHOSTAKOVICH, DMITRI
Quartet No. 12, Op. 133. Arr. by N. Tsyganova.
IM (1972).

Symphony No. 1, Op. 10, F Major. Arr. by E.
Slavinsky. IMC.

SIBELIUS, JEAN
    The Swan of Tuonela (from 4 Legends, Op. 22).   Arr.
by Otto Taubmann.   Br&H (1908).

STRAUSS, RICHARD
    Also sprach Zarathustra.   Arr. by O. Singer.   JAV
(1896).

    Aus Italien; sinfonische Fantasie (G Major).   Arr. by
the composer.   JAV (19?).

    Don Quixote.   Arr. by O. Singer.   JAV (1898).

    Der Rosenkavalier, Concert Waltz for Piano Duet.
Arr. by O. Singer.   B&H (1911).

    Serenade.   Woodwinds and Brasses, Op. 7, E-flat
Major.   Arr. by the composer.   JAV (19?).

    Till Eulenspiegel's Merry Pranks.   Arr. for piano, 4
hands.   JAV (1895).

STRAVINSKY, IGOR
    Concertino.   Arr. by the composer.   WH (1923).

    Feu d'artifice, Op. 4.   Arr. by O. Singer.   BSS (1924).

    Petrouchka, Burlesque in Four Scenes.   Arr. by the
composer.   B&H (1947).

    The Rite of Spring.   Arr. by the composer.   B&H
(1926).

TAILLEFERRE, GERMAINE
    Image, pour huit instruments.   Tr. by the composer.
J&WC (1921).

TANEYEV, SERGEY
    String Quartet, No. 6, Op. 19, B-flat Major.   Arr.
for piano, 4 hands.   MPB (1906).

    Symphony No. 1, Op. 12, C Minor.   Arr. by the com-
poser.   MPB (1901).

TANSMAN, ALEXANDER
    Le jardin du paradis.   La danse de la sorcière.   Arr.
by the composer.   ME (1924).

TCHAIKOVSKY, PETER
    Capriccio Italien, Op. 45.   Arr. by the composer.
PJ (1880).

    1812 Overture.   Arr. for piano, 4 hands.   DR (1898).

    50 Russian Folk Songs.   Arr. by the composer.   LPC
(1949).

    Marche Miniature, Suite for Orchestra, Op. 43.   Arr.
by A. Siloti.   DR (189?).

    The Nutcracker Suite, Op. 71a.   Arr. by E. Langer.
GS (1918).   Arr. by S. Esipoff.   Aug, BMC (1904).

    Russian Folk Songs.   Arr. by K. Hermann.   CFP
(1940).

    Symphonies, Selections (Manfred, symphony; Sym-
phony No. 6).   Arr. by the composer.   IM (1964).

    Symphony No. 2, Op. 17, C Minor.   Arr. by the
composer.   WB (19?).

    Waltz (from "Serenade for Strings" Op. 48).   Tr. by
M. Castelnuovo-Tedesco).   LPC (1965).

VAUGHAN WILLIAMS, RALPH
    Fantasia on Greensleeves.   Arr. by Hubert J. Foss.
OxU (1942).

WAGNER, RICHARD
    Kaisermarsch.   Arr. by H. Ulrich.   CFP (189?).

    Overtures (Selections).   Arr. by O. Singer.   CFP.

    Parcifal.   Arr. by E. Humperdink.   BSS (1883).

    Vorspiel zu Tristan und Isolde.   Arr. by Hans von
Bülow.   Br&H (186?).

WALTON, WILLIAM TURNER
    Facade, Second Suite for Orchestra.   Arr. for piano,
4 hands.   OxU (1938).

    Facade, Suite for Orchestra.   Arr. by C. Lambert.
OxU (1927).

WEBER, K. MARIA
    Oberon, Overture. Arr. by L. M. Gottschalk. OD (1873).

WOLF, HUGO
    Penthesilea. Arr. by Max Reger. L&K (1903).

2. FOR TWO PIANOS, FOUR HANDS

ADDINSELL, RICHARD
    Festival. Arr. by Percy Grainger. Ch.

ALBENIZ, ISAAC
    Rapsodia española. Arr. for 2 pianos. UME (1962).

    Spanish Rhapsody. Arr. for 2 pianos. BMC (1916).

    Triana. Arr. by E. G. Miller. GS (1965).

ALEXANDER, HAIM
    Six Israeli Dances. Arr. by the composer. LPC
(1960).

ARGENTO, DOMINICK
    Divertimento for Piano and Strings. Arr. for 2 pi-
anos. B&H (1969).

ARMA, PAUL
    Sept transparences, pour deux pianos. Arr. from
string quartet by the composer. EHL (1969).

BACH, J. S.
    Ah! How Ephemeral (from The Wise Virgins, arr. by
William Walton). Arr. for 2 pianos by Walter Goehr. OxU
(1960).

    Air in D Major (Air for the G String). Arr. by Guy
Maier. JF (1940). Arr. by Marjory Moore. B&H.

    Andante (from the Brandenburg Concerto No. 2). Tr.
by A. Siloti. CF.

    Andante (from Concerto No. 3 for Two Pianos and Or-
chestra). Tr. by A. Siloti. CF.

The Art of the Fugue. Tr. by Schwebsch. EFK.

Be Contented, O My Soul. Arr. by H. Cohen. OxU.

Beloved Jesus, We are Here. Arr. by H. Cohen.
OxU.

Brandenburg Concerti, Nos. 2, 4, 5, 6. Arr. by Krug.
B&H.

Fantasia and Fugue in A Minor. Arr. by Harold Bauer.
OD (1918).

Fantasia and Fugue in G Minor. Tr. by R. Burmeister. IMC. Arr. by O. Singer. SV.

Humble Us by Thy Goodness. Arr. by R. Burmeister.
BMC. Arr. by B. Williams. OxU.

Inventions. Second piano part to the fifteen Two-part
Inventions, by R. Vené. TP (1944). Five Two-part Inventions arr. by G. Maier. JF.

It Is a True Saying (from Cantata No. 141). Arr. by
Mary Howe. OxU (1935).

Italian Concerto. Arr. by Harold Bauer. GS (1931).
Arr. by A. Siloti. JF.

Jesus, Joy of Man's Desiring (from Cantata No. 147).
Arr. by Victor Babin. BMC (1965). Arr. by Myra Hess.
OxU (1934).

Jig Fugue in G. Tr. by Cyril Scott. Elk, GMC
(1936).

Komm, süsser Tod. Tr. by Mary Howe. GR (1942).
Tr. by S. B. Kohn. SMC (1964).

Now Comes the Gentle Savior. Tr. by P. Luboshutz.
JF.

Passacaglia in C Minor. Tr. by Abram Chasins.
JF (1933). Arr. by G. Tagliapietra. GR (1956). Arr. by
I. Philipp. Dur.

Prelude and Fugue for Organ, S. 543. Arr. by I.
Philipp. Dur (1902).

Prelude and Fugue for Organ, S. 546.   Arr. by Harold Bauer.   OD (1918).

Prelude and Fugue in A Minor.   Arr. by O. Singer. SV.

Prelude and Fugue in E Minor for Organ.   Arr. by Henri Duparc.   IMC.

Prelude in G for Organ.   Arr. by John Odom.   JC (1951).

See What His Love Can Do (from Cantata No. 85). Arr. by H. Foss.   OxU (1936).

Selected Compositions (12 v.).   Arr. by I. Philipp. GR.

Sheep May Safely Graze.   Arr. by Mary Howe.   OxU (1936).   Arr. by P. Grainger (as Blithe Bells).   GS (1932).

Siciliene.   Arr. by G. Maier.   JF.

Sleepers Wake.   Arr. by W. G. Whittaker.   OxP (1935).

Thy Birthday Is Come (from Cantata No. 142).   Tr. by Mary Howe.   OxU (1937).

Trio Sonatas for Organ (3rd, in d; 4th, in e; 5th, in C, 6th, in G).   Arr. by Victor Babin.   B&H.

Well-tempered Clavier (selections).   Arr. by E. Humperdinck.   Scho (1900).

BACH, WILHELM FRIEDEMANN
    Sonate.   Arr. by Johannes Brahms.   CFP (1939).

BARBER, SAMUEL
    Souvenirs.   Arr. by Arthur Gold and Robert Fizdale. GS (1964).

BARTOK, BELA
    Rhapsodie for Piano and Orchestra.   Arr. by the composer.   Roz.

Seven Pieces from "Mikrokosmos. "   Arr. by the composer.   B&H (1947).

BEETHOVEN, LUDWIG VAN
Grosse Fuge, Op. 133. Arr. by Harold Bauer (from the composer's own arrangement for piano, 4 hands, op. 134). GS (1927).

Seven Variations on a Theme from Mozart's Magic Flute. Arr. by P. Luboschutz. JF (1948).

Variations on a Theme by Count von Waldstein. Arr. by V. Babin. EV (1946).

BENJAMIN, ARTHUR
From San Domingo. Arr. for 2 pianos. B&H (1946).

BERLIOZ, HECTOR
Marche hongroise de la damnation de Faust. Tr. by E. Redon. ECo (190?).

Rokoczy March. Arr. by Hutcheson. JF.

BIZET, GEORGES
Carillon. Arr. by B. Easdale. OxU.

Galop (from "Jeux d'enfants). Arr. by J. Lovell. OxU.

Minuet from "L'Arlesienne Suite." Arr. by Castel-nuovo-Tedesco. MCA.

BLOCH, ERNEST
Evocations. Arr. for 2 pianos. GS.

BORODIN, ALEXANDER
Notturno from String Quartet in D. Arr. by R. Stern-dale-Bennett. JC, GS (1952).

Polovetsian Dances from "Prince Igor." Arr. by V. Babin. LPC (1954), MAC.

BRAHMS, JOHANNES
Five Waltzes from Op. 39 (Nos. 1, 2, 11, 14, 15). Arr. by the composer. CFP.

How Lovely Are Thy Dwellings (from the "German Requiem"). Tr. by C. Kramer. PRP (1938).

Liebeslieder Waltzes, Set 1 and 2, Op. 52. Tr. by G. Maier. JF (1928).

Symphony No. 3, Op. 90.   Tr. by the composer.

Symphony No. 4, Op. 98.   Tr. by the composer.

BRITTEN, BENJAMIN
Scottish Ballad for 2 Pianos and Orchestra, Op. 26.
Arr. for 2 pianos.   B&H (1946).

Soirees Musicales, Op. 9.   Tr. by B. Easdale.   B&H.

BUXTEHUDE, DIETRICH
Prelude and Fugue for Organ, G Minor.   Arr. by C.
Dougherty.   GS (1944).

BYRD, WILLIAM
The Bells.   Arr. by M. Penny.   OxU (1948).

CHABRIER, EMMANUEL
España Rhapsody.   Arr. for 2 pianos by the composer.
BM.

CHANCE, JOHN BARNES
Introduction and Capriccio, for Piano and 24 Winds.
Reduction for 2 pianos.   B&H (1966).

CHASINS, ABRAM
Parade.   Arr. by the composer.   JF (1934).

Rush Hour in Hong Kong.   Arr. by the composer.   JF
(1934).

Serenade.   Arr. by the composer.   JF (1934).

CHERUBINI. LUIGI
Scherzo in C Major (from String Quartet No. 2).   Tr.
by R. Berkowitz.   EV (1943).

COPLAND, AARON
Billy the Kid (excerpts from the ballet).   Arr. by the
composer.   B&H (1946).

Dance of the Adolescent (from Dance Symphony, 1930).
Arr. by the composer.   B&H (1968).

Danza de Jalisco.   Arr. by the composer.   B&H
(1968).

Hoe-Down and Saturday Night Waltz (from Rodeo).
Arr. by A. Gold and R. Fizdale.   B&H (1950).

El Salon Mexico.   Arr. by Leonard Bernstein.   B&H
(1943).

COUPERIN, FRANCOIS
Fanfare.   Tr. by Paul Schwartz.   B&H (1957).

D'ALBERT, EUGEN
Allemande, Gavotte and Musette (from Suite. Op. 1).
Arr. by B. Dieter.   CFS (1948).

DEBUSSY, CLAUDE
Arabesque No. 2.   Tr. by L. Rogues.   Dur (1910).

Le Martyre de Saint Sebastien; fragments symphoniques.
Tr. by L. Garban.   Dur (1919).

La Mer.   Arr. by Caplet.   Dur.

Nocturnes.   Tr. by M. Ravel.   JJ.

Petite Suite.   Tr. by H. Busser.   Dur (1908).

Prelude to the Afternoon of a Faun.   Arr. by the composer.   GS.

Printemps, suite symphonique.   Arr. by A. Benfeld.
Dur.

String Quartet, Op. 10.   Arr. by G. Samazeuieh.
Dur (1915).

DELIUS, FREDERICK
A Dance Rhapsody.   Tr. by P. Grainger.   LPC

Fantastic Dance.   Arr. by E. Bartlett and R. Robertson.   B&H (1936).

DINICU, GRIGORAS
Hora Staccato.   Tr. by Jascha Heifetz.   CF (1930).

DOHNANYI, ERNST VON
Variations on a Nursery Tune, Op. 25.   Arr. by
Kodula.   Sim.

DUPARC, HENRI
    Lénore; poème symphonique pour orchestre d'après la
ballade de Bürger.   Arr. by Camille Saint-Saëns.   RL (1905).

FALLA, MANUEL DE
    Dance of the Miller's Wife, Fandango (from the Three
Cornered Hat ballet).   Arr. by C. Dougherty.   J&WC (1949).

    Pantomime (from El Amor Brujo).   Arr. by C.
Dougherty.   J&WC (1944).

    Ritual Fire Dance.   Arr. by Braggiotti.

FELDMAN, MORTON
    Ixion, for 10 instruments.   Arr. for 2 pianos.   CFP
(1965).

FRANCK, CESAR
    Pastorale, no. 4 des 6 pièces pour orgue, op. 19.
Arr. by J. Griset.   Dur (1912).

    Prelude, fugue et variation.   Tr. by Rudolph Gruen.
AMP (1934).   Arr. by E. Bartlett and R. Robertson.   OxU.

    Preludio, aria e finale, per pianoforte.   Tr. by R.
Silvestri.   GR.

GERSHWIN, GEORGE
    Cuban Overture.   Tr. by Gregory Stone.   NWM.

    Fantasy on George Gershwin's Porgy and Bess.   By
P. Grainger.   Ch (1951).

    I Got Rhythm.   Tr. by the composer.   NWM (1934).

    Preludes.   Tr. by Gregory Stone.   NWM (1927).

    Second Rhapsody.   Tr. for 2 pianos.   NWM (1932).

    Short Story.   Tr. by Al and Lee Reiser.   Scho (1943).

GLIERE, REINHOLD M.
    Russian Sailors' Dance (from the ballet the Red Poppy).
Tr. by Rudolph Gruen.   AMP (1938).

GLINKA, MIKHAIL
    The Lark.   Arr. by P. Luboshutz.   JF (1941).

GLUCK, CHRISTOPH
      Melody; second ballet from Orpheus. Arr. by Abram
Chasins. CR (1939).

GODOWSKY, LEOPOLD
      Alt Wien. Old Vienna. Tr. by the composer. GS
(1935).

GOTTSCHALK, LOUIS
      Bamboula; West Indies drum dance. Arr. by Eliza-
beth Gest. EV (1943).

      The Banjo. Arr. by Jerome Moross. GS (1962).

GRAINGER, PERCY
      English Waltz (Last movement of Youthful Suite for
orchestra). Arr. by the composer. Scho (1947).

      Hill-songs I and II. Arr. for 2 pianos. GS (1922).

GRANADOS, ENRIQUE
      The Lover and the Nightingale (from Goyescas). Arr.
by Bartlett and Robertson. J&WC (1944).

HAHN, REYNOLD
      Le Bal de Béatrice d'Este; suite for wind instruments,
2 harps and one piano. Arr. by the composer. Heu (1905).

HANDEL, GEORGE FRIDERIC
      Andante from Organ Concerto. Arr. by Phyllis Tate.
OxU.

      Arrival of the Queen of Sheba. Arr. by B. Easdale.
OxU.

      The Harmonious Blacksmith. Arr. by B. Easdale.
OxU. Arr. by R. Palmer. WMC (1920).

      Suite. Tr. by Thurston Dart. OxU (1950).

HAYDN, JOSEPH
      Concertino (Divertimento) in C Major. Arr. by
George Anson. CFP (1964).

      Two Pieces for a Musical Clock. Arr. by Joan Lovell.
Elk, GMC (1956).

HINDEMITH, PAUL
Sinfonische metamorphosen Carl Maria von Weber'scher Themen, 1943.　Tr. by Jon Thorarinsson.　AMP (1952), BSS.

HÖLLER, KARL
Two Sonatas for 2 Pianos, Op. 41 (from Kleine Sonaten, No. 2-3).　Arr. by the composer.　MHS (1967).

HOLST, GUSTAV
The Planets.　Tr. by the composer.　JC (1949).

HUMPERDINCK, ENGELBERT
Hansel and Gretel.　Overture.　Arr. by C. T. Griffes. GS (1951).

INDY, VINCENT D'
Wallenstein, Op. 12.　Arr. by Marcel Labey.　Dur (1909).

KHACHATURIAN, ARAM
Dance of the Rose Maidens (from Gayne Ballet).　Tr. for 2 pianos.　LPC.

Lesginka (from Gayne Ballet).　Tr. by V. Babin. LPC (1948).

Lullaby (from Gayne Ballet).　Tr. by A. Gotlieb. LPC (1948).

Sabre Dance (from Gayne Ballet).　Tr. by P. Luboshutz.　LPC (1948).

Waltz (from Masquerade Suite).　Arr. by M. Castelnuovo-Tedesco.　LPC (1951).

KUHLAU, FRIEDRICK
Sonatinas, Op. 20, No. 1-3, Op. 55, No. 1-3.　Second Piano Part by August Riedel.　CFP (1927).

LALO, EDOUARD
Symphonie espanole, pour violon et orchestre, op. 21. Arr. by A. Benfeld.　Dur (1905).

LECUONA, ERNESTO
Andalucia (from the Spanish Suite Andalucia).　Arr. by Grace Helen Nash.　MaM (1932).

Gitaneria (from the Spanish Suite Andalucia).   Arr. by Morton Gould and Bert Shefter.   MaM (1934).

Malaguena (from the Spanish Suite Andalucia).   Arr. by Grace Helen Nash.   MaM (1932).

LISZT, FRANZ
Rhapsodie hongroise pour le piano, no. 11.   Arr. by R. Kleinmichel.   BSe (1879?).

Symphonic Poems Nos. 1-12.   Arr. by the composer. Br&H (186?).

MCPHEE, COLIN
Balinese Ceremonial Music.   Tr. by Colin McPhee. GS (1940).

MALIPIERO, GIAN FRANCESCO
Dialoghi I: Con Manuel de Falla, in memoria, per piccola orchestra.   Tr. by the composer.   GR (1957).

MARTIN, FRANK
Come to the Fair (Valse Caprice).   Tr. by Samuelson.   B&H.

Etudes (for string orchestra).   Tr. by the composer. UE (1969).

MASSENET, JULES
Air de Ballet.   Tr. by Otto Singer.   SS.

Angelus.   Tr. by O. Singer.   SS.

March.   Tr. by O. Singer.   SS.

Scenes Pittoresques.   Tr. by O. Singer.   SS.

Suite.   Tr. by O. Singer.   SS.

MENDELSSOHN, FELIX
Midsummer Night's Dream. Overture.   Arr. by the composer.   Paris, A. Ikelmer.

On Wings of Song.   Tr. by Rudolph Gruen.   AMP (1934).

Scherzo (from Fantasia for Piano, Op. 16, No. 2, E Minor).   Arr. by E. Bartlett.   OxU (1950).

Scherzo (from Incidental Music to A Midsummer Night's Dream). Arr. by I. Philipp. GS (1943).

Sonatas 1-6, Op. 65 (for Organ). Arr. by I. Philipp. Dur.

MOLDENHAUER, HANS
Prelude and Waltz "Night Must Fall." Tr. for 2 pianos.

MORGENSTERN, SAM
Toccata Guatemala. Arr. by Whittemore and Lowe. CF (1954).

MOSZKOWSKI, MORITZ
Spanish Dance, Op. 12, No. 3, 4. Arr. by Bernhard Wolff. Sim (1884).

Valse Brillante in A-flat Major. Arr. by Silver. JF.

MOUSSORGSKY, MODEST
Coronation Scene from "Boris Godounoff." Arr. by L. Pattison. GS (1928).

Intermezzo (genre classique). Arr. by C. Tschernow. WB (1895).

A Night on the Bald Mountains. Arr. by Eustafieff. Bes.

MOZART, WOLFGANG AMADEUS
Adagio and Allegro for Mechanical Organ, K. 594. Arr. by Silvio Omizzolo. GR (1954).

Adagio and Fugue in C Minor, for Two Pianos (K. 546 and 426). Adagio arr. and Fugue ed. by Victor Babin. Aug (1955). Arr. by Paul Badura-Skoda. GS (1973).

Fantasia and Sonata in C Minor, K. 475. Second piano part by Edvard Grieg. GS (1921).

Fantasia for Musical Clock Work, K. 608. Arr. by F. Busoni. IMC (1943).

Magic Flute Overture. Tr. by F. Busoni. IMC.

Sonata in C Major, K. 545. Second piano part by Edvard Grieg. GS (1921), CFP.

Sonata in F Major, K. 533 and 494.   Second piano part by Edvard Grieg.   GS (1921).

Sonata in G Major, K 189h.   Second piano part by Edvard Grieg.   GS (1921).

NEVIN, MARK
Deep River Fantasy.   Tr. based on the negro spiritual, "Deep River," by Mark Nevin.   S&G (1957).

PADEREWSKI, IGNACE JAN
Fantasie Polonaise sur des thèmes originaux pour piano et orchestre, op. 19.   Arr. by the composer.   B&B (1895).

PIERNE, GABRIEL
March of the Little Lead Soldiers.   Arr. by Wallingfold Riegger.   HF (1942).

PINTO, OCTAVIO
Scenas Infantis.   Tr. for 2 pianos.   GS.

POULENC, FRANCIS
Aubade; concerto pour piano et dix-huit instruments. Arr. by the composer.   RL (1931).

Concerto in D Minor for Two Pianos and Orchestra (1932).   Arr. by the composer.   RL (1949).

POWELL, JOHN
Natchez-on-the-hill; Three Virginian Country-dances. Arr. by John Powell.   GS (1933).

PROKOFIEFF, SERGE
Cinderella's Waltz (from the ballet Cinderella).   Tr. by Castelnuovo-Tedesco.   LPC (1954).

March, Band, Op. 99.   Arr. by P. Luboshutz.   LPC (1948).

PURCELL, HENRY
Sonata III (from Sonatas in Four Parts).   Arr. by C. Dougherty.   CF (1952).

Two Bourées.   Arr. by Catharine Dickinson.   GS (1966).

RACHMANINOFF, SERGEI
     Concerto No. 2, Op. 18. Arr. for 2 pianos by the composer. CFo (1938).

     Italian Polka. Tr. by the composer. CFo (1938), BM.

     It's Lovely Here (Originally for voice and piano). Arr. by V. Babin. UMC (1942).

     Morceaux de Fantasie, Op. 3, Prelude. Arr. by Richard Lange. Moscow, A. Gutheil (191?).

     Prelude in C-sharp Minor. Arr. by the composer. CFo (1938).

     Symphonic Dances, Op. 45. Arr. by the composer. CFo (1942).

RAFF, JOACHIM
     The Mill. Arr. by George Anson. EV (1948).

RAMEAU, JEAN PHILIPPE
     La Bourrée de Vincent. Arr. by Charles Ross. Nov (1938).

     Gavotte with Variations in A Minor. Tr. by J. Doebber. IMC (1957).

     A Gay Melody (Air Trés Gai). Arr. by P. Luboshutz. JF (1937).

RAPHLING, SAM
     Square Dance, from American Album. Arr. by the composer. EMu (1946).

RAVEL, MAURICE
     Bolero. Arr. by the composer. Dur (1930).

     Ma mere l'oye. Arr. by Gaston Choisnel. Dur (1911).

     Pavan, pour une enfante défunte. Tr. by M. Castlenuovo-Tedesco. LPC (1950).

     Rapsodie espagnole. Tr. by the composer. Dur (1907).

La Valse.   Tr. by the composer.   Dur (1920).

REGER, MAX
Variations and Fugue on a Theme of J. S. Bach.
Arr. by K. H. Pillney.   B&B (1926).

Variations and Fugue on a Theme of Mozart, Op. 132a.
Arr. by the composer.   CFP

REINECKE, CARL
Festival Overture, Op. 148.   Arr. by the composer.
B&H.

Pictures from the South, Op. 86.   Arr. for 2 pianos.
JMRB.

RESPIGHI, OTTORINO
The Pines of Rome.   Arr. for 2 pianos.   GR.

RIEGGER, WALLINGFORD
Evocation, Op. 17.   Arr. by the composer.   PIC
(1953).

Variations for Two Pianos, Op. 54a.   Tr. by the
composer.   AMP (1955).

RIMSKI-KORSAKOV, NIKOLAI
Capriccio Espanol, op. 34.   Arr. by Schaefer.   MPB.

Cradle Song.   Arr. by V. Babin.   B&H.

Scheherazade, Op. 35.   Arr. by G. Humbert.   MPB
(1910).

ROSSINI, GIOACCHINO
Largo al factotum (from the opera Barber of Seville).
Arr. by A. Diabelli.   D&B (18?).

ROUSSEL, ALBERT CHARLES PAUL
Evocations.   Arr. by the composer.   Dur (1911).

RUBINSTEIN, ANTON
Ballade (Léonore de Burger) for Piano.   Arr. by J.
Pomerantzeff.   WB (1902?).

Fantaisie hongroise.   Arr. by H. Gobbi.   WB (1900).

SAINT-SAËNS, CAMILLE
Caprice pour le piano sur les airs de ballet a'Alceste
de Gluck. Arr. by C. A. Debussy. Dur (1900).

Le carnaval des animaux. Tr. by Ralph Berkowitz.
EV (1947), Dur

Danse Macabre, Op. 40. Tr. by the composer. Dur.

Introduction and Rondo Capriccioso, Op. 28. Tr. by
Claude Debussy. IMC (1963).

Menuet et gavotte du septuor, op. 65. Arr. by the
composer. IMC (1954).

Le Rouet d'Omphale. Arr. for 2 pianos. Dur.

Rhapsodie de Auvergne. Arr. for 2 pianos. Dur.

Suite Alzarinne, Op. 60. Arr. for 2 pianos. Dur.

SCARLATTI, DOMENICO
Pastorale. Tr. by J. Doebber. IMC.

SCHOENBERG, ARNOLD
Five Pieces for Orchestra, Op. 16. Arr. by Anton
von Webern. CFP (1918).

Variations on a Recitative. Arr. by C. Dougherty.
HWG (1955).

SCHUBERT, FRANZ
Andantino varie, op. 84, no. 1 (for piano, four hands).
Arr. for 2 pianos by Harold Bauer. GS (1928).

Fantasia in F Minor, Op. 103 (for piano, four hands).
Arr. for 2 pianos by Harold Bauer. GS (1928).

Marche Militaire, Op. 51, No. 1 (for piano, four
hands). Arr. for 2 pianos by Harold Bauer. GS (1931).

Rondo Brillante, Op. 84, No. 2 (for piano, four hands).
Arr. for 2 pianos by Harold Bauer. GS (1928).

Theme and Variations from the Piano Quintet, Op. 114,
The Trout. Arr. by R. Sterndale Bennet. Aug (1951).

SCHUMANN, ROBERT
Six Etudes in the Form of a Canon. Tr. by Claude
Debussy. IMC (1952).

SCOTT, CYRIL
Danse Negre. Tr. for 2 pianos. GMC.

Lento from "Two Pierrot Pieces." Arr. by I. Arnold.
B&H.

Three Symphonic Dances for Orchestra. Arr. by P.
Grainger. BSS (1922).

SCRIABIN, ALEXANDER
Poem of Ecstacy, Op. 54. Arr. by Conus. MPB.

Prometheus, Op. 60. Arr. by Labaniew. RM.

SHOSTAKOVICH, DMITRI
Polka from Ballet "L'age d'or." Arr. by P. Luboshutz. JF (1941).

Waltz from the film "Golden Mountains." Tr. by P.
Luboshutz. LPC (1948).

SMETANA, BEDRICH
Aus meinem Leben. Arr. by Otto Vrieslander. Hei
(1959).

My Fatherland. Arr. by Trnecek. Urb.

STRAUSS, JOHANN
The Bat, a Fantasy on Themes from Johann Strauss'
Die Fledermaus. By P. Luboshutz. JF (1951).

The Blue Danube Waltze. Tr. by Abram Chasins.
JF (1933).

Kuenstlerleben (Artist's Life) waltz. Arr. by A.
Chasins. JF.

Moto Perpetuo. Arr. by Rae Robertson. OxU (1950).

STRAUSS, RICHARD
Eine Alpensinfonie, Op. 64. Arr. by O. Singer.
FECL (1951).

Aus Italien. Arr. by O. Singer. JAV (1904).

Ein Heldenleben. Arr. by O. Singer. FECL (1899).

Der Rosenkavalier, Concert Waltze. Arr. by O. Singer. B&H (1911).

Salome's Dance. Arr. by J. Doebber. B&H.

Serenade. Arr. by Abram Chasins. JF.

STRAVINSKY, IGOR
Agon; Ballet for Twelve Dancers. Tr. by the composer. B&H (1957).

Circus Polka (1942). Tr. by V. Babin. B&H.

Concerto in E-flat Major (Dumbarton Oaks). Tr. by
the composer. AMP (1938), BSS.

Danses Concertantes. Arr. by Ingolf Dahl. AMP
(1944).

Madrid, from Four Studies for Orchestra. Arr. by
Soulima Stravinsky. B&H (1951).

Scherzo à la russe. Tr. by the composer. AMP
(1945).

Tango. Arr. by Victor Babin. MeM (1962).

Three Movements from Petrouchka. 1. Russian
Dance. 2. Petrouchka. 3. The Shrove-tide Fair. Arr. by
Victor Babin. B&H (1953).

TAYLOR, DEEMS
Through the Looking Glass; Five Pictures from Lewis
Carroll. Arr. by James Whittaker. JF (1936).

TCHAIKOVSKY, PETER
Roméo et Juliette Overture. Arr. by K. Klindworth.
WB (1900).

VAUGHAN WILLIAMS, RALPH
Fantasia on Greensleeves. Arr. by H. Foss. OxU
(1942).

The Running Set; Founded on Traditional Dance Tunes.
Arr. by V. Lasker and H. Bidder.   OxU (1936).

VILLA-LOBOS, HECTOR
     Moreninha (from A próle do bébé, no. 1).   Arr. by
A. Whittemore and J. Lowe.   AMP (1943).

VIVALDI, ANTONIO
     Concertó in A Minor.   Tr. by Wendell Nelson.   GS
(1968).

VORISEK, JAN HUGO
     Grande ouverture in c, op. 16.   Tr. for 2 pianos.
Bar (1971).

WAGNER, RICHARD
     Parcifal.   Arr. by E. Humperdink.   BSS (1884?).

WALTON, WILLIAM
     Facade (Polda, Old Sir Faulk, Swiss Jodelling Song,
Tarantella, Valse).   Arr. by H. Murrill.   OxU (1934).

     Portsmouth Point; an Overture.   Arr. by the composer.
OxU (1927).

     Sinfornia concertante.   Arr. by Roy Douglas.   OxU
(1943).

WEBER, CARL MARIA VON
     Allegro di bravure.   Arr. by C. Czerny.   CPS (1840).

     Concertpiece (Konzertstuck) in f, Op. 79.   Arr. by
Beveridge Webster.   IMC.

     Grand Duo Concertant, Op. 48.   Arr. by A. Henselt.
Schl (1873).

     Invitation to the Dance.   Arr. by Weingartner.   B&H
(1943).   Contrapuntal paraphrase for 2 pianos with an optional
accompaniment of a third piano, by Leopold Godowsky.   CF
(1922).

     Rondo.   Arr. by Pierre Luboshutz.   JF.

     Rondo Brillant, Op. 62.   Arr. by M. Penny.   OxU.

     Rondo in C.   Freely transcribed by Vivian Langrish.
Elk (1950).

WEINBERGER, JAROMIR
    Polka and Fugue from the opera Shvanda.   Tr. by
the composer.   AMP (1940).

WIDOR, CHARLES MARIE
    Toccata from the Fifth Symphony for Organ.   Tr. by
Isidor Philipp.   GS (1943).

3.   FOR TWO PIANOS, SIX HANDS

GRAINGER, PERCY
    English Dance, for 2 pianos, 6 hands.   Tr. by P.
Grainger.   GS (1924).

    Green Bushes; Passacaglia.   Arr. for 2 pianos, 6
hands.   (1st pianist at 1st piano, 2nd and 3rd pianists at
2nd piano.)   GS (1921).

4.   FOR TWO PIANOS, EIGHT HANDS

BACH, J. S.
    Five Chorales.   Arr. by Dorothy Connor.   GS (1944).

    Fugue in A Minor.   Arr. by Percy A. Grainger.   GS
(1930).

    Passacaglia.   Arr. by C. Burchard.   GH (186?).

    Ten Chorales.   Tr. by E. M. Ohley.   S&G (1942).

BEETHOVEN, LUDWIG VAN
    Egmont Overture, Op. 84.   Arr. by Otto Lessmann.
Schl (1871).

    Grande Polonaise, Op. 56.   Arr. by C. Burchard.
GH (1868).

    Leonore Overture.   Arr. by G. M. Schmidt.   Br&H
(1843).

    Phantasie für Pianoforte, Chor und Orchester, Op. 80
Arr. for 2 pianos, 8 hands.   Br&H (1857).

GLINKA, MIKHAIL
Rousslan et Ludmila, Ouverture.   Arr. by S. Liapounow.   PJ (1910).

GRIEG, EDVARD
Peer Gynt Suite No. 1.   Arr. by A. Ruthardt.   CFP (19?).

MAHLER, GUSTAV
Symphony No. 2, C Minor.   Arr. by Heinrich von Bocklet.   UE (1914).

MENDELSSOHN, FELIX
Overtures, Selections.   Arr. by F. Hermann.   CFP.

MOSCHELES, IGNAZ
Les contrastes, op. 115.   Arr. for 2 pianos, 8 hands. FK (1844).

MOSZKOWSKI, MORITZ
Valse brillante.   Arr. by C. Gurlitt.   GS (1902).

MOZART, WOLFGANG AMADEUS
Quintett für Pianoforte, Hoboe, Clarinette, Horn und Fagott.   Arr. by C. T. Brunner.   FH (1862).

RIMSKI-KORSAKOV, NIKOLAI
Sadko; tableau musical pour orchestre.   Arr. by E. Langer.   PJ (1893).

ROSSINI, GIOACCHINO
Overture to William Tell.   Arr. by G. M. Schmidt. OD (18?).

RUBINSTEIN, ANTON
Trot de cavalerie, morceau de salon pour piano.   Arr. by E. Langer.   JP (1890?).

SAINT-SAËNS, CAMILLE
Suite algérienne.   Arr. by the composer.   Dur.

SCHUBERT, FRANZ
Ouverture zu Rosamunde.   Arr. by F. G. Jansen. Schl (1885).

SCHUMANN, ROBERT
Ouverturen zu Genoveva, Op. 81, und Manfred, Op. 115.   Arr. by Theodor Kirchner.   CFP (1888).

TCHAIKOVSKY, PETER
　　　　Capriccio Italien.　Arr. by E. Langer.　PJ (189?).

　　　　Marche slave; slavonic march, Op. 31.　Arr. by E.
Langer.　GS.

　　　　Sleeping Beauty, Waltz.　Arr. by E. Langer.　PJ
(1888).

　　　　Symphony No. 3, D Major, Op. 29.　Arr. by E.
Langer.　PJ (1903).

　　　　La Tempete, op. 18.　Arr. by E. Langer.　PJ
(1898).

WAGNER, RICHARD
　　　　Overture to Tannhäuser.　Arr. by C. Burchard.
CFM (1859).

　　　　Der Ritt der Walküren.　Arr. by C. Chevillard.
Scho (1901).

5.   FOR THREE PIANOS

BACH, J. S.
　　　　Concerto, 3 Harpsichords and String Orchestra, C
Major.　Arr. by Harold Bauer.　GS (1929).

　　　　Toccata in F for Organ.　Arr. for 3 pianos, or any
multiple of 3, with one or more players at each piano, by
Percy Grainger.　GS (1940).

PART 6

RECORDINGS

1. ABBREVIATIONS FOR RECORD MANUFACTURERS

Candide	Can.
Collectors Guild	CG
Columbia	Col.
Command	Com.
Composers Recordings, Inc.	CRI
Connoisseur Society	Conn.
Deutsche Grammophon	DGG
Everest	Ever.
Friends of Four-Hand Music	FFHM
GWM Records	GWM
Golden Crest	GC
Gravure Universelle	Grav.
Kapell	Kap.
Klavier	Kla.
London	Lon.
Music Guild	MG
Music Library Recordings	MLR
Mercury	Mer.
Monitor	Mon.
Odyssey	Odys.
Philips	Phi.
Qualiton	Qua.
Seraphim	Sera.
SPA Records	SPA
Supraphon	SUA
Turnabout	Turn.
Vanguard	Van.
Veritas	Ver.
Westminster	West.
World Series	WS

2. RECORDINGS FOR ONE PIANO, FOUR HANDS

BEETHOVEN, LUDWIG VAN
Eight Variations in C Major, WoO 67, on a Theme by
Count Waldstein.
  Joerg Demus and Norman Shetler.   DGG SLPM 139448.
  Hans Kann and Rosario Marciano.   MHS 1096 (1970).

Grosse Fugue, in B-flat Major, Op. 134 (Beethoven's own
arrangement).
  Hans Kann and Rosario Marciano.   MHS 1096 (1970).

Six Variations in D Major, WoO 74, on the Song Ich denk
dein
  Hans Kann and Rosario Marciano.   MHS 1096 (1970).

Sonata in D Major, Op. 6.
  Joerg Demus and Norman Shetler.   DGG SLPM 139448.
  Hans Kann and Rosario Marciano.   MHS 1096 (1970).

Three Marches, Op. 45.
  Hans Kann and Rosario Marciano.   MHS 1096 (1970).

BENNETT, RICHARD RODNEY
Capriccio for Piano Duet.
  The composer as one of the pianists.   Argo ZRG 704
  (1972).

BIZET, GEORGES
Jeux d'enfants, op. 22.
  Arthur Gold and Robert Fizdale.   Odys. 32 16 0334.
  Beatriz and Walter Klien.   Turn. TV34241; Vox STPL
  512,590 (1964).
  Allinon Nelson and Harry Neal.   Kap. SKR 4026 (1970).
  Vitya Vronsky and Victor Babin.   Col. ML 2107 (1950);
  Sera. S 60053 (1967); RCA ALP 2065 (1962).

BRAHMS, JOHANNES
Hungarian Dances, for Piano, Four Hands, No. 1-21.

Alfred Brendel and Walter Klien.   Vox PL 9640 (1956?).
Bracha Eden and Alexander Tamir (Nos. 1-10).   Lon.
CS 6614 (1969).
Richard and John Contiguglia (Nos. 5 and 6).   Conn. CS
2037 (1971).
Julius Katchen and Jean-Pierre Marty.   Lon. CS 6410,
6473-6474, 6477 (196?) (Brahms: The Complete Piano
Works).
Walter and Beatriz Klien.   Turn. TV 4068, TV 34068S.
Allinon Nelson and Harry Neal (No. 5).   Kap. SKR 3041.
Helen Schnabel and Karl Ulrich Schnabel (Nos. 1-4, 11-
13 and 17).   Epic LC 3183 (195?).

Neue Liebeslieder Walzer, Op. 65.
    Yaltah Menuhin and Joel Ryce.   Ever. LPBR 6130,
    SDBR 3130 (1965).

Variations on a Theme by Schumann, Op. 23.
    Sharon Gunderson and Jo Ann Smith.   Orion 7151.

Waltzes, Op. 39.
    Abram Chasins and Constance Keene.   Mer. MG 10135.
    Richard and John Contiguglia.   Conn. CS 2037 (1971).
    Bracha Eden and Alexander Tamir (Nos. 9, 10, 16).
    Lon. CS 6694 (1971).
    Walter and Beatriz Klien.   Turn. TV 34041S (1965).
    Allinon Nelson and Harry Neal (No. 5, in A-Flat).
    Kap. SKR 3041.

CHABRIER, EMMANUEL
    Cortége burlesque.
    Rena Kyriakou and Walter Klien.   Vox VBX 400; Turn.
    TV 34241.

Souvenirs de Munich.
    Rena Kyriakou and Walter Klien.   Vox VBX 400; Turn.
    TV 34241.

CHOPIN, FREDERIC
Variations sur un air national de Moore.
    Allinon Nelson and Harry Neal.   Kap. SKR 5101 (1970).

DEBUSSY, CLAUDE
    Ballade.
    Alfons and Aloys Kontarsky.   DGG 2707 072 (1974).

Cortége et air de danse, from L'Enfant prodigue.

Alfons and Aloys Kontarsky. DGG 2707 072 (1974).

Marche écossaise.
Alfons and Aloys Kontarsky. DGG 2707 072 (1974).

Petite Suite.
Ethel Bartlett and Rae Robertson. MGM E161.
Robert and Gaby Casadesus. Col. ML 5723; MS 6323
(1962).
Bracha Eden and Alexander Tamir. Lon. CS 6754
(1972).
Walter and Beatriz Klien. Turn. TV 34234.
Alfons and Aloys Kontarsky. DGG 2707 072 (1974).

Six épigraphes antiques (1914).
Robert and Gaby Casadesus. Col. ML 6041; MS 6641
(1964).
Arthur Gold and Robert Fizdale. Col. ML 4854 (in SL
198) (1954).
Walter and Beatriz Klien. Turn. TV 34235.
Alfons and Aloys Kontarsky. DGG 2707 072 (1974).

Symphony in B Minor for Piano, Four Hands (1880).
Phillips and Renzulli. Harl. 3805.

DEL TREDICI, DAVID
Scherzo.
Robert Helps and the composer. CRI SD 294 (1973).

DIABELLI, ANTON
Sonatina, Op. 24, No. 2.
Hans Kann and Rosario Marciano. MHS 916.

Sonatina, Op. 150, No. 2.
Hans Kann and Rosario Marciano. MHS 916.

DVOŘAK, ANTONIN
Legends, Op. 59, No. 1-3.
Walter and Beatriz Klien. Turn. TV 34041S (1965).

Slavonic Dances, for Piano, Four Hands, Op. 46 and 72.
Alfred Brendel and Walter Klien. Vox PL 11620 (1959);
Turn. TV 34060S (1966).
Bracha Eden and Alexander Tamir (Op. 46). Lon. CS
6614 (1969).
Allinon Nelson and Harry Neal (Op. 72, No. 2). Kap.
SKR 3041.

Vitya Vronsky and Victor Babin (Op. 72, No. 10).
Decca DL 9791, 1956.

FAURE, GABRIEL
Dolly, Op. 56.
Robert and Gaby Casadesus.   Col. ML 5723; MS 6323
(1962).
Walter and Beatrice Klien.   Vox STPL 512, 590 (1964);
Turn. 34234.

GRIEG, EDVARD
Norwegische Tänze, Op. 35.
Walter and Beatrice Klien.   Turn. TV 34041S (1965).

HAYDN, JOSEPH
Maestro e scolare.
Arthur and Ruth Balsam.   MHS OR H115.

HINDEMITH, PAUL
Sonata for Piano, Four Hands (1938).
Arthur Gold and Robert Fizdale.   Col. ML 4853 (in SL
198) (1954).
Yaltah Menuhin and Joel Ryce.   Ever. LPBR 6130;
SDBR 3130 (1965).
Milton and Peggy Salkind.   FFHM SKD 1027 (1965).

INFANTE, MANUEL
Andalusian Dance No. 1 and No. 2.
José and Amparo Iturbi.   RCA LM 36 (1951?).

JANACEK, LEOS
Narodni tance na Morave (National Dances of Moravia).
Hans Kann and Rosario Marciano.   MHS 1272.

KŘENEK, ERNST
Four Bagatelles (Sonata) for Piano, Four Hands, Op. 70
(1931).
Maro Ajemian and the composer.   MLR 7014 (1952).

LISZT, FRANZ
Festkantate, G 584 for Piano, Four Hands.
Richard and John Contiguglia.   Conn. CSQ 2052.

MENDELSSOHN, FELIX
Allegro brillant, in A major, op. 92.
Rena Kyriakou and Walter Klien.   Vox VBX 413.
Helen and Karl Ulrich Schnabel.   SPA 50 (195?).

Variations in B-flat, Op. 83a.
 Rena Kyriakou and Walter Klien.   Vox VBX 413.
 Helen and Karl Ulrich Schnabel.   SPA 50 (195?).

MOSCHELES, I
Hommage à Händel.
 Jane Smisor and James Bastien.   GWM 100 (1967).

MOSS, LAWRENCE
Omaggio (1966) (Eng. "Homage").
 Jean and Kenneth Wentworth.   Desto Stereo DC-7131.

MOZART, WOLFGANG AMADEUS
Adagio and allegro in F Minor, K. 594.
 Lilly Berger and Fritz Neumeyer.   Decca ARC 3101.
 Nadia Reisenberg and Artur Balsam.   MHS 632-, 632S-
 (1966-).

Andante and Variations in G Major, K. 501.
 Paul Badura-Skoda and Joerg Demus.   West. WST 17156;
 MG MS867 (1970).
 Robert and Gaby Casadesus.   Col. ML 5046 (1955).
 Ingrid Haebler and Ludwig Hoffmann.   Vox SVBX 566.

Complete works for piano, four hands.
 Joerg Demus and Paul Badura-Skoda.   MHS 1293-1296
 (1972).
 Yaltah Menuhin and Joel Ryce.   Ever, SDBR 3168/3
 (1967).

"Jugend" Sonata in C Major, K. 19d.
 Ingrid Haebler and Ludwig Hoffmann.   Vox SVBX 566.

Sonata in G Major, K. 357.
 Ingrid Haebler and Ludwig Hoffmann.   Vox SVBX 566.

Sonata in B-flat Major, K. 358.
 Ingrid Haebler and Ludwig Hoffmann.   Vox SVBX 566.
 Nadia Reisenberg and Artur Balsam.   MHS 632-, 632S-
 (1966-).
 Vitya Vronsky and Victor Babin.   Col. ML 4667 (1953).

Sonata in D Major, K. 381.
 Ingrid Haebler and Ludwig Hoffmann.   Vox SVBX 566.
 Nadia Reisenberg and Artur Balsam.   MHS 718S.
 Vitya Vronsky and Victor Babin.   Col. ML 4667 (1953).

Sonata in F Major, K. 497.
  Lilly Berger and Fritz Neymeyer. Decca ARC 3101.
  Ingrid Haebler and Ludwig Hoffmann. Vox SVBX 566.
  Nadia Reisenberg and Artur Balsam. MHS 632-, 632S-
  (1966-).

Sonata in C Major, K. 521.
  Artur Balsam and Nadia Reisenberg. MHS 718 S.
  Christoph Eschenbach and Justus Frantz. DGG 2530
  285.
  Ingrid Haebler and Ludwig Hoffmann. Vox SVBX 566.

MUETHEL, JOHANN G.
  Sonata (duetto) for Two Pianos.
    Victor Bouchard and Renée Morisset. RCA CCS 1021
    (1967).

PERSICHETTI, VINCENT
  Concerto, for Piano, Four Hands, Op. 56.
    Dorothea and Vincent Persichetti. Col. ML 4989 (1955).

PIERNE, GABRIEL
  March of the Little Lead Soldiers, Op. 28, No. 8.
    Myra Hess and Harold Bauer. Kla. KS 102 (1970).

POULENC, FRANCIS
  Sonate for Piano, Four Hands (1918).
    Arthur Gold and Robert Fizdale. Col. ML 4854 (in
    SL 198).

RACHMANINOFF, SERGEI
  Six Pieces, Op. 11.
    Sharon Gunderson and Jo Ann Smith. Orion ORS 7151
    (1971).

RAVEL, MAURICE
  Habañera.
    Robert and Gaby Casadesus. Col. ML 5213 (1957);
    ML 4519 (1952).

Ma mère l'oye.
  Ethel Bartlett and Rae Robertson. MGM E161.
  Robert and Gaby Casadesus. Col. ML 4519 (1952).
  Philippe Entremont and Dennis Lee. Col. D3M 33311
  (1974).
  Arthur Ferrante and Louis Teicher. ABC 454 (1963).
  Samson François and Pierre Barbizet. Sera. SIC 6046.

Walter and Beatriz Klien.   Vox STPL 512,590 (1964);
Turn. TV 34235.
Alfons and Aloys Kontarsky.   DGG 2707 072 (1974).

REGER, MAX
Deutsche Tänze, Op. 10a.
 Karl-Heinz and Michael Schlüter.   MHS 1487, 1618
(1972-1973).

5 Piéces pittoresques, op. 34.
 Sharon Gunderson and Jo Ann Smith.   Orion ORS 73130.
Karl-Heinz and Michael Schlüter.   MHS 1487, 1618
(1972-1973).

Sechs Burlesken, Op. 58.
 Karl-Heinz and Michael Schlüter.   MHS 1487, 1618
(1972-1973).

Sechs Stücke, Op. 94.
 Sharon Gunderson and Jo Ann Smith.   Orion ORS 73130.
Karl-Heinz and Michael Schlüter.   MHS 1487, 1618
(1972-1973).

Sechs Waltzer, Op. 22.
 Sharon Gunderson and Jo Ann Smith.   Orion ORS 73130.
Karl-Heinz and Michael Schlüter.   MHS 1487, 1618
(1972-1973).

RODRIGO, JOAQUIN
Gran marcha de los Subsecretarios.
 Joaquin and Victoria Camhi de Rodrigo.   Odeon LALP
581 (1960).

SATIE, ERIK
Aperçus Désagréables.
 Frank Glazer and Richard Deas.   Can. CE 31041.

En habit de cheval (1911).
 Frank Glazer and Richard Deas.   Can. CE 31041.
Arthur Gold and Robert Fizdale.   Col. ML 4854 (in SL
198) (1954).

Trois morceaux en forme de poire.
 Robert and Gaby Casadesus.   Col. ML 5723; MS 6323
(1962).
Bracha Eden and Alexander Tamir.   Lon. CS 6754
(1972).

Jacques Février and Georges Auric.   Ever. SDBR 3221
(1968).
Frank Glazer and Richard Deas.   Can. CE 31041.

Trois petites pièces montées.
Aldo Ciccolini, both parts.   Angel S 36811 (1968?).

SCHMITT, FLORENT
Une semaine du petit elfe ferme-l'oeil, op. 58.
Robert and Gaby Casadesus.   Col. ML 5259 (1958).

SCHUBERT, FRANZ
Allegro in A Minor, Op. 144, D947 (Lebensstürme).
Paul Badura-Skoda and Joerg Demus.   West. WL 5147
(1952); WST 14344-14345 (1968); DGG LPM 39107 (1966).
Alfred Brendel and Evelyne Crochet.   Turn. TV 34141S -
34144S; Also TV S 34516 (1973).
Maureen Jones and Dario de Rosa.   MHS 1576 (1973).

Andantino Varié in B Minor, Op. 84, No. 1.
Paul Badura-Skoda and Joerg Demus.   West. XWN
18790 (1958).
Robert and Gaby Casadesus.   Col. ML 5046 (1955).
Maureen Jones and Dario de Rosa.   MHS 1576 (1973).

Chamber works for piano duo; contains D. 617, 823 (no. 2),
940 and 886 (no. 2).
Eleanor Hancock and Caroline Norwood.   CG 641 (1965).

Deutsche Tänze und Ecossaisen, Op. 33.
Vitya Vronsky and Victor Babin.   Decca DL 9791 (1956).

2 Marches caractéristiques in C Major, Op. 121.
Paul Badura-Skoda and Joerg Demus.   DGG LPM 39107
(1966); West WST 14344-14345, WL 5047, XWN 18790
(1958).
Ingrid Haebler and Ludwig Hoffmann.   Phi. 802817 LY
(SAL 3745).
Milton and Peggy Salkind (No. 2).   FFHM SKD 1027
(1965).

Divertissement à la hongroise, in G Minor, Op. 54.
Joerg Demus and Paul Badura-Skoda.   RCA VIC 1329
(1968); West. XWN 18790 (1958).
Vitya Vronsky and Victor Babin.   Col. ML 2125 (1950).

Fantasy in F Minor, Op. 103.

Paul Badura-Skoda and Joerg Demus. West. WST
14344-14345 (1968); WST 17156; WL 5047; MG MS867
(1970); DGG LPM 39107 (1966).
Alfred Brendel and Evelyne Crochet. Vox STDL 501,
050 (1964); Turn TV 34141S-34144S.
Robert and Gaby Casadesus. Col. ML 5046 (1955).
Richard and John Contiguglia. Conn. CS 2037 (1971).
Ingrid Haebler and Ludwig Hoffmann. Phi. 802817 LY
(SAL 3745).
Maureen Jones and Dario de Rosa. MHS 1576 (1973).
Milton and Peggy Salkind. FFHM SKD 1027.
Helen and Karl Ulrich Schnabel. Epic LC 3185 (195?).
Vitya Vronsky and Victor Babin. Decca DL 9790 (1956).

Grand Duo for Piano, Four Hands, Op. 140, D. 812.
Alfred Brendel and Evelyne Crochet. Vox STDL 501,
050 (1964).
Arthur Gold and Robert Fizdale. Col. ML 5717 (1962);
MS 6317 (1962).

Grand Rondo in A Major, Op. 107.
Paul Badura-Skoda and Joerg Demus. West. WST
17156; WL 5047; WST 14344-14345 (1968); MG MS867;
DGG LPM 39107 (1966).

Grande marche in E Major, Op. 40, No. 6.
Paul Badura-Skoda and Joerg Demus. West. XWN
18790 (1958).

Marche militaire in D Major, Op. 51, No. 1.
Paul Badura-Skoda and Joerg Bemus. DGG LPM 39107
(1966); West. XWN 18790 (1958).
Harold Bauer and Ossip Gabrilowitsch. Kla. KS 102
(1970).
Richard and John Contiguglia. Conn. CS 2037 (1971).
Walter and Beatriz Klien. Turn. TV 34041S (1965).
Allinon Nelson and Harry Neal. Kap. SKR 3041.

Rondo in D Major, Op. 138.
Paul Badura-Skoda and Joerg Demus. West. WST 17156;
WST 14344-14345 (1968); MG MS867 (1970).
Bracha Eden and Alexander Tamir. Lon. CS 6694
(1971).
Ingrid Haebler and Ludwig Hoffmann. Phi. 802817
LY (SAL 3745).
Maureen Jones and Dario de Rosa. MHS 1576 (1973).

Variations in A-flat Major, Op. 35.
Joerg Demus and Paul Badura-Skoda. RCA VIC 1329
(1968); West. WL 5147 (1952); WST 14344-14345 (1968).

Variations in B-flat Major, Op. 82, No. 2.
Paul Badura-Skoda and Joerg Demus.   West. WL 5147
(1952); WST 14344-14345 (1968).
Ingrid Haebler and Ludwig Hoffmann.   Phi. 802817
LY (SAL 3745).

Vierhändige Klaviermusik, Compositions for Piano Duet.
(Contains D.947, 940, 733, 951, 886).
Paul Badura-Skoda and Joerg Demus.   DGG LPM 39107
(1966); SLPM 139107 (1966).

SCHUMANN, ROBERT
Kinderball, Op. 130, for Piano, Four Hands.
Joerg Demus and Norman Shetler.   MHS OR 400-402.

SCOTT, CYRIL
Symphonic Dance, D Minor.
Cyril Scott and Percy Grainger.   Kla. KS 102 (1970).

SHAPEY, RALPH
Seven for Piano, 4 Hands.
Milton and Peggy Salkind.   FFHM SKD 1027 (1965).

SPIEGELMAN, JOEL
Kousochki (1966), (Eng. "Morsels").
Jean and Kenneth Wentworth.   Desto DC-7131.

STRAUSS, RICHARD
Till Eulenspiegel's Merry Pranks, Op. 28.
Percy Grainger and Ralph Leopold.   Kla. KS 102 (1970).

STRAVINSKY, IGOR
Easy Pieces for Piano, Four Hands.
Arthur Gold and Robert Fizdale.   Col. ML 5733; MS
6333 (1962).

Five Easy Pieces (1917).
Ethel Bartlett and Rae Robertson.   MGM E3038 (1953).
Bracha Eden and Alexander Tamir.   Lon. CS 6626
(1969).
Alfons and Aloys Kontarsky.   MACE MXX 9092.

Petrouchka, adapted in 1947 by the composer.

Yaltah Menuhin and Joel Ryce.   Ever. LPBR 6130;
SDBR 3130 (1965).

The Rite of Spring.
Bracha Eden and Alexander Tamir.   Lon. CS 6626
(1969).

Three Easy Pieces (1915).
Ethel Bartlett and Rae Robertson.   MGM E 3038 (1953).
Bracha Eden and Alexander Tamir.   Lon. CS 6626
(1969).
Arthur Gold and Robert Fizdale.   Col. MS 6333 (1962).
Alfons and Aloys Kontarsky.   MACE MXX 9092.

TCHAIKOVSKY, PETER
Romeo et Juliette, fantasy overture.
Percy Grainger and Ralph Leopold.   Kla. KS 102
(1970).

WEBER, CARL MARIA VON
Eight Pieces for Piano, Four Hands, op. 60.
Hans Kann and Rosario Marciano.   Vox SVBX 5450-
5451.
Helen and Karl Ulrich Schnabel (Selections).   SPA 50
(195?).

Six Pieces for Piano, Four Hands, Op. 3.
Arthur Gold and Robert Fizdale.   Col. ML 4968 (1955).
Hans Kann and Rosario Marciano.   Vox SVBX 5450-5451.

Six Pieces for Piano, Four Hands, Op. 10.
Hans Kann and Rosario Marciano.   Vox SVBX 5450-5451.

WUORINEN, CHARLES
Making Ends Meet (1966).
Jean and Kenneth Wentworth.   Desto DC-7131.

3.   RECORDINGS FOR TWO PIANOS

ARENSKY, ANTON
Waltz from Suite for Two Pianos, Op. 15.
Harold Bauer and Ossip Gabrilowitsch.   RCA SP-33-143
(LM 2585) (1961); Kla. KS 102 (1970).
Bracha Eden and Alexander Tamir.   Lon. CS 6694 (1971).

Judith and Dorothy Lang. GC CR 4070 (1963).
Allinon Nelson and Harry Neal. Kap. SKR 3041.
Vitya Vronsky and Victor Babin. RCA LSC 2417 (1960);
VICS 1419 (1969); Col. ML 4157 (1949).

AURIC, GEORGES
Une valse.
Arthur Gold and Robert Fizdale. Col. ML 2147 (1950).

BABIN, VICTOR
Russian Village.
Vitya Vronsky and Victor Babin. Col. ML 4157 (1949).

BACH, J. S.
Concerto, Harpsichord, S.1065, A Minor, arranged.
Genia Nemenoff and Pierre Luboshutz. RCA WDM
1378.

Nun kommt der heiden Heiland, arranged by P. Luboshutz.
Genia Nemenoff and Pierre Luboshutz. RCA WDM 1378.

Siciliano, from Sonata for Flute and Clavier in E-flat.
Arthur Wittemore and Jack Lowe. RCA LM 1926 (1955).

BARBER, SAMUEL
Souvenirs, Op. 28 (1952), tr. from four-hand version.
Arthur Gold and Robert Fizdale. Col. ML 4855 (in
SL 198) (1954).

BARTOK, BELA
Mikrokosmos.
Richard and John Contiguglia (Fourteen Pieces from
Mikrokosmos). Conn. CS 2033 (1971).
Lajos Dévényi and Tibor Dévai (Seven Pieces, and other
selections). Qua LP 1577.
Liselotte Gierth and Gerd Lohmeyer (Selections). Odeon
C 80816 (196?).
Katia and Marielle Labeque (Seven Pieces from Micro-
kosmos). MHS 1499 (1973).
Arthur Whittemore and Jack Lowe (Nos. 1, 3, 5, from
Seven Pieces). RCA LM 1705 (1952).

Suite, Op. 4b.
Richard and John Contiguglia. Conn. CS 2033 (1971).

BAX, ARNOLD E. TREVOR
The Poisoned Fountain.

Arthur Whittemore and Jack Lowe. RCA LM 1705 (1952).

BEETHOVEN, LUDWIG VAN
Symphony No. 9 in D Minor, Op. 125, arr. by F. Liszt for 2 pianos.
   Richard and John Contiguglia. Conn. CSQ 2052.

BENJAMIN, ARTHUR
Jamaicalypso.
   Vitya Vronsky and Victor Babin. RCA LSC 2417 (1960); RCA VICS 1419 (1969).

Jamaican Rumba.
   Judith and Dorothy Lane. GC CR4070 (1963).
   Allinon Nelson and Harry Neal. Kap. SKP 3041.
   Jane Smisor and James Bastien. GWM 100 (1967).

BEREZOWSKY, NICOLAI
Fantasy for Two Pianos, Op. 9 (1930).
   Yarbrough and Cowan. CRI S-279.

BERGER, ARTHUR VICTOR
Three Pieces for Two Pianos.
   Paul Jacobs and Gilbert Kalish. Col. ML 6359, MS 6359 (1967).

BRITTEN, BENJAMIN
Two compositions for Piano Duet, Op. 23 (Rondo alla burlesca, and Mazurka elegiaca).
   Vera and Vlastimil Lejsek. SUA 10694; SUA ST 50694.

BUSONI, FERRUCCIO
Duettino concertante nach Mozart, for two pianos.
   Kurt Bauer and Heidi Bung. DGG LPEM 19158 (1960).

Fantasia contrappuntistica, for two pianos.
   Peter Serkin and Richard Goode. Col. ML 6291; MS 6891 (1966).

CASADESUS, ROBERT
Danses Mediterranéennes, Op. 36 (1944).
   Robert and Gaby Casadesus. Col. ML 2146 (1950).

Six Pieces for Two Pianos.
   Judith and Dorothy Lang. GC CR4070 (1963).

CHABRIER, EMMANUEL
  Trois valses romantiques.
    Robert and Gaby Casadesus.   Col. ML 5723, MS 6323
    (1962).
    Edith Henrici and Hans-Helmut Schwarz.   MHS 1225
    (1971).
    Geneviéve Joy and Jacqueline Robin-Bonneau.   MHS
    849S-850S (1968).
    Walter Klien and Rena Kyriakou.   Turn. TV 34241;
    Vox VBX 400

CHOPIN, FREDERIC
  Rondo for Two Pianos in C Major, Op. 73.
    Kurt Bauer and Heidi Bung.   DGG LPEM 19158 (1960).
    Samson François and Pierre Barbizet.   Sera. S 60109.
    Pierre Luboshutz and Genia Nemenoff.   Ever. M 6076,
    S 3076.
    Allinon Nelson and Harry Neal.   Kap. SKR 3041.
    Jane Smisor and James Bastien.   GWM 100 (1967).
    Melvin Stecher and Norman Horowitz.   Ever. LPBR
    6147.
    Vitya Vronsky and Victor Babin.   Decca DL 9790 (1956).

CLEMENTI, MUZIO
  Sonata for Two Pianos, No. 1, in B-flat Major.
    Liselotte Gierth and Gerd Lohmeyer.   Odeon C 80816
    (196?).

COPLAND, AARON
  Billy the Kid (Celebration Dance, Billy's Demise and The
  Open Prairie Again).
    Arthur Whittemore and Jack Lowe.   RCA LM 1705;
    RCA LM 1926 (1955) (Celebration Dance only).

  Danzón Cubano.
    Vitya Vronsky and Victor Babin.   RCA LSC 2417 (1960),
    VICS 1419 (1969).

DEBUSSY, CLAUDE
  En blanc et noir.
    Robert and Gaby Casadesus.   Col. ML 6041, MS 6641
    (1964).
    Leonid Hambro and Jascha Zayde.   Com. CC 11013 SD
    (1962).
    José and Amparo Iturbi.   RCA LM 36 (1951).
    Geneviéve Joy and Jacqueline Robin-Bonneau.   MHS
    849S-850S (1968).

Walter and Beatriz Klien.   Turn. TV 34234.
Alfons and Aloys Kontarsky. DGG 2707 072 (1974).
Vitya Vronsky and Victor Babin.   Col. ML 4470 (1952).

Lindaraja.
Geneviéve Joy and Jacqueline Robin-Bonneau.   MHS
849S-850S (1968).
Alfons and Aloys Kontarsky. DGG 2707 072 (1974).
Phillips and Renzulli.   Harl. 3805.

Nocturnes: Nuages and Fêtes.
Arthur Ferrante and Louis Teicher.   ABC 454 (1963).

Prélude à l'après-midi d'un faune.
Bracha Eden and Alexander Tamir.   Lon. CS 6754
(1972).
Alfons and Aloys Kontarsky. DGG 2707 072 (1974).

Symphony in B Minor (for 2 pianos).
Alfons and Aloys Kontarsky. DGG 2707 072 (1974).

DONOVAN, RICHARD FRANK
Three Pieces for Two Pianos.
Paul Jacobs and Gilbert Kalish.   Col. ML 6359.

DVOŘAK, ANTONIN
Slavonic Dances.
Leonid Hambro and Jascha Zayde (No. 10).   Comm.
CC 11023 SD (1964).
Arthur Whittemore and Jack Lowe (Nos. 1, 6, 8, 10).
RCA LM 1926 (1955).

ENESCO, GEORGES
Roumanian Rhapsody, No. 1, in A, Op. 11, arr. for 2
pianos by Whittemore and Lowe.
Arthur Whittemore and Jack Lowe.   RCA ERB 7010
(549-0019 - 549-0020).

FALLA, MANUEL DE
El amor brujo.
Arthur Whittemore and Jack Lowe.   RCA ERB 7010
(549-0019 - 549-0020).

Danza ritual del fuego.
Arthur Whittemore and Jack Lowe.   RCA ERB 7010
(549-0019 - 549-0020).

Ritual Fire Dance, arr. by Braggiotti.
Judith and Dorothy Lane. GC CR4070 (1963).

FRANÇAIX, JEAN
Six danses exotiques.
Geneviéve Joy and Jacqueline Robin-Bonneau. MHS
849S-850S (1968).

FRANK, CESAR
Prelude, Fugue and Variation (Originally for organ, tran-
scribed by Patrick Williams).
Leonid Hambro and Jascha Zayde. Comm. CC 11013
SD 1962.

GLINKA, MIKHAIL
The Lark - Romance (Transcribed by Pierre Luboshutz).
Pierre Luboshutz and Genia Nemenoff. Van. VRS 1096
(1963), VSD 2128.

GLUCK, CHRISTOPH WILLIBALD
Mélodie from Orfeo and Euridice.
Arthur Whittemore and Jack Lowe. RCA LM 1926
(1955).

GODOWSKY, LEOPOLD
Alt Wien.
Allinon Nelson and Harry Neal. Kap. SKR 3041.

GOULD, MORTON
Guaracha.
Arthur Whittemore and Jack Lowe. RCA LM 1926
(1955).

HAIEFF, ALEXEI
Sonata for Two Pianos (1945).
Col. ML 4855 (in SL 198) (1954). Arthur Gold and
Robert Fizdale.

HETU, JACQUES
Sonata pour deux pianos.
Victor Bouchard and Renée Morisset. RCA CCS 1021
(1967).

IVES, CHARLES
Three Quarter-tone Pieces, for 2 Pianos.
George C. Pappastravrou and Stuart Warren Lanning.
Odys. 32 16 0162.

KHACHATURIAN, ARAM
Fantastic waltz (from Three Dances).
Bracha Eden and Alexander Tamir. Lon. CS 6694
(1971).

Suite for Two Pianos.
Pierre Luboshutz and Genia Nemenoff. Van. VRS 1096
(1963) VSD 2128.

KREISLER, FRITZ
Liebeslied, La gitana, and others.
Arthur Whittemore and Jack Lowe. RCA LM-1989
(1956); RCA ERA-95.

KUPFERMAN, MEYER
Sonata for 2 Pianos (1958).
Jean and Kenneth Wentworth. Sere. 12044.

LECUONA, ERNESTO
Malagueña.
Arthur Whittemore and Jack Lowe. RCA LM 1926
(1955).

LISZT, FRANZ
Concerto pathétique in E minor.
Edith Henrici and Hans-Helmut Schwarz. MHS 1225
(1971).
Louis Kentner and Joan Havill. Turn. TV-S 34444.
Vitya Vronsky and Victor Babin. Decca DL 9790 (1956).

LUBOSHUTZ, PIERRE
"The Bat" A Fantasy from Johann Strauss' "Die Fleder-
maus."
Pierre Luboshutz and Genia Nemenoff. Ever. M 6076,
S 3076.

LUTOSLAWSKI, WITOLD
Variations on a Theme of Paganini (1941).
Bracha Eden and Alexander Tamir. Lon. 6434.
Liselotte Gierth and Gerd Lohmeyer. Odeon C 80816
(196?).
Vera and Vlastimil Lejsek. SUA 10694, SUA ST50694.
Vitya Vronsky and Victor Babin. RCA ALP 2065 (1962);
Sera. S 60053 (1967).

MENDELSSOHN, FELIX
Allegro brillant, in A, Op. 92, arranged for two pianos.

Leonid Hambro and Jascha Zayde. Com. CC11010 SD
(1963).
Pierre Luboshutz and Genia Nemenoff. Van. VRS 1096
(1963), VSD 2128.

MESSIAEN, OLIVIER
Visions de l'amen.
John Ogden and Brenda Lucas. Argo ZRG 665 (1971).
Peter Serkin and Yuji Takahashi. RCA ARLI 0363
(1973).

MILHAUD, DARIUS
Scaramouche.
Bracha Eden and Alexander Tamir. Lon. 6434.
Liselotte Gierth and Gerd Lohmeyer. Odeon C 80816
(196?).
José and Amparo Iturbi. RCA LRM-7038 (1954).
Genevieve Joy and Jacqueline Robin-Bonneau. MHS
854S.
Walter and Beatriz Klien. Turn. TV 34235.
Judith and Dorothy Lane. GC CR 4070 (1963).
Pierre Luboshutz and Genia Nemenoff. Van. VRS 1096
(1963), VSD 2128.
Allinon Nelson and Harry Neal. Kap. SKR 3041.
Jane Smisor and James Bastien. GWM 100 (1967).
Melvin Stecher and Norman Horowitz. Ever. LPBR
6147.
Vitya Vronsky and Victor Babin. Decca DL 9790 (1956).

MOZART, WOLFGANG AMADEUS
Fugue in C Minor, K. 426.
Alfred Brendel and Walter Klien. Vox SVBX 566.

Piano Sonata in F, for Four Hands, K. 497, arranged for
2 pianos.
Leonid Hambro and Jascha Zayde. Com. CC 11010 SD
(1963).

Sonata in D Major for Two Pianos, K. 448.
Robert and Gaby Casadesus. Col. ML 5046 (1955).
Liselotte Gierth and Gerd Lohmeyer. Odeon C 80816
(196?).
Walter and Beatriz Klien. Vox SVBX 566.
Pierre Luboshutz and Genia Nemenoff. Ever. M 6076,
S 3076.

MUSSORGSKY, MODEST

Boris Godounoff, Coronation Scene (Arr. by Whittemore and Lowe).
　　Arthur Whittemore and Jack Lowe.　RCA 49-0405.

NEPOMUCENO, ALBERTO
　　La siesta, arr. by Amparo and José Iturbi.
　　　Amparo and José Iturbi.　RCA LRM-7038 (1954).

PASQUINI, BERNARDO
　　Sonata in D Minor.
　　　Arthur Whittemore and Jack Lowe.　RCA 49-0917.

PERSICHETTI, VINCENT
　　Sonata for 2 Pianos, Op. 13 (1940).
　　　Yarbrough and Cowan.　CRI S-279.

POULENC, FRANCIS
　　L'embarquement pour Cythère.
　　　Bracha Eden and Alexander Tamir.　Lon. CS 6694
　　　(1971).
　　　Vitya Vronsky and Victor Babin.　Decca DL 9791 (1956).

　　Sonata for Piano, Four Hands (1918), arr. for 2 pianos.
　　　Leonid Hambro and Jascha Zayde.　Com. CC 11013
　　　SD (1962).
　　　Arthur Whittemore and Jack Lowe.　RCA LM 1705
　　　(1952).

　　Sonata for Two Pianos (1953).
　　　Bracha Eden and Alexander Tamir.　Lon. 6434.
　　　Liselotte Gierth and Gerd Lohmeyer.　Odeon C 80816
　　　(196?).
　　　Arthur Gold and Robert Fizdale.　Col. ML 5068 (1955),
　　　ML 5918 (1964), MS 6518 (1963).
　　　Leonid Hambro and Jascha Zayde.　Com. CC 11013 SD.
　　　Genevieve Joy and Jacqueline Robin-Bonneau.　MHS
　　　854S.
　　　Judith and Dorothy Lane.　GC CR 4070 (1963).

RACHMANINOFF, SERGEI
　　Fantasia (Suite No. 1), Op. 5.
　　　Bracha Eden and Alexander Tamir.　Lon. 6434; Lon.
　　　CS 6694 (1971) (Barcarolle)
　　　Arthur Ferrante and Louis Teicher.　West. WN 18059
　　　(1955?).
　　　Allinon Nelson and Harry Neal.　Kap. SKR 4026 (1970).
　　　Vitya Vronsky and Victor Babin.　RCA LM 2648, LSC
　　　2648 (1963); Col. ML 4379.

Italian Polka, for 2 Pianos.
  Sergei and Natalie Rachmaninoff.   Ver. VM 102 (1967).
  Hans-Helmut Schwarz and Edith Henrici.   MHS 1147
  (1971).
  Vitya Vronsky and Victor Babin.   Decca DL 9719 (1956).

Prelude in G Minor, Op. 23, No. 5, adapted and arranged
by Jascha Zayde.
  Leonid Hambro and Jascha Zayde.   Com. CC 11023
  SD (1964).

Suite No. 2, Op. 17.
  Bracha Eden and Alexander Tamir.   Lon. 6434.
  Arthur Ferrante and Louis Teicher.   West. WN 18059
  (1955).
  Edith Henrici and Hans-Helmut Schwarz (Tarantella).
  MHS 1225 (1971).
  Vitya Vronsky and Victor Babin.   RCA LM2648, LSC
  2648 (1963); Col. ML 4379.

Symphonic Dances, Op. 45.
  Vitya Vronsky and Victor Babin.   RCA ALP 2065 (1962);
  Sera. S 60053 (1967).

RAVEL, MAURICE
  Bolero.
    Arthur Ferrante and Louis Teicher.   ABC 454 (1963).

  Frontispice (for 2 pianos).
    Alfons and Aloys Kontarsky.   DGG 2707 072 (1974).

  Habañera.
    Philippe Enremont and Dennis Lee.   Col. D3M 33311
    (1974).
    Génevíéve Joy and Jacqueline Robin-Bonneau.   MHS
    849S-850S (1968).

  Rapsodie espanole (for 2 pianos).
    Alfons and Aloys Kontarsky.   DGG 2707 072 (1974).
    Allinon Nelson and Harry Neal.   Kap. SKR 5101 (1970).

  La Valse.
    Arthur Ferrante and Louis Teicher.   ABC 454 (1963).
    Arthur Whittemore and Jack Lowe.   RCA LM 1705
    (1952).

REGER, MAX

Introduction, Passacaglia and Fugue in B Minor, Op. 96.
 Alfons and Aloys Kontarsky. MHS 1292 (1972).

Valse d'amour.
 Arthur Whittemore and Jack Lowe. RCA LM1926
 (1955).

Variations and Fugue in B-flat Major, Op. 86, on a Theme
of Beethoven.
 Alfons and Aloys Kontarsky. MHS 1292 (1972).

Variations and Fugue on a Theme of Wolfgang Amadeus
Mozart, Op. 132a.
 Alfons and Aloys Kontarsky. MHS 1268 (1972).

RIEGGER, WALLINGFORD
 Variations for 2 Pianos, Op. 54a (1952).
 Yarbrough and Cowan. CRI S-279.

RIETI, VITTORIO
 Suite champêtre (1948).
 Arthur Gold and Robert Fizdale. Col. ML 4853 (in
 SL 198) (1954).

Second Avenue Waltzes.
 Arthur Gold and Robert Fizdale. Col. ML 2147 (1950).

RIMSKI-KORSAKOV, NIKOLAI
 Dance of the Tumblers.
 Vitya Vronsky and Victor Babin. RCA LSC 2417 (1960);
 RCA VICS 1419 (1969); Col. ML 4157 (1949).

Sadko; Cradle Song.
 Vitya Vronsky and Victor Babin. Col. ML 4157 (1949).

SAINT-SAËNS, CAMILLE
 Caprice Héroique, Op. 106.
 Marie-José Billard and Julien Azais. Grav. S/M:
 6525 005.

Danse Macabre, Op. 40.
 Edith Henrici and Hans-Helmut Schwarz. MHS 1225
 (1971).
 Arthur Whittemore and Jack Lowe. RCA ERB 7010
 (549-0019 - 549-0020).

Minuet and Gavotte, Op. 65 (Tr. by the composer for 2

pianos)
>Leonid Hambro and Jascha Zayde. Comm. CC 11013
>SD (1962).

Polonaise, Op. 77.
>Marie-José Billard and Julien Azais.   Grav. S/M 6525
>005.

Scherzo, Op. 87.
>Marie-José Billard and Julien Azais.   Grav. S/M 6525
>005.

Variations sur un thème de Beethoven, 2 pianos, Op. 35.
>Kurt Bauer and Heidi Bung. DGG LPEM 19158 (1960).
>Marie-Jose Billard and Julien Azais.   Grav. S/M:
>6526 005.

SATIE, ERIC
Gymnopédie no. 2.
>Arthur Whittemore and Jack Lowe.   RCA LM 1926
>(1955).

SAUGUET, HENRI
Valse brève.
>Arthur Gold and Robert Fizdale.   Col. ML 2147 (1950).

SCHMITT, FLORENT
Trois Rapsodies, op. 53.
>Robert and Gaby Casadesus.   Col. ML 5259 (1958).

SCHUBERT, FRANZ
Fantasy in F Minor, Op. 103, arr. for 2 pianos.
>Leonid Hambro and Jascha Zayde.   Com. CC 11010
>SD (1963).

Valses nobles.
>Arthur Whittemore and Jack Lowe.   RCA LM 1926
>(1955).

SCHUMANN, ROBERT
Andante und Variationen, Op. 46, B-flat Major.
>Kurt Bauer and Heidi Bung.   DGG LPEM 19158 (1960).
>Lajos Dévényi and Tibor Dévai.   Qua. LP 1577.

Etudes en forme de canon, op. 56, no. 2-4, arr. by Debussy.
>Bracha Eden and Alexander Tamir.   Lon. CS 6694 (1971).

SCRIABIN, ALEXANDER
  Phantasie for Two Pianos, Op. posth.
    Hans-Helmut Schwarz and Edith Henrici.   MHS 1147
    Michael Ponti and R. Leonardi.   Vox SVBX 5474.

  Sonata No. 4 in F-sharp Minor, Op. 30.
    Hans-Helmut Schwarz and Edith Henrici.   MHS 1147
    (1971).

SHAW, CLIFFORD
  Third Street Rhumba.
    Arthur Whittemore and Jack Lowe.   RCA LM 1926
    (1955).

SHOSTAKOVICH, DMITRI
  Age of Gold.   Polka, arranged.
    Pierre Luboshutz and Genia Nemenoff.   Van. VRS 1096
    (1963), VSD 2128.
    Arthur Whittemore and Jack Lowe.   RCA 49-0405.

  Concertino for Two Pianos.
    Allinon Nelson and Harry Neal.   Kap. SKR 5101 (1970).
    Hans-Helmut Schwarz and Edith Henrici.   MHS 1147
    (1971).
    Maxim and Dmitri Shostakovich.   Bruno BR 14057
    (1964); Mon. MC 2040 (1959).

  Three Fantastic Dances, Op. 1.
    Hans-Helmut Schwarz and Edith Henrici.   MHS 1147
    (1971).

  Waltz from "Golden Mountains," tr. by P. Luboshutz.
    Pierre Luboshutz and Genia Nemenoff.   Van. VRS 1096
    (1963), VSD 2128.

SIMMONS, H.
  Scherzino.
    Jane Smisor and James Bastien.   GWM 100 (1967).

STOCKHAUSEN, KARLHEINZ
  Mantra.
    Alfons and Aloys Kontarsky.   DGG 2530 208 (1972).

STRAUSS, JOHANN
  Die Fledermaus; adapted and arranged by Jascha Zayde.
    Leonid Hambro and Jascha Zayde.   Com. CC 11023 SD
    (1964).

Waltz Fantasy.
> Arthur Whittemore and Jack Lowe. RCA LM 1926
> (1955).

STRAUSS, RICHARD
Der Rosenkavalier: Concert Waltz, arr. by O. Singer.
> Vitya Vronsky and Victor Babin. RCA LSC 2417 (1960);
> RCA VICS 1419 (1969).

Rosenkavalier Waltzes, tr. by Victor Babin.
> Vitya Vronsky and Victor Babin. Decca DL 9791 (1956).

STRAVINSKI, IGOR
Circus Polka.
> Vitya Vronsky and Victor Babin. Col. ML 4157 (1949);
> RCA LSC 2417 (1960); RCA VICS 1419 (1969).

Concerto for Two Solo Pianos (1935).
> Ethel Bartlett and Rae Robertson. MGM E3038 (1953).
> Arthur Gold and Robert Fizdale. Col. ML 4853 (in
> SL 198) (1954); ML 5733, MS 6333 (1962).
> Alfons and Aloys Kontarsky. MACE MXX9092.
> Vera and Vlastimil Lejsek. SUA 10694, SUA ST 50694.
> Vitya Vronsky and Victor Babin. Col. ML 4157 (1949).
> Charlotte Zelka and Alfred Brendel. Vox PL 10,660
> (1958).

The Rite of Spring.
> Michael Tilson Thomas and Ralph Grierson. Angel
> S 36024 (1969).

Scherzo à la russe.
> Michael Tilson Thomas and Ralph Grierson. Angel
> S36024 (1969).

Sonata for Two Pianos (1943-4).
> Ethel Bartlett and Rae Robertson. MGM E3038 (1953).
> Arthur Gold and Robert Fizdale. Col. ML 5733, MS
> 6333 (1962).
> Arthur Whittemore and Jack Lowe. RCA LM 1705.

Three Movements from Petrouchka, arr. for 2 pianos.
> Hans-Helmut Schwarz and Edith Henrici. MHS 1147
> (1971).
> Vitya Vronsky and Victor Babin. Col. ML 4470 (1952).

Variations on In den fernern Tälern.

Hans-Helmut Schwarz and Edith Henrici.   MHS 1147
(1971).

TAILLEFERRE, GERMAINE
Valses I and II.
Arthur Gold and Robert Fizdale.   Col. ML 2147 (1950).

TCHAIKOVSKY, PETER
Dances from Swan Lake.
Vitya Vronsky and Victor Babin.   RCA VICS 1419 (1969).

Eugen Onegin: Waltz, arr. by V. Babin.
Vitya Vronsky and Victor Babin.   RCA LSC 2417 (1960).

The Nutcracker: Waltz of the Flowers, arr. by V. Babin.
Vitya Vronsky and Victor Babin.   RCA LSC 2417 (1960).

Serenade, Op. 48: Waltz, arr. by V. Babin.
Vitya Vronsky and Victor Babin.   RCA LSC 2417 (1960).

Swan Lake: Waltz, arr. by V. Babin.
Vitya Vronsky and Victor Babin.   RCA LSC 2417 (1960).

THOMPSON, L.
Two Masques.
Judith and Dorothy Lane.   GC CR4070 (1963).

THOMSON, VIRGIL
Synthetic waltzes.
Arthur Gold and Robert Fizdale.   Col. ML 2147 (1950).

VAUGHAN WILLIAMS, RALPH
Fantasia on Greensleeves, arr. by H. Foss.
Judith and Dorothy Lane.   GC CR 4070 (1963).

WEBER, CARL MARIA VON
Invitation to the Dance, Op. 65, adapted and arr. by
Jascha Zayde.
Com. CC 11023 SD (1964).

WEINBERGER, JAROMIR
Polka and fugue from Schwanda.
Bracha Eden and Alexander Tamir.   Lon. CS 6694
(1971).

WILLIAMSON, MALCOLM
Sonata for Two Pianos.

The composer as one of the pianists.   Argo ZRG 704
(1972).

ZAYDE, JASCHA
   Variations on a Theme by Paganini.
        Leonid Hambro and Jascha Zayde.   Com. CC 11023
        SD (1964).

4.   RECORDINGS FOR THREE AND FOUR PIANOS

FELDMAN, MORTON
   Extension 4 for Three Pianos.
        David Tudor, Russell Sherman, Edwin Hywovitz.   Colum-
        bia ML 5403.

   Piece for Four Pianos.
        David Tudor, Russell Sherman, Edwin Hywovitz, Morton
        Feldman.   Columbia ML 5403.

HAMPTON, CALVIN
   Catch-up.
        G. C. Pappastavrou and S. W. Lanning.   Odys.
        32160161-2.